The Elvis Movies

The Elvis Movies

James L. Neibaur

ROWMAN & LITTLEFIELD
Lanham • Boulder • New York • Toronto • Plymouth, UK

Published by Rowman & Littlefield
4501 Forbes Boulevard, Suite 200, Lanham, Maryland 20706
www.rowman.com

10 Thornbury Road, Plymouth PL6 7PP, United Kingdom

Copyright © 2014 by Rowman & Littlefield

All images courtesy of the author

All rights reserved. No part of this book may be reproduced in any form or by any electronic or mechanical means, including information storage and retrieval systems, without written permission from the publisher, except by a reviewer who may quote passages in a review.

British Library Cataloguing in Publication Information Available

Library of Congress Cataloging-in-Publication Data

Neibaur, James L., 1958–
  The Elvis movies / James L. Neibaur.
    pages cm
  Includes bibliographical references and index.
  ISBN 978-1-4422-3073-6 (cloth : alk. paper) — ISBN 978-1-4422-3074-3 (ebook)
 1. Presley, Elvis, 1935-1977—Criticism and interpretation. 2. Musical films—United States—History and criticism. I. Title.
  ML420.P96N45 2014
  791.43'75—dc23   2013045779

∞™ The paper used in this publication meets the minimum requirements of American National Standard for Information Sciences—Permanence of Paper for Printed Library Materials, ANSI/NISO Z39.48-1992. Printed in the United States of America

To my friend Eddie Deezen,
actor, comedian, voice artist, Elvis fan

Contents

Acknowledgments ix

Introduction xi

1	The Rise of Elvis Presley	1
2	*Love Me Tender*	9
3	*Loving You*	16
4	*Jailhouse Rock*	27
5	*King Creole*	38
6	Elvis in the Army	49
7	*G.I. Blues*	54
8	*Flaming Star*	63
9	*Wild in the Country*	71
10	*Blue Hawaii*	80
11	*Follow That Dream*	89
12	*Kid Galahad*	100
13	*Girls! Girls! Girls!*	109
14	*It Happened at the World's Fair*	118
15	*Fun in Acapulco*	127
16	*Kissin' Cousins*	134
17	*Viva Las Vegas*	143
18	*Roustabout*	152
19	*Girl Happy*	162
20	*Tickle Me*	171
21	*Harum Scarum*	180
22	*Frankie and Johnny*	186
23	*Paradise, Hawaiian Style*	192

24	*Spinout*	199
25	*Easy Come, Easy Go*	206
26	*Double Trouble*	211
27	*Clambake*	216
28	*Stay Away, Joe*	222
29	*Speedway*	227
30	*Live a Little, Love a Little*	234
31	*Elvis*: The Elvis Comeback Special	238
32	*Charro!*	242
33	*The Trouble with Girls*	247
34	*Change of Habit*	252
35	The Concert Films	257
36	The Final Years	262

Notes	265
Bibliography	269
Index	271
About the Author	281

Acknowledgments

Thanks to these people for providing graphics, research materials, and material from their books or interviews, as well as offering constant encouragement and support: Bob Furmanek, Terri Niemi, Ted Okuda, Katie Carter, Christopher Riordan, Chris Noel, Marlyn Mason, Francine York, Edward Faulkner, Donna Butterworth, Vicky Tiu, Tuesday Weld, the late Edward Bernds, Marty Lacker, Eliot Underhill, Alanna Nash, Jerry Lewis, the late Lamar Fike, Priscilla Presley, Paul McCartney, Keith Richards, Shelley Fabares, Hal Kanter, David Stanley, Billy Smith, Eddie Deezen.

Introduction

Elvis Presley's impact on popular culture is quite vast and far reaching, making him among the most important entertainers of the twentieth century. Influenced by the myriad of musical styles he had gravitated toward as a youth, including gospel, country, and blues, Presley's creative mind fused them together and offered a new and different sound that was strong enough to alter the course of entertainment in far-reaching ways. From the primitive yearning of his initial Sun recordings, to the raucous triumph of his early RCA material, Elvis Presley paved the way for an explosion of youth-oriented music that altered the cultural progression of the 1950s. After quickly achieving superstardom while redefining popular music, Elvis Presley then embarked upon a movie career that, for the most part, traded on what eventually became a manufactured image.

While there have been countless books trying to ferret out the "real Elvis" tucked deeply beneath layers of showbiz mythology, and just as many examining the enormous impact of his music, his motion picture career is either dismissed as insignificant or overlooked entirely. Elvis Presley starred in 31 feature films and two concert documentaries from 1956 to 1972. Most of these were star vehicles tailor made for his image. While he had a real interest in being a good actor, his initial promise was soon thwarted by his management's anticreative decisions. However, Elvis Presley's star power ensured box office success even after he had lapsed into a predictable formula of lightweight musicals.

Elvis made his film debut in the pedestrian western *Love Me Tender* (1956), creating an initial impact by exhibiting promise for a future in acting. While he had no intention to reinvent cinema the way he had popular music, he wanted to learn more about acting, and to work in good films with talented directors. For his first few movies, Elvis had that opportunity.

Elvis Presley made his best films while he was creating some of his finest music, from 1956 to 1958. Films like the semibiographical *Loving You* (1957),

Early Elvis in performance

and the heavy dramas *Jailhouse Rock* (1957) and *King Creole* (1958), offer solid narratives, thoughtful direction, and increasingly improving performances by the hardworking young newcomer, determined to do his best in the new medium. Inspired by such actors as Humphrey Bogart, Tony Curtis, James Dean, and Marlon Brando, Presley decided that the less he smiled, the more effective his acting work would be. However, this also further solidified the image conservative America had of Elvis Presley—that he was an angry, sullen, dangerous, sexually motivated deviant who was responsible for whatever decadence was perceived in regard to American youth. The despicable character he played in *Jailhouse Rock* seemed to perpetuate this idea.

A two-year stint in the army, the tragic death of his mother, and a more sanitized, family-friendly image helped Elvis Presley's career success immensely, but some believe it was at a cost to his creative freedom. The pleasant lightweight musical *G.I. Blues*, Presley's first film after serving in the army, was a box office smash. The similar *Blue Hawaii*, released the next year, was the biggest moneymaker of Presley's movie career. Stints in more dramatic pictures offered less box office success, and his management only saw things in financial terms. Thus, from 1965, the Elvis Presley movies settled into a pat formula of pretty girls, beaches, race cars, snappy songs, and light comedy. Sometimes these movies were disarming, harmless fun; they nearly always made piles of money at the box office, and continued to soften Presley's initial image. Occasionally during the earlier 1960s, Presley would have an opportunity to do a more serious film like *Flaming Star*, with a top-level director like Don Siegel, but when the drama *Wild in the Country* (1961) became the only Elvis movie to lose money, the decision makers sacrificed art for artifice.

Elvis Presley's motion picture career parallels his simultaneous music career. First there is the music of 1954–1956 that had such an enormous impact and caused the stardom that led to a movie contract. Then there were the continued great songs of 1956–1958 during which he also made his best movies. A backlog of already recorded songs sustained Presley's career while in the army, and when he came out, he reminded everyone of his range and power with the phenomenal *Elvis Is Back* album, containing some of the finest music he'd ever recorded.

From 1960 to 1965 Presley continued to enjoy a succession of hit songs both from his movie soundtracks and studio recordings. Even the initial impact of the Beatles was not enough to diminish his success on the charts. However, once the Beatles introduced an even greater range of music and exhibited the songwriting prowess that Presley did not have, his status on the charts plummeted. In 1965 he had a Top 10 hit with a gospel song, *Crying in the Chapel*, that he'd recorded five years earlier. He would have no major hits in 1966, 1967, or 1968 during which the Beatles released such albums as *Rubber Soul, Revolver,* and *Sergeant Pepper's Lonely Hearts Club Band,* while the Rolling Stones recorded *Aftermath* and Bob Dylan offered *Blonde on Blonde*. These landmark albums allowed the basis of rock and roll that Presley had helped to create achieve even greater progression.

Despite being eclipsed on the charts and shrugging off his ability in lightweight star vehicles, Elvis Presley's movies during this period remained consistently popular. Theater owners reported success when a Presley movie played, critics did not always pan the films but often found them quaint and harmlessly amusing, while the same young people who were not buying his records still appeared to be attending his films. It was not until the sixties had gone past their halfway point that the movies became so numbingly formulaic, and Elvis so disillusioned, that their box office success dwindled considerably.

In 1968 Presley was hired to do a network Christmas special. His management expected a conventional program with Yuletide standards, but Elvis had other ideas. Clad in a leather outfit, sitting in a circle among old musician friends on a center stage surrounded by eager fans, Elvis jammed on a guitar and belted out nearly all of his biggest hits from the 1950s to the present. Some call the 1968 TV special the finest performance of his career. It was at that point that Presley decided to abandon his film career, finish out the terms of his contract, and return to live performance. Since his formulaic films were no longer as lucrative, Elvis was allowed to stretch a bit as an actor, and his last productions, including *Charro!, The Trouble with Girls,* and *Change of Habit* were an interesting departure and, ultimately, an improvement. But by this time Elvis was completely disillusioned with Hollywood.

In 1969 Presley went back into the recording studio in Memphis, cutting some of his strongest material in decades, and returning to the top of the charts with such hits as "Suspicious Minds" and "Kentucky Rain" during what are now known as the fabled Memphis sessions. Covering gospel, country, and rock, fusing them as only he knew how, Elvis Presley enjoyed another creative and commercial milestone. But his movie career was over. He had other opportunities to appear in films, but did no more movie acting after 1970.

Looking at the Presley movies film by film, we are able to examine the promise, the achievement, the commercial success, the successful use of formula, the power of marketing, and the lasting impact. This book assesses, discusses, and reveals the most overlooked and neglected portion of Elvis Presley's magnificent career. The text also covers Presley's frustration with creatively numbing misfires like *Clambake* and *Harum Scarum* that did well enough at the box office to help finance the studio's more prestigious films—movies Elvis would like to have done.

The importance of Elvis Presley to music is so all-encompassing that it is easy to look at his movie career as a mere tangent worth little if any discussion. This book argues that Presley's film career is yet another extension of his talent, does merit serious discussion, and is better than its unfortunate reputation.

CHAPTER 1
The Rise of Elvis Presley
(1954–1956)

Many studies have attempted to understand and explain the creative dynamic that existed between Elvis Presley, guitarist Scotty Moore, and bassist Bill Black in July 1954 when they stood in the Sun recording studios in Memphis, Tennessee, and covered the Arthur Crudup song "That's All Right." The essence of rock and roll as we know it was invented at this session, so its significance is beyond measure.

Moore and Black were talented session musicians, and Elvis was making his fifth appearance at the recording studios, so they were not completely unfamiliar with each other. Previously, Elvis had been there to make private recordings and his unique vocal sound caused others to take notice. Sun Studio was owned by Sam Phillips, who used his facilities to record two earthy forms of music that were well outside the mainstream in the 1950s. At the time, what we recognize as country music was called "hillbilly" and what we would now identify as blues or rhythm and blues (R&B) was known as "race music." These are the styles that Phillips's studio specialized in, allowing him to discover such noted artists as Howlin' Wolf, Johnny Cash, Jerry Lee Lewis, and Carl Perkins.

According to legend, during a break at the uneventful session in July 1954, Elvis started noodling around on the guitar, playing the old Crudup song, which had been recorded in 1946 and released a few years later by RCA. As someone whose taste ran to the race and hillbilly music that rested outside the mainstream, as well as the pop of easy listening stylists like Dean Martin and Frank Sinatra, Presley already had quite a musical vocabulary to draw from. As he went into an up-tempo version of "That's All Right," Scotty and Bill joined in. The improvisation caught the attention of Sam Phillips, and he asked the three to start over so he could record it. It was recorded on one track, with only the three of them and no drummer present. The backup music maintained an up-tempo rhythm as it supported Presley's soaring vocals. Even when compared to the brilliant purity of Arthur Crudup's original recording, it is easy to understand how Elvis built on the composition and added his own unique perspective. Along with the rich diversity of music his mind was able to fuse, Presley's singing conveyed all of the emotional anxieties and feelings of social isolation the man himself had. Growing up in extreme poverty as an only child whose twin brother was stillborn, Elvis came from a sheltered dirt-poor background with a father who did jail time and a doting mother. His talent and vision were purely innate.

According to most accounts, this recording is the very first rock and roll record. Upon completing it Bill Black was said to have stated, "Get that on the radio and they'll run us out of town." Sam Phillips understood the restlessness of the lower working class in postwar America, those who were not benefiting from the prosperity of the era. The intelligence of bop jazz and the raw power of country and blues were overshadowed by the well-marketed mainstream success of pop balladeers that, for the most part, were only significant as to their sameness.

Disc jockey Dewey Phillips (no relation to Sam) had a show on Memphis radio that specialized in playing race music. Sam Phillips delivered to Dewey a recording of "That's All Right" (the flipside was an up-tempo version of Bill Monroe's "Blue Moon of Kentucky," which Elvis, Scotty, and Bill recorded at Sun the very next night). Dewey Phillips played the song, resulting in over 40 calls to the radio station asking about the singer and where to obtain the record. Elvis, who was said to be at the theater seeing the movie *High Noon*, was brought to the radio station for a live impromptu interview before Dewey Phillips's program ended. It was during the interview, when Elvis told which high school he had attended in the segregated city, that listeners realized he was white. Elvis would soon sign an exclusive recording contract with Sam Phillips and Sun Records.

During 1954 and 1955 Elvis Presley, backed by Scotty Moore and Bill Black, released several Sun records. Sam Phillips was always careful to spotlight Presley's abilities in both R&B and country, while Elvis continued to develop a sound he'd created from the basic compositions he'd been provided. His second release was what would be the definitive version of Roy Brown's 1947 R&B shouter "Good Rockin' Tonight," even surpassing Wynonie Harris's more raucous version, which had been released in 1949. Phillips backed this record with the rollicking version of a traditional country song, "I Don't Care if the Sun Don't Shine." Presley's third Sun record, a rocking interpretation of Junior Walker's 1953 record "Mystery Train," also had a more traditional country song as its B side, the Charlie Feathers–Stan Kesler composition "I Forgot to Remember to Forget."

Creating a regional sensation with radio play and live performances throughout the area, Presley caught the attention of Colonel Tom Parker, who recognized that Elvis had a unique and distinctive sound and realized its impact on listeners. Parker had been in the talent management business since 1938, with Gene Austin, Eddy Arnold, and Hank Snow numbering among his clients. Scotty Moore was initially managing the gigs, after which disc jockey Bob Neal arranged with Sam Phillips to take over as Presley's manager. Neal found the massive success of his new client to be difficult to maintain, and allowed Colonel Parker to help control some of the bookings. Parker became more and more involved throughout 1955, realizing that Presley's talent required signing to a major label in order to achieve more than the regional success he was currently enjoying.

Sam Phillips also realized that his record label was too small an operation for a performer of Presley's talent, but refused to let Elvis out of his contract for less than $40,000 (at that time an unprecedented amount for such a deal). Parker shopped around various record labels, and although some became interested due to Presley's regional impact, all of them balked at the $40,000 signing fee. RCA Victor producer Steve Shoals realized that Presley's style could generate the same success at the national level as it had regionally. Bill Haley and the Comets' song "Rock Around the Clock," combining country swing with an R&B style, had become a sensation when used over the end credits of the movie *Blackboard Jungle* in March 1955, and the song became the first rock and roll record[1] to enter the Billboard charts that July. Since Presley's Sun records were earthier and had greater substance than the Haley record, Shoals understood that his superior ability would build on the initial distraction caused by "Rock Around the Clock." RCA obtained Elvis Presley's contract from Sun Records in November 1955 for the $40,000 required by Sam Phillips. Phillips has often been chided for having lost out on the millions Presley's music would later make, but since he soon became one of the original investors in the Holiday Inn motel franchise, the financial outcome turned out to be about the same.

Elvis Presley's first record for RCA Victor, "Heartbreak Hotel," was released on January 27, 1956. No longer limited to regional airplay, "Heartbreak Hotel" was distributed nationwide by a major record label, and quickly became a fixture on the radio. The story behind the song, written by Mae Axton and Thomas Durden, was based on a newspaper article about a young man who jumped to his death from a hotel window, leaving behind a note that stated, "I walk a lonely street." The emotional power of Elvis Presley's vocal, the noisy, angry strumming of Scotty Moore's electric guitar, the backup of Chet Atkins's acoustic, the echo of Bill Black's bass, and Floyd Cramer's quiet, creeping piano combined to produce what has been called the single greatest recording of the twentieth century. George Harrison of the Beatles recalled that hearing the song transformed him from an obedient thirteen-year-old into a guitar-wielding truant who would join John Lennon's group the Quarrymen a year later. Lennon himself stated in a 1975 interview for *The Beatles Anthology*:

> When I first heard "Heartbreak Hotel," I could hardly make out what was being said. It was just the experience of hearing it and having my hair stand on end. We'd never heard American voices singing like that. They always sang like Sinatra and enunciate very well. Suddenly, there's this hillbilly hiccupping on tape echo and all this bluesy stuff going on. And we didn't know what Elvis was singing about. . . . It took us a long time to work what was going on. To us, it just sounded as a noise that was great.

Paul McCartney later owned the stand-up bass that Bill Black plays on the recording, and stated in *The Beatles Anthology*, "It's the perfect example of a singer being in command of a song." Rolling Stones guitarist Keith Richards recalled in his 2010 autobiography, *Life*:

> Good records just get better with age. But the one that really turned me on, like an explosion one night, listening to Radio Luxembourg on my little radio when I was supposed to be in bed and asleep, was "Heartbreak Hotel." That was the stunner. I'd never heard it before, or anything like it. I'd never heard of Elvis before. It was almost as if I'd been waiting for it to happen. When I woke up the next day I was a different guy.

"Heartbreak Hotel" caused Elvis Presley's fame to explode across the nation, being helped by TV appearances that Colonel Parker lined up on popular shows hosted by the Dorsey Brothers, Milton Berle, and Ed Sullivan. "Heartbreak Hotel" topped the Billboard pop chart and country chart, while rising to number five on the R&B chart. It became the biggest selling record of 1956. Its success paved the way for the mainstream success of R&B artists like Chuck Berry, Fats Domino, and Little Richard to racially integrate radio stations throughout the nation.

Much of the song's success stems from the restless culture of postwar youth who instinctively rebelled against the relaxed pace of their parents' lifestyle. After living through the Depression and a world war, adults of the fifties built houses in the suburbs, enjoyed their prosperity, and avoided the sort of cultural tumult that rock and roll music provided. The youth culture had embraced everything from comic books to horror movies to ill-fated youth icon James Dean, who was tragically killed only months before Elvis hit the national charts. Presley was their pop culture savior. They all reacted in much the same manner as John Lennon or Keith Richards have described. At his live performances, young audiences screamed, cried, leaped, and danced in a frenzy that confused and appalled their elders.

Dave Marsh stated in his 1982 book, *Elvis:*

> Hardly a single critic had any idea of the musical base from which Elvis was working. What the uproar really revealed was the vast American ignorance of its own culture. No critic pointed out the importance of Elvis' synthesis and fusion of various American popular music styles, because it was considered inconceivable that such purely American products could be worthwhile. The notion that Elvis was in fact that most vital cultural phenomenon of the post-war era would have been greeted with laughter and derision.

Elvis onstage

By March 1956, Bob Neal's contract with Elvis had expired, so Colonel Parker became the exclusive manager. Parker signed a deal with a merchandiser to make Elvis Presley a brand name. The resulting charm bracelets, guitars, and record players that bore the Elvis Presley name resulted in earnings of $22 million by the end of 1956. Meanwhile Elvis continued recording. His first album, the self-titled *Elvis Presley* containing some of the unreleased Sun material acquired by RCA in the contract buyout, as well as some newly recorded tracks, is a brilliant example of Presley's diversity. The timeless rock of "Blue Suede Shoes," the upbeat blues of "I Got a Woman," the haunting ballad "Blue Moon," and the passionate yearning of "Trying to Get to You" caused *Elvis Presley* to be the first rock and roll album to top the Billboard charts.

Elvis topped the charts again with the beautiful ballad "I Want You, I Need You, I Love You," but when he released the double-sided hit "Hound Dog" backed by "Don't Be Cruel," rock and roll music had reached its pinnacle. Nobody has topped the pure power and excellence of this two-sided recording in the subsequent history of rock music, and few have matched it. "Hound Dog," written by Jerry Leiber and Mike Stoller, had originally been a hard-driving R&B number recorded by Willie Mae Thornton. Presley reinvented it completely and defined it as the ultimate rock and roll song that was accusatory, demanding, and triumphant. Its flipside, "Don't Be Cruel," was written by Otis Blackwell, an R&B artist Presley greatly admired. Blackwell would go on to write or cowrite many Elvis Presley songs, including such classics as "All Shook Up" and "Return to Sender." Although Steve Shoals is listed as producer, Elvis is said to have been the one who arranged the music, ran the sessions, and chose the best take (out of nearly 30 for "Don't Be Cruel" and over 30 for "Hound Dog"). The single "Hound Dog" with "Don't Be Cruel" remained at the top of the charts for 11 weeks, a record that remained unbroken until the 1990s.

Elvis Presley's tremendous impact on international pop culture exploded onto the scene and rose very quickly, and the controversy increased among the older generation. Critics throughout the nation were immediately against Presley and against rock and roll. To those who had no understanding of the heritage of country or blues music, rock and roll was merely a lot of noise, and Elvis's gyrations were the actions of a dangerous deviant. Jack Gould of the *New York Times* wrote:

> Mr. Presley has no discernible singing ability. . . . His phrasing, if it can be called that, consists of the stereotyped variations that go with a beginner's aria in a bathtub. . . . His one specialty is an accented movement of the body . . . primarily identified with the repertoire of the blond bombshells of the burlesque runway.

Ben Gross of the *New York Daily News* opined that popular music

> has reached its lowest depths in the "grunt and groan" antics of one Elvis Presley. . . . Elvis, who rotates his pelvis . . . gave an exhibition that was suggestive and vulgar, tinged with the kind of animalism that should be confined to dives and bordellos.

Singer Frank Sinatra stated in *Western World* magazine, "His kind of music is deplorable, a rancid smelling aphrodisiac. It fosters almost totally negative and destructive reactions in young people."

None of this controversy mattered to his record sales; in fact, it may have helped increase them. In a television interview with Hy Gardner on *Hy Gardner Calling*, Elvis stated he had no plans to change his style because "I don't see how I'm doing anything wrong." He also dismissed the pejorative Elvis the Pelvis name that the press tagged him with as "the most childish thing I ever heard from an adult."

According to Dave Marsh in his book, *Elvis*:

> It was Elvis' performance of "Hound Dog" the second time he appeared on *The Milton Berle Show* that created outrage in the papers and pulpits across the land. "Hound Dog" itself, although written as an exercise in black vernacular by a pair of hustling white leftists from Hollywood, Jerry Leiber and Mike Stoller, was greeted as the worst kind of hillbilly barbarism. That is, "You ain't nothin' but a hound dog. Cryin' all the time" was regarded as culturally retarded by a nation that only months before found "How much is that doggie in the window. The one with the waggily tail" perfectly acceptable.

Elvis Presley's superstardom was such that he began being courted for movie appearances. Not content with merely doing a song spot in a film, Elvis genuinely wanted to be an actor. Colonel Parker saw it as an opportunity to use the movies to promote his latest songs, so he investigated the possibilities, finally landing at the Paramount Pictures studio. After several screen tests for producer Hal Wallis, who had been behind such productions as *The Maltese Falcon* (1941) and *Casablanca* (1942), it was up to the studio heads to decide how to best utilize Elvis Presley's talents for movies. He was considered for a role in the Katherine Hepburn–Burt Lancaster starrer *The Rainmaker*, and there was even some brief talk of pairing him with comedian Jerry Lewis, who had just split from his partner Dean Martin.[2] Finally, the decision was made to loan Elvis out to 20th Century Fox for a supporting role in the western *The Reno Brothers*.

Filming began in August while Elvis continued recording. His second album, entitled simply *Elvis*, was every bit as good as his first. Unlike *Elvis Presley*, this second album contained all newly recorded material for RCA, with no Sun recordings. Some were recorded at the initial January sessions, while others were done in September while he was filming *The Reno Brothers*. The album was another exhilarating mixture of different styles, from the hard-rocking "Rip It Up" and "Ready Teddy" to the emotionally stirring ballads "Love Me" and "Old Shep," continuing Presley's triumphant assault on the music industry. By the end of 1956, the pop charts were filled with the sort of rock, country, and R&B styles the mainstream had ignored.

With the 1956 release of Elvis Presley's latest hit, "Love Me Tender," a song recorded for *The Reno Brothers*, the movie's title was also changed to *Love Me Tender* in order to capitalize on the single's runaway success. The song featured Elvis Presley's beautiful vocal performance backed by a guitar and warm backup harmonies. When it quickly soared to the top of the charts, the song succeeded "Hound Dog" and "Don't Be Cruel" and remained at number one for five weeks. This set another record in that it allowed Elvis to achieve the longest stay at number one for a single artist—for a total of 16 weeks. First "Hound Dog" / "Don't Be Cruel" rested at the number one position, and then "Love Me Tender" remained on top. This accomplishment would not be surpassed until 2004.

The movie *Love Me Tender* was released to theaters in November 1956. Having completely overtaken the music industry as well as becoming a sensation for his television appearances, Elvis Presley set out to conquer motion pictures.

CHAPTER 2

Love Me Tender

(20TH CENTURY FOX, 1956)

Director: Robert D. Webb
Screenplay: Robert Buckner
Producer: David Weisbart
Art directors: Lyle R. Wheeler and Maurice Ransford
Music: Lionel Newman
Vocal supervision: Ken Darby
Orchestration: Edward B. Powell
Technical advisor: Colonel Tom Parker
Cast: Richard Egan, Debra Paget, Elvis Presley, Robert Middleton, William Campbell, Neville Brand, Mildred Dunnock, Bruce Bennett, James Drury, Russ Conway, Robert Adler, Barry Coe, Ken Clark, Paul E. Burns, Heinie Conklin, Joe Di Reda,[1] L. Q. Jones, Frank Mills, Dick Sargent, Steve Darrell, Tom Greenway, Dorothy Hack, Jay Jostyn, Frank Griffin, Jack Kenny, Edward Mundy, Jerry Sheldon, James Stone, Jack Tornek, Bob Rose
Songs:[2]
   "Love Me Tender" (adapted by the 1861 song "Aura Lee"; music by George Poulton and new lyrics by Ken Darby; performed by Elvis Presley)
   "Let Me" (composed by Ken Darby; performed by Elvis Presley)
   "Poor Boy" (composed by Ken Darby; performed by Elvis Presley)
   "We're Gonna Move" (composed by Ken Darby; performed by Elvis Presley)

"Love Me Tender" spent five weeks at number one in 1956
"Poor Boy" reached number 24 on the Billboard charts
Love Me Tender soundtrack album peaked at number one in October 1956

Released November 15, 1956
89 minutes
Black and white
Aspect ratio: 2.35:1; sound mixed in 4-track stereo
Budget estimate: $1,250,000 (of which Elvis received $100,000); box office gross: $4.5 million
Released on DVD by 20th Century Fox

Little has been said about Elvis Presley's movies, even in the more detailed studies of his career. It is significant that in his film debut Elvis is given an actual movie role that makes no attempt to trade off of his growing image in music. It is also noteworthy that Elvis is billed third—he does not star in the movie. Finally, throughout the course of *Love Me Tender* Elvis is called on to register a gamut of emotions, playing a character with great vulnerability who is susceptible to making the wrong decisions, and, somewhat surprisingly, he is shot dead at the film's conclusion.³

Love Me Tender is certainly not in the upper class of westerns like *High Noon* (1952), *The Searchers* (1956), and *Rio Bravo* (1959). It is also not a bad movie. It is simply an average western, the type of which was quite popular during the 1950s, and, due to his massive and continually expanding popularity, Elvis Presley is given a supporting role in the film. The music (only four songs) is incidental, not organic to the plot.

The basic western plot deals with three Confederate brothers, thought dead, who return home at the end of the Civil War after stealing a Union payroll. The robbery occurred during the war as part of the war effort, but once the battle has ended, the brothers decide to split the money.

Poster for *Love Me Tender*

There are two different dynamics that the film's narrative attempts to follow, both dealing with the oldest brother, Vance, played by Richard Egan. Vance begins to feel some level of remorse for the robbery now that the war is over, and plans to return the money. He has the support of his brothers, but not others who were in on the robbery. The second dynamic deals with a conflict between Vance and his hero-worshipping younger brother Clint, played by Elvis Presley. When Vance was reported dead, Clint married Vance's fiancée, Cathy (Debra Paget).

Elvis Presley's supporting role was in a decidedly tangential portion of the film's narrative, while the main part of the story dealt with the robbery and Vance's attempt to gather and return the money. However, we are continually reminded of this plot point not only because it involves Elvis (who, despite his supporting role, remains the most distracting member of the cast). Egan exhibits tension, Paget displays confusion, while Elvis is so completely trusting, he remains naively ignorant.

Presley's performance is energetic and committed but his enthusiasm causes him to overact in nearly every scene. Along with Egan and Paget, Elvis is surrounded by actors who have experience in western films, including James Drury, who would later become famous on TV's *The Virginian*, and Neville Brand, who would go on to star on television in *Laredo*. When compared to their measured performances, Presley's high-pitched shouting for every line tends to stand out. Elvis is sometimes called on to convey a level of performance that could be a bit challenging to a newcomer. He must convey Clint's initial hero worship slowly evolving into a suppressed suspicion that the romance between Vance and Cathy is not over. When one of the bandits with whom his brothers robbed the Union payroll starts feeding Clint more reasons to doubt his brother and Cathy's honesty, Elvis must silently display a smoldering anger and feelings of vengeance. When he confronts Cathy and violently shakes her, his character is exhibiting behaviors that may have been startling to his fan base. By all accounts, Elvis was very friendly and compliant on the set of his first film, and even had romantic feelings for Paget. His ability to convey Clint's sense of betrayed rage in so believable a manner is quite impressive. Finally, filming a death scene—often challenging even to a seasoned actor—and pulling it off as effectively as he does, is even more remarkable.

Newspaper columnists chortled with delight at the prospect of Elvis, whom they perceived as a noisy diva, being placed among veteran actors in a Hollywood movie and realizing that all of the performers on the film had the experience to steal every scene from the newcomer. But Elvis was the polar opposite of the diva he'd been labeled by the press. He confided in Richard Egan that he was "plenty scared" about acting in his first feature. Egan was a former acting teacher, and took Elvis under his wing. The other actors were equally benevolent, and found him friendly and cooperative throughout the filming, as did the director. Along with developing a bit of a crush on Debra Paget, Elvis also gushed over producer David Weisbart, who produced one of Presley's favorite movies, *Rebel without a Cause* with James Dean, the previous year.

The music in *Love Me Tender,* composed by Ken Darby, manages to pretty neatly balance between its Civil War setting and the rock and roll persona Presley had quickly developed. The title song not only reminded everyone that he was a brilliant ballad singer, it had authentic roots in that it was based on "Aura Lee," a Civil War–era ballad. The other songs, "Let Me," "We're Gonna Move," and "Poor Boy" have a solid country base and depict Elvis at his hip-swiveling, leg-shaking best. While overacting during the dramatic scenes, Presley's comfort level during the song sequences is certainly palpable.

Supporting actor William Campbell recalled for Tom Weaver in *Classic Images*:

> We were invited to go down and have a sandwich and a soft drink, a highball if we wanted it. I got myself a sandwich and a soft drink, and I was standing there chatting with Richard Egan and Jim Drury. All of a sudden I got a tap on the shoulder, and when I turned around, it was Elvis. He said, "You did one of the pictures that I love." I asked, "What is that?" He said, "I've seen it 18 times: *Man Without a Star*," which was a [1955] picture I did with Kirk Douglas. He continued, "Listen, could I talk to you a minute?" So I excused myself and I walked with him, and he said, "Bill, could you do me a big favor? This is my first picture. I don't know a damn thing about acting. Now, if you see me doin' anything that's wrong, would you just inform me and help me out a little bit?" I thought he was really putting me on. I said, "Elvis, let me tell you something. They are going to shoot you from your toes to your head, inside, outside, back, front, sideways, at an angle, closeups—they're gonna do whatever it takes to make you a movie star. So you're not gonna have to worry about anything."
>
> "No, that isn't what I mean," he said. "I wanna do a good job."
>
> And I could see that there was some sincerity there. So I said, "Look, Elvis, if I saw that there was something blatant, of course I would let you know, if you won't be offended by it." As it turned out, we had a lot of that on the picture [Elvis doing things blatantly wrong]. He had a hell of a time, as many actors do if they've not been trained at all (and he had not), figuring out what to do with his hands. I used to go to him and say, "What you're doing is, you're doing your lines standing like a soldier. That gets a little tiresome. So do something with your hands—put 'em in your pockets but don't move them too much. People'll think you're playing with yourself and you don't want to get into that!" I told him, "There are lots of

things you can do with your hands and be a little expressive with 'em." Then he would think about it, and he would do it.

Love Me Tender was a diverting, enjoyable western drama with good performances by a cast of veterans. And despite his enthusiastic overacting, Elvis Presley displayed genuine potential that would be honed as he made more serious films. Elvis realized he was "green as a gourd" as far as acting was concerned, but believed he learned a lot from the patience of his director and the benevolence of his costars. Elvis even considered attending acting school to better hone his craft, but his recording and touring schedule did not allow for such a diversion. Even during the filming of *Love Me Tender*, Elvis was recording new songs, appearing on television, and giving live concerts.

One has to marvel at the twenty-three-year-old performer's energy, especially since, in his enthusiasm, he had also memorized the entire script of *Love Me Tender*, including everyone else's lines.

William Campbell further recalled:

> I've been gifted in that I've met great people. Having Spencer Tracy get me under contract, working with Humphrey Bogart, William Holden, Edward G. Robinson, I could go on and on, name dozens of people I've had the opportunity to work with over the course of my career. And no one that I can think of was any greater than Elvis.

A few weeks prior to the film's release, reports out of Hollywood were indicating that Elvis had potential as an actor, and could develop some genuine skills given the innate ability he exhibited in his film debut. On November 16, 1956, *Love Me Tender* premiered at the Paramount Theater in New York City. Press photos showed massive crowds lining up to see the movie as early as seven o'clock in the morning. A 40-foot-tall Elvis cutout towered over the marquee. *Love Me Tender* opened nationally during Thanksgiving weekend, on November 21, 1956.

Reviews of the film were mixed, most agreeing it was a rather pedestrian western drama and its success was due to Elvis Presley's tremendous popularity. Most critics begrudgingly admitted to Presley's raw talent as an actor, but others took a perverse delight in issuing cheap shots, mostly due to their inability to comprehend the cultural revolution that Elvis was ushering in.

The *New Yorker* stated:

> It is my relentless duty to report that Elvis Presley is now on view in a movie called *Love Me Tender*. Thick lipped, droopy-eyed, and indefatigably sullen, Mr. Presley, whose talents are meager but whose earnings are gross, excites a large part of the young female population as nobody has ever done.

14 CHAPTER 2

The opening for *Love Me Tender*

Films in Review opined: "How a society as dynamic as ours throws up such a monstrosity is beyond the scope of this review."

In order to keep up with the number of theaters wanting to show *Love Me Tender*, 20th Century Fox's print order for the feature was a staggering 500 prints (200 was roughly the average for a film of this sort).

The studio was initially concerned with the $100,000 flat fee it gave Elvis for his supporting role, and the $1 million budget that was quite high by 1956 standards, especially for an average western. The entire million was earned back during the film's opening weekend (movie admission prices were roughly 35 to 40 cents in 1956). Despite being little more than a standard western, *Love Me Tender* was one of the top box office hits of its year, due almost completely to Elvis Presley's presence in the cast.

A Minnesota theater owner reported this to *Box Office* magazine:

> Our east seating wing was filled to capacity with students at the Sunday night show of *Love Me Tender* and the adults, not to be outdone,

came out in good numbers. This was a happy ending to a long day's work. The student boys showed their jealousy at times during the picture, and one must have carried it too far because when the show was over he had to use some mighty "friendly persuasion" to convince his girl friend to come home with him. Earlier, after the matinee when I was ready to lock up, I heard somebody crying in the auditorium. Went in and there were ten student girls crying out loud. After about ten minutes they left. I didn't have a tissue left in the house. Then they were back for the night show. So let us take heed. Next time, keep Elvis alive!

The success of *Love Me Tender* proved to Presley's home studio of Paramount that he could handily sustain a leading role. Based on the box office success of this film debut, Colonel Parker began negotiating with producer Hal Wallis for a larger salary and a cut of the profits for Presley's next movie.

Approximately a week after the release of *Love Me Tender,* Elvis was back home in Memphis and stopped by Sun Studio to say hello. In a truly momentous occasion, Sun recording artists Johnny Cash, Jerry Lee Lewis, and Carl Perkins all happened to be there at the same time. The four men began to improvise a few songs and the session was recorded. It remained in Sam Phillips's vault until 1977 when it was released on record as *The Million Dollar Quartet.*

By the end of 1956, Elvis was reported to have the most songs in the Billboard Top 100 since the chart began. It had been a whirlwind year of hard work, recording, touring, doing TV appearances, and making his first movie, and his popularity continued to soar to astronomical heights. In October, Elvis received his draft status announcement from the U.S. military. On January 4, 1957, he reported to Kennedy Veteran's Hospital for his pre-induction physical, which he passed. After receiving his draft number, Elvis prepared to start work on his next movie, *Loving You*, with principal photography beginning on January 21, 1957.

CHAPTER 3
Loving You
(PARAMOUNT, 1957)

Director: Hal Kanter
Screenplay: Hal Kanter and Herbert Baker, from a story by Mary Agnes Thompson
Producer: Hal B. Wallis
Cinematographer: Charles Lang, Jr.
Editor: Howard A. Smith
Assistant directors: James A. Rosenberger and Charles C. Coleman
Costumes: Edith Head
Music conductor: Walter Scharf
Vocal accompaniment: The Jordanaires
Makeup: Wally Westmore
Hairstyle supervisor: Nellie Manley
Technical advisor: Colonel Tom Parker
Cast: Elvis Presley, Lizabeth Scott, Wendell Corey, Dolores Hart, James Gleason, Ralph Dumke, Paul Smith, Ken Becker, Jana Lund, Skip Young, Madge Blake, Timothy Butler, Irene Tedrow, Almira Sessions, Julius Tannen, Scotty Moore, Bill Black, D. J. Fontana, Vernon Presley, Gladys Presley, Heather Ames, Joan Bradshaw, Kathie Anderson, Yvonne Federson, Les Clark, Harry Cheshire, Melinda Byron, Drew Cahill, Eane DuPont, Sue England, Sydney Chatton, Gwen Caldwell, Beach Dickerson, Myrna Fahey, Hal K. Dawson, David Cameron, Florine Carlan, Leo Castillo, Mike Mahoney, Audrey Lowell, Jack Latham, Kenner G. Kemp, Jerry Hunter, James Horan, Helene Hatch, Donna Jo Gribble, Joe Gray, Michael Hodge, Grace Hayle, Hugh Jarrett, Nancy Kilgas, Brenda Lomas, Gail Lund, Carla Merey, Steve Pendelton, Vernon Rich, Dick Ryan, Jeffrey Sayre, Karen Scott, Joy Reynolds, Linda Rivera, Cecile Rogers, Joy Stoner, Steffi Sidney, Trude and Maida Severn, William H. O'Brien, Jeanette Taylor, Buck Young, Dave White, Heather Tuscany, Gary Troy
Songs (in the order performed in the film):
"Got a Lot o' Livin' to Do" (written by Aaron Schröder [as Aaron Schroeder] and Ben Weisman; performed by Elvis Presley)

> "(Let's Have a) Party" (written by Jessie Mae Robinson; performed by Elvis Presley)
> "(Let Me Be Your) Teddy Bear" (written by Kal Mann and Bernie Lowe; performed by Elvis Presley)
> "Hot Dog" (written by Jerry Leiber and Mike Stoller; performed by Elvis Presley)
> "Lonesome Cowboy" (written by Sid Tepper and Roy C. Bennett; performed by Elvis Presley)
> "Mean Woman Blues" (written by Claude Demetri; performed by Elvis Presley)
> "Loving You" (written by Jerry Leiber and Mike Stoller; performed by Elvis Presley)
>
> *Loving You* soundtrack album spent ten weeks at number one in 1957
> "(Let Me Be Your) Teddy Bear" spent seven weeks at number one
> "Loving You" reached number 20 on the charts
>
> Released July 9, 1957
> Filmed January 21–March 8, 1957
> 101 minutes
> Technicolor
> Aspect ratio: 1.85:1
> U.S. gross: $3.7 million
> Released on DVD by Paramount Home Video

It is quite impressive how much Elvis Presley's natural acting ability had been honed in the months between the conclusion of filming on *Love Me Tender* and the outset of shooting *Loving You*. Where he had been prone to jittery overacting in his first movie, Elvis now appeared relaxed, confident, and at one with his role as an orphaned drifter whose singing and ability to captivate a crowd gets him involved with a traveling country band. Unlike the four country-oriented songs offered in *Love Me Tender,* there several solid rockers and ballads in *Loving You*. Elvis dyed his blondish-brown hair jet black for this role, believing it gave him a more dramatic appearance in the manner of favorite actors Rudolph Valentino and Tony Curtis. He would continue to dye his hair this color for the remainder of his career.

Loving You has been called semiautobiographical, due to some very general similarities to the Presley story. It appears that producer Hal Wallis was interested in trading on the public image Presley already had. His talent as a singer, his animal magnetism, the cool defiance, and the well-bred politeness are all part of the complex Deke Rivers character he plays in the movie. Once again seeming most at ease during the musical sequences, Presley also rises to the occasion during an emotionally stirring scene when he candidly reveals his true identity to a friend and mentor. Where critics were primed to attack and to seek out any

18 CHAPTER 3

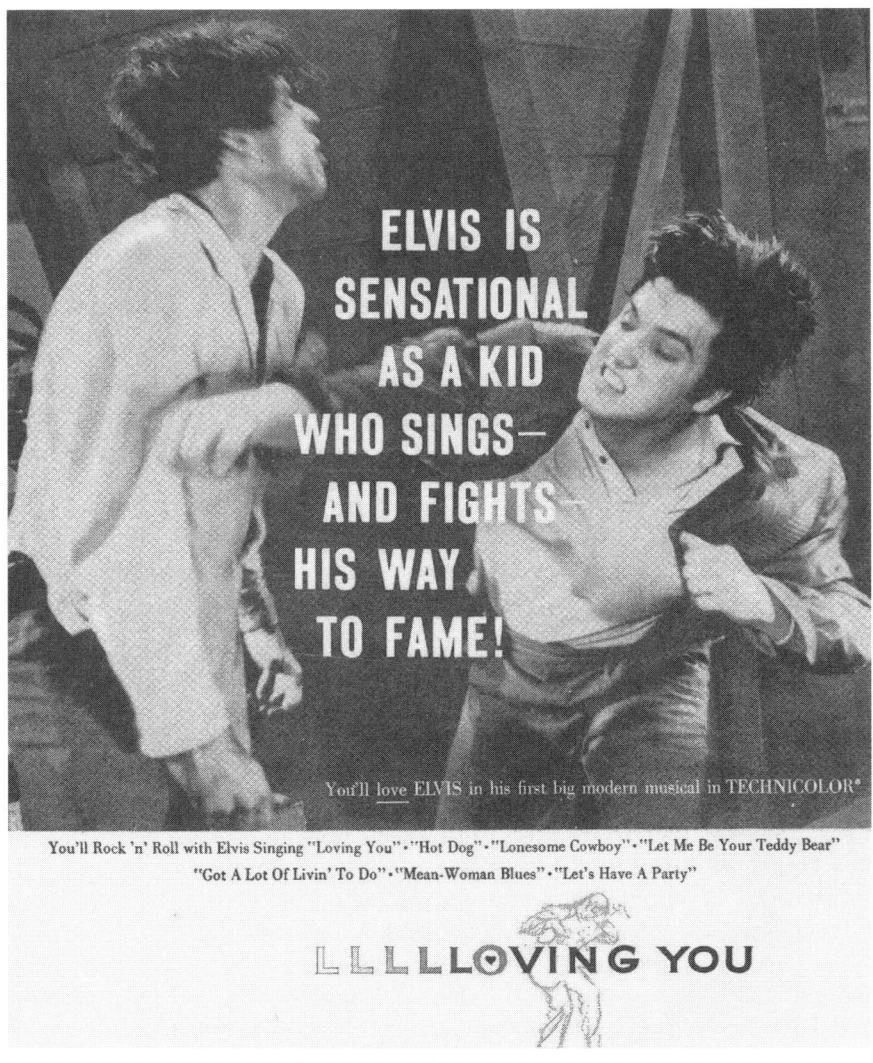

Press kit ad for *Loving You*

acting imperfections in *Love Me Tender*, they were forced by *Loving You* to admit that Elvis Presley's talents were already evident by his second movie.

Deke Rivers is a delivery man who happens upon an outdoor concert where a country band is playing, He and his comical partner start dancing to the music and are noticed by Glenda (Lizabeth Scott), the agent who handles the band. She asks if either can sing, and Deke is recruited by his friend and goaded by the agent into stepping up onstage.

Prior to this scene, the opening footage establishes the band as toiling with little success in small-town venues and the group's leader, Walter (Wendell Corey), is chagrined at having to play country music and wear attire appropriate to this music. Apparently he is a talented musician and feels limited by both the music and his having to foster a "hick" status and the nickname of Tex in order to maintain a country facade.

Loving You quickly puts the spotlight on Elvis when he finally allows himself to be talked into going onstage. The band gives him a generic boogie-woogie beat as he jumps into the rocking "Got a Lot o' Livin' to Do." Director Hal Kanter's showcasing of this scene is interesting. He cuts from a medium shot of Elvis onstage, full body, shaking to the music and strumming a borrowed guitar. His actual backup band—Scotty Moore, Bill Black, and D. J. Fontana—are part of the setup, framing him as they would during live performances. Kanter cuts to the crowd, and back to the band, with the same rhythm as the song, but holds his shots of the audience just long enough to register their reaction. The younger ones are swaying and clapping. The older ones look confused and dismayed.

One of the more intriguing cutaways during this nicely edited sequence is Kanter's choice to occasionally shoot Elvis singing in close-up. This reminds one of the Ed Sullivan appearance where Sullivan, feeling the singer's gyrations were too suggestive for a family show, insisted he be shown only from the waist up.[1] Even one reviewer would later compliment Kanter's choice in doing this, stating in *Box Office*, "The film judiciously cuts periodically to close-ups of [Presley's] face to avoid further blatant bad taste on the giant-sized screen."

This difference in the reactions of young and old is pointed out in the movie as well. When the song concludes, Tex, who is not impressed, says to Glenda, "If he sang one more song they'd be throwing things at him." "Yes," replies an impressed Glenda, "their door keys!" While Deke is clearly disgruntled at having to perform on the spot, his performance was strong and he seemed at ease in the position. He is offered a spot with the band, where he would tour with them and step up from the audience for one number. The rocking Elvis style creates a real dichotomy when placed within the lighter country fare being otherwise presented by the band, and it causes increased success. Soon, Deke is promoted to a regular member of the group who sings several songs, and finally is elevated to the position of costar, sharing the billing with Tex.

Enhancing this narrative basis is the dynamic between Tex and Glenda and the one between Deke and Susan (Dolores Hart), a sweet vocalist. Glenda is attracted to Deke, which is reciprocated. Deke also is attracted to Susan, which is also reciprocated. While Deke is torn between the mature, accomplished woman and the sweet younger one, Tex (Walter) is always relaxed, understanding, and never exhibits any jealousy. Even when Glenda arranges top-level bookings based on elevating Deke to Tex's level of billing, the advancement is accepted. In

20 CHAPTER 3

Elvis Presley, Lizabeth Scott, Wendell Corey, and Dolores Hart

fact, Tex even becomes angry with Glenda when he believes she is merely using Deke, leading him on, in order to advance the group's success.

While the drama is fairly standard, it is well played by old pros, and Presley's improved acting helps with his central role. In a 1992 interview with this writer, Lizabeth Scott recalled Elvis as very shy on the set, eager to please, friendly, and charming: "Everybody liked him, even those who were skeptical about working in his first starring movie."

Director Hal Kanter recalled in his 1998 autobiography, *So Far, So Funny*:

> Wendell Corey's children were more excited about Elvis than any of the actors Wendell had already starred with. Shooting the film was a joy. Alice Corey, Wendell's wife, confessed to me that it was the first time in years the actor looked forward to coming to work. And Elvis was such an attraction, it was the first time Alice visited Wendell while he was working. And the first time my own wife came with friends, after she had brought our girls to meet Elvis.

Loving You concentrates on the musical performances that are strewn about the movie and that is when the most impressive cinematic aspects are displayed. Along with the rocking performances Elvis gives to "Let's Have a Party" and "Teddy Bear," the stillness he projects as he sings the ballads "Lonesome Cowboy" and "Loving You" are equally impressive. This being a Technicolor production, Kanter's use of color and lighting in the "Lonesome Cowboy" performance makes it one of the most striking scenes in the film. The scene opens with Elvis, under a spotlight in a long shot, surrounding by pure darkness. As the song progresses, the camera moves closer. After a cutaway from a backstage vantage point, the film cuts to a close-up of Elvis continuing with the ballad. Kanter's framing of this sequence, his choice of shots and edits, matches the starkness of the song perfectly.

Perhaps the best scene in *Loving You* features Elvis being accosted by a town bully in a diner: "My girlfriend wants to hear you sing!" His friend and fellow bandmate Skeeter (Paul Smith, who often played comic sidekicks) tries to come to his defense, but Deke saves Skeeter from the much bigger man and agrees to do one number. Presley's performance of "Mean Woman Blues" is exhilarating and the diner setting frames the action perfectly. Kanter builds the momentum of the scene by having younger people from different parts of the diner coming nearer to hear Elvis sing. Elvis had begun singing near the jukebox (which is accompanying him, justifying the background instruments more so than the typical Hollywood musical), but once the crowd builds, his performance extends to dancing up and down the aisle, framed by diners on either side. The sea of bodies extends several rows by the end of the song, each one moving to the rhythm. Elvis is in the foreground, the center of attention at all times. Again the use of Technicolor is impressive, as the color blue is decidedly predominant among the outfits of the spectators, bringing out Elvis's red jacket and grey pants.

When the song concludes and the bullying continues, Elvis engages in the first of many fight scenes he will have in his movies. His Deke Rivers character has already been established as an orphaned drifter, so naturally Deke is presented as fully capable of defending himself. However, rather than have him handily put the bully away, the fight is staged as being more even. Deke has a pretty tough time with the larger man before finally defeating him.

The most emotionally stirring scene, and perhaps the most challenging for the rookie actor, is when Deke takes Glenda to a cemetery and shows her the tombstone of a Deke Rivers which reads, "He was alone, except for his friends." Deke then reveals his name is actually Jimmy Tompkins and that he ran away from home as a child and ended up in this graveyard, taking the Rivers name. While just an added element to the character's backstory, the scene in which this information is conveyed calls on Presley to conjure up a higher level of emotion, and he tempers it nicely. None of the overacting that permeated his performance in *Love Me Tender* is evident here.

Hal Kanter recalled in his autobiography *So Far, So Funny*:

> Gaining entrance to our set was not easy because I wanted to give Elvis enough privacy to work without distractions. But I soon learned he was a fast study, had a photographic memory and enjoyed meeting his fans. Even before I relaxed my rules about a closed set, studio executives, major exhibitors and other producers used their clout to keep us over-supplied with visitors. Elvis willingly posed for photographs, shook hundreds of hands, and kissed dozens of little girls and old ladies, but when he was called for the camera, he was on his mark and ready for "Action!"

Due to the success of *Love Me Tender*, Colonel Parker was able to cut a good deal for Presley's second movie. Being offered a $150,000 up-front payment and 50 percent of the profits, Parker insisted on $250,000 up front with the same profit margin. Since *Loving You* was an even bigger box office hit than *Love Me Tender*, Presley's fortune grew considerably from this deal.

Loving You is a good musical drama, much more serious in tone and nicely mounted than Presley's future musicals would be. The songs here are far more authentic to the singer's established style than those in *Love Me Tender*, since in the former film they had to seem at least somewhat appropriate to the era being depicted. The similarities to Elvis Presley's actual story include the character being a delivery man who became a singer (Elvis had a job driving a truck when he first started to visit Sun Studio), his rapid rise to prominence from smaller towns to bigger cities, and the range of reactions from listeners. The fight scene highlight also rings true; Elvis frequently had to defend himself in real life from jealous men who wanted to take a poke at the singer and prove something to their girlfriends. Two noted real-life incidents include a fight with a gas station attendant who accosted Elvis as he was signing autographs for gathering fans, and a jealous husband who challenged the singer because his wife kept Presley's photograph in her purse.

Other areas of this film's authenticity have been challenged, however. Dave Marsh pointed out in his book *Elvis* that Wendell Corey's character playing a saxophone is inauthentic, as "horns are totally inappropriate to the type of country and western music he is playing." This is indeed true, but since it was established that Corey is a bandleader who has worked in larger mainstream clubs and is relegated to country music because that was the only band he could get together for small Southern venues, it would seem relevant that he would somehow incorporate his "inappropriate" instrument into the music.

Marsh made another point, perhaps unwittingly. Assessments of Elvis Presley's career always seem to view his films as the venue that took him away from the insightful music that had effectively touched off a cultural revolution.

There are those who angrily expect Elvis to have continued in a more creative vein, breaking from his management and trying his luck on freely exploring the depths of his creativity. They want his films to celebrate the purity and substance of the roots music that inspired Elvis to be creative. As Presley stated to an interviewer for *Life* who told him to attend college rather than sign a movie contract: "I expect you've never been poor, have you sir?" Movies were Presley's job, and he worked hard to accomplish what he was assigned, especially early on. He benefited from benevolent fellow actors and directors who offered guidance. Friendly and affable, Elvis was committed to doing his best.

In *So Far, So Funny*, Hal Kanter recalled meeting Elvis before production began, and recognizing his apprehension: "Elvis allowed that he might not be up to the demands of starring in such a big picture as [this one]. I sensed his 'aw shucks' shit-kicker demeanor was no act and assured him he had nothing to fear."

One of the more charming incidents to occur during the filming of *Loving You* was a studio visit from Vernon and Gladys Presley, Elvis's parents, who were staying with him at the Beverly Wilshire (where Elvis was given an entire floor of rooms). One day these homespun Southerners dropped by Paramount Studios and greeted the guard at the gate with "Howdy, can we come in? Our boy works in there." When the bemused guard finally identified who these people were, the Presleys were given top-level treatment, including a tour of the studio and introduction to several Hollywood stars on the lot. Director Hal Kanter found the Presleys to be lovely people, and asked them to sit in the audience during one of the song sequences. While Vernon was delighted to be asked, Gladys had to be coaxed, feeling she would look too fat. Elvis Presley's parents can be spotted in the audience during the sequence when Elvis is singing "(Let Me Be Your) Teddy Bear," with Vernon snapping his fingers to the beat, and Gladys looking on proudly at her boy.[2]

Elvis also gets his first screen kiss in *Loving You*. However, it is not from Dolores Hart, as has been indicated elsewhere. Hart does kiss Elvis, but not before Jana Lund, who plays a fan that accosts him in his dressing room. Hart recalled in an interview: "I knew Elvis when he was shy, and so was I. When it was time for a kissing scene, we were blushing so much they had to apply extra makeup!"

When *Loving You* was released in July 1957 it did capacity business in theaters throughout the nation, from big cities to small towns. Teenagers were its strongest draw, but enough curious adults came out to the nighttime showings and were made to realize that Elvis Presley was a developing actor and the movie was a solid drama with music. Presley's hip swinging and leg shaking continued to concern the more conservative elements of society, while jealous boyfriends still abounded as well. While the review in *Box Office* admitted to the film's value at the box office, it continued to dismiss the entire rock and roll revolution as a passing fad:

> No matter what an exhibitor's personal opinion may be of Elvis Presley, he can't afford to pass this one up. Presley and rock and roll are riding the crest and until both he and the tempo pass into oblivion, it's a safe bet that this picture will make money. A sneak preview audience of all ages responded warmly to the film, but let's face it: the squeals came from the teenagers every time there was a close-up of Presley. The star does a nice acting job and is ably supported. Presley sings nine songs.

Only days after shooting completed on *Loving You* in March 1957, Elvis released the single "All Shook Up," which remains, in the twenty-first century, one of his most enduring songs. At the time, its unbridled lyrics about adolescent sexual passion—where the only cure for trembling and being tongue-tied is to have "that girl" and "a love so fine"—increased the continued negative reaction to Presley's music among most American adults. On an episode of the Groucho Marx TV quiz program *You Bet Your Life*, one of two contestants, a middle-aged man, is a musician who tells Groucho about his work during the segment when the host asks the players about their background. Groucho brings up Elvis and the contestant sarcastically states, "No, I prefer to play music." The other contestant, a young girl, defends Elvis and even sings a few bars of his latest hit, "All Shook Up," accompanied by the house band. There are likely other examples on television shows during this time that show how Presley's music was permeating the culture. A double-sided pair of hits from *Loving You*, the film's title song[3] and "(Let Me Be Your) Teddy Bear," sold 12.5 million copies in one week.

Another of the more noted events in Elvis Presley's life upon completing *Loving You* was his purchase of Graceland, the mansion in which he would live for the rest of his life. The 1957 purchase price was only $100,000. Making more money than he could possibly spend, the extravagant singer had already purchased a custom-made pink Cadillac for his mother, which remained in the family and later was on display at Graceland when the home became a tourist attraction after Presley's death. Throughout his career, Elvis would notoriously buy expensive gifts, sometimes even for strangers.

Although he enjoyed being an actor and wanted to continue to improve in this field, the Hollywood scene was not for Elvis. One of his associates, Marty Lacker, told Alanna Nash in an interview for her book *Elvis Aaron Presley: Revelations from the Memphis Mafia*:

> Elvis didn't like Hollywood. He didn't like the people. He didn't like the phoniness. And he never really changed his opinion. Although he became more polished as the years went on, and more educated in people in general, he was still a country boy at heart with simple tastes. He didn't want to go to parties. He didn't want to go out and be seen. It made him uncomfortable.

In *So Far, So Funny*, Hal Kanter echoed Marty Lacker's statements:

> Even after he became an authentic name-above-the-title movie star, Elvis avoided the social life of show business to hide from his peers under the security blanket provided by his home boys from the Delta country. Somewhere deep within, the King still considered himself a commoner just visiting from Mississippi.

Presley's closest friend in Hollywood appeared to be actor Nick Adams, who had supported both James Dean in *Rebel without a Cause* and Andy Griffith in the bucolic comedy *No Time for Sergeants,* as well as starring on television in *The Rebel* as Johnny Yuma. Lacker told Nash in *Elvis Aaron Presley*:

> [Nick Adams] was really his only actor friend. He liked him a lot. In fact when Nick was more or less blacklisted in Hollywood, Elvis took him on the road as an opening act. He was a great imitator. When Elvis first went out to Hollywood, he was tremendously excited about being an actor. He wanted it more than anything.

At this time Hollywood noticed that Elvis Presley had expanded on his initial potential and showed greater innate ability as an actor. With *Loving You* he proved he could hold his own in the lead role of a dramatic feature, not only owning the song sequences, but commanding his dialog and action scenes as well. And despite the diva reputation that preceded him, the director, the crew, and the other actors found him to be genuine, affable, and hardworking.

Due to his immediate box office success, the prestigious Metro-Goldwyn-Mayer studio beckoned for his services, willing to pay the high loan-out fee to Paramount and Hal Wallis so that Elvis could star in a prison drama penned by screenwriter Guy Trosper. Richard Thorpe, the director lined up, was a Hollywood veteran who had helmed everything from *Tarzan* and *Thin Man* movies to the lavish spectacles *Quo Vadis* (1952) and *The Prisoner of Zenda* (1953). The producer, Pandro S. Berman, had a career dating back to the dawn of talking pictures. He was no stranger to musicals, having produced Fred Astaire–Ginger Rogers movies as well as *Blackboard Jungle* (1955), the first film to use a rock and roll song (during the closing credits). What is more significant about this next film, which was to be called *Jailhouse Rock*, is that its score would be penned by two of Presley's best songwriters—Jerry Leiber and Mike Stoller, who had composed "Hound Dog," "Loving You," and "(Let Me Be Your) Teddy Bear."

When Elvis read the script he was intrigued. His character in *Jailhouse Rock* was an arrogant, often downright mean individual who used people throughout the course of the film before finally learning his lesson at the end. It was nothing like he was in real life, but a lot like the way he was being depicted in many press stories, and how he was perceived in certain parts of the establishment. A recent midwestern tour resulted in prayer meetings and picketing by clergymen and church congregations to keep the hip-swiveling deviant out of their community. Interested in exploring the type of character others had envisioned him, while wanting the challenge of playing a role that was unlike his true nature, Elvis was excited to use what he'd learned on his first two films and make an even greater impact with his third.

CHAPTER 4
Jailhouse Rock
(MGM, 1957)

Director: Richard Thorpe
Screenplay: Guy Trosper, from a story by Ned Young
Cinematography: Robert J. Bronner
Producer: Pandro S. Berman
Editor: Ralph E. Winters
Associate producer: Kathryn Hereford
Assistant directors: Robert E. Relyea and Hank Moonjean
Original music: Jeff Alexander
Art direction: Randall Duell and William A. Horning
Set decoration: Keogh Gleason and Henry Grace
Makeup: William Tuttle
Sound: Dr. Wesley C. Miller
Choreography: Alex Romero and Elvis Presley
Special effects: A. Arnold Gillespie
Stunts: Joe Gray (also Elvis Presley's stand-in) and Loren James
Technical advisor: Colonel Tom Parker
Cast: Elvis Presley, Judy Tyler, Mickey Shaughnessy, Vaughn Taylor, Jennifer Holden, Dean Jones, Anne Neyland, Percy Helton, Peter Adams, Robert Bice, Scotty Moore, Bill Black, D. J. Fontana, Bill Hickman, Joan Dupuis, S. John Launer, Walter Johnson, Harry Hines, Donald Kerr, John Logan, Lamar Fike, Cliff Gleaves, Alyn Lockwood, Tom Mayton, Jack Herrin, Bess Flowers, William Forrest, Jo Gilbert, Elaine Dupont, Francis DeSales, Tracey Morgan, Robin Raymond, Granton Rhodes, Charles Postal, Joe Ploski, Orve Mohler, John Dennis, Frank Mills, John Daheim, Fred Coby, Carl Milletaire, George Cisar, Tom McKee, Jack Chefe, Joe McGuinn, Don Burnett, Bill Hale, Francois Andre, Dorothy Abbott.
Songs (in the order performed in the film):
 "One More Day" (written by Sid Tepper and Roy C. Bennett; performed by Mickey Shaughnessy)
 "Young and Beautiful" (written by Abner Silver and Aaron Schröder; performed by Elvis Presley)

> "I Want to Be Free" (written by Jerry Leiber and Mike Stoller; performed by Elvis Presley)
> "Don't Leave Me Now" (written by Aaron Schröder and Ben Weisman; performed by Elvis Presley)
> "Treat Me Nice" (written by Jerry Leiber and Mike Stoller; performed by Elvis Presley)
> "Jailhouse Rock" (written by Jerry Leiber and Mike Stoller; performed by Elvis Presley)
> "(You're So Square) Baby I Don't Care" (written by Jerry Leiber and Mike Stoller; performed by Elvis Presley)
>
> "Jailhouse Rock" spent seven weeks at number one in October–November 1957
> "Treat Me Nice" peaked at number 18 in November 1957
>
> Released November 8, 1957
> Filmed May 13–June 14, 1957
> 96 minutes
> Black and white
> Aspect ratio: 2.35:1
> Budget: $400,000. Estimated gross: $4 million
> DVD: Deluxe edition and Blu-ray released by Warner Home Video

One of best films of Elvis Presley's career, *Jailhouse Rock* was an improvement over *Loving You*, which was better than his debut, *Love Me Tender*. The narrative is once again inspired by Presley's own story, although it appears to define his persona based on negative traits perceived in some quarters. In *Jailhouse Rock*, Elvis plays a character that is sullen, egotistical, uncaring, and sometimes cruel. However, what is most interesting about this character is how it develops within the course of the narrative, and how Presley effectively conveys the evolution of the character's personality. He is initially shown as quick tempered and prone to violence, and then environmental factors cause other negative traits. Curiously, it is the positive things, the triumph and success, that are most instrumental in shaping his personality.

Elvis plays Vince Everett, who kills a man in self-defense during a barroom brawl. While serving time in jail with Hunk Houghton, a former country-western singer, Vince picks up some tricks on the guitar, and discovers he has a natural talent for singing. At a prison show, which is televised, Vince's appearance nets sacks of fan mail. Upon being released, Vince embarks on a singing career, meets up with Peggy, a publicity woman, and the two eventually start their own record label. His records become a hit, but Vince's already substantial ego grows even larger. He treats Peggy shabbily, and when Hunk gets out of prison, all promises Vince had made are forgotten and the man who gave him his start is demoted to flunky status.

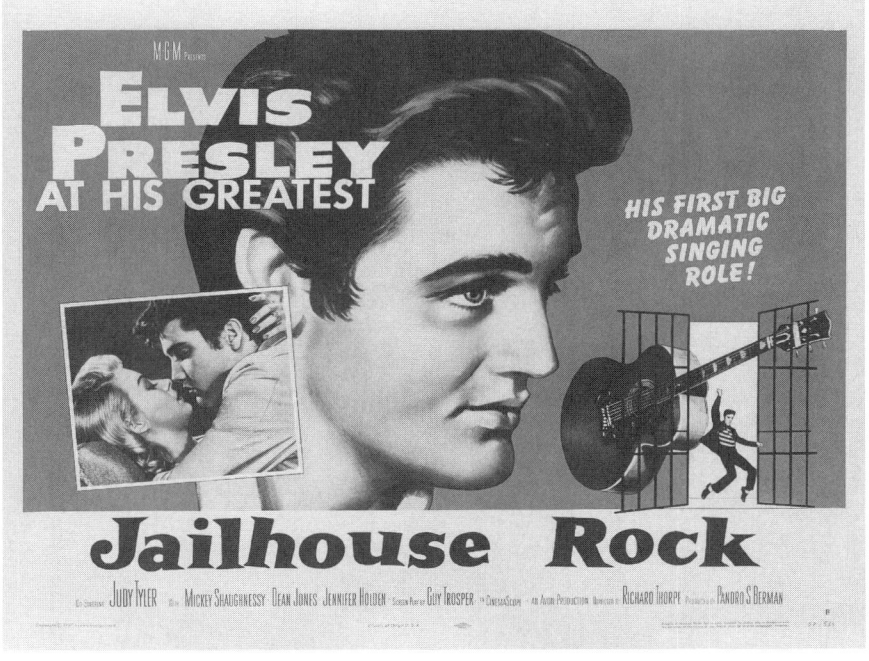

Jailhouse Rock featured Elvis in an unsympathetic role

The expedience with which the story puts Presley's character in jail is rather remarkable. His obtaining his paycheck at work, ordering drinks for everyone in a bar, getting in a fight that proves fatal to his opponent, and being tried and convicted in court, all take place in the first five minutes of the movie. Also, not a great deal of the film's running time occurs in the prison setting. All of the prison scenes are completed in the first half hour. Thus, *Jailhouse Rock* is not a typical prison drama in the same manner as *The Big House, Each Dawn I Die,* or *Brute Force*. The prison sentence is just a catalyst for Vince's realization that his natural singing ability can be parlayed into monetary success. Hunk Houghton, Vince's cellmate, is presented as the archetype of the laid-back country singer whose music was rendered obsolete by rock and roll. Hunk had enjoyed some level of success before being sent to prison, and is unable to realize that the music industry has since changed. Oddly, the man who changed it is playing a role in this film. The reason for the actual change in musical direction is never credited to anyone in the context of the movie, but referred to as something that is simply a part of the prevailing culture. Hunk, who brags about having worked with the likes of Eddy Arnold and Roy Acuff, is confident his work will continue to achieve success upon his release from prison. Vince knows better.

The *Jailhouse Rock* dance number is considered a portent to the music video

When the prison show where each man performs nets Vince an enormous amount of fan mail, Hunk, who works in the mail room, is amazed. Hunk also realizes that the warden will not release the letters to Vince until he leaves prison. Hunk never tells Vince of his popularity, but instead talks him into signing an exclusive contract allowing a 50-50 split between either's future earnings. Vince, skeptical but naive, signs the contract, not realizing that Hunk is taking advantage of him. Vince's sentence is concluding, while Hunk has months to go. It is up to Vince to get things started in the music business.

The entirety of the prison portion of the film is a setup to later events, establishing Vince's understanding of his own ability and his recognition that money can be earned from this talent. He has no understanding of how to obtain employment as a singer except from whatever out-of-date methods Hunk may have shared. The continued expedience of the narrative places a newly released Vince in a tavern on the same night that Peggy, a music publicist, is present.

As with the exposition at the outset of the film, the dynamic between Vince and Peggy develops very quickly when she sees a failed audition at a tavern and instinctively recognizes his potential. It is at this point that *Jailhouse Rock* takes on some particularly intriguing developments. First, Vince cuts a record and when it is played back, he recognizes how limited it is. Sounding a bit too much like the archaic style Hunk utilizes, Vince restructures his approach and creates a better sound. However, when a record company executive accepts it, the song is given to an established star to re-record using Vince's arrangement. Vince responds more to the fact that the singer not only recorded the song, but did so in the manner of Vince's demo. Vince confronts the record executive in his office and demands, "What about my arrangement?" The executive responds, "You can't copyright an arrangement." Vince lifts the executive out of his chair and slaps him a few times across the face before shoving him back down and storming out of the office. The violent streak inherent in Vince, the one that got him sent to prison, is only one ingredient of a complex character. He is confident enough to talk Peggy into the two of them starting their own record label, even investigating some of the necessary steps that need to be taken. However when he attends a gathering at her parents' house, he feels inferior and out of his element as the well-dressed guests talk intelligently about a jazz recording. When Vince is asked his opinion he responds with a sullen "I don't know what the hell you're talking about," and characteristically storms out of the home. Peggy is offended, but cannot resist his animal magnetism, even as he treats her even more cruelly after their label, and his records, enjoy continued success.

From here the narrative follows Vince's continued descent into uncaring arrogance. Hunk, released from prison, expects Vince to honor their contract. Vince's lawyer points out that it is invalid. Hunk is hired to be a flunky whose main duty is to walk Vince's dogs. Peggy's caring for Vince starts to wane as his womanizing and unfeeling loftiness at his success pushes her further and further away. Having a controlling interest, he plans to sell their record company to a conglomerate against Peggy's wishes. Quietly holding in his rage when Vince treats him shabbily, Hunk cannot bear to see Peggy so upset. Once she leaves, an angry Hunk throws a punch, which lands on Vince's throat and seriously injures him. It is only this incident and his gradual recovery that allows him to realize what he had become.

The complexities of Vince's character, and Presley's exceptional performance in the role, are the axis of *Jailhouse Rock*. The supporting players are led by newcomer Judy Tyler as Peggy and veteran character actor Mickey Shaughnessy as Hunk. Hunk represents the old guard, telling himself that his outdated style will be on top once the newer style fades away. The culture has passed him by, and rather than being supportive, Vince treats him as insignificant. Even when Vince pretends benevolence by allowing Hunk a spot on a TV special, it turns out to be an ugly lesson as Hunk's segment is cut by producers. Vince is willing to throw some money his way by demoting him to the most menial tasks. While Hunk has already been established as untrustworthy by hiding Vince's fan mail popularity from him, he comes off as a pathetic character rather than a crooked or dangerous one (he was in prison for a bank robbery that had been necessitated by bookings becoming less frequent).

Vince's response to Peggy appears to be a hostile masking of his affection toward her. He continually reminds her that money is the only thing that matters, and they are simply partners. Peggy is a savvy veteran of the business and the big city, able to coolly handle such a reaction. Vince is never violent toward her, but treats her with the sort of cruel disdain that he tends to reserve for those who have assisted him. The complexity of Vince's descending personality is shown being prompted by success, not failure.

While *Jailhouse Rock* deals with growing success in somewhat the same manner as shown in *Loving You*, its perspective is far different. *Loving You*'s Deke Rivers was pleased with his success and appreciated those who helped make it possible. Vince Everett evolves into a veritable monster of abject egomania. Rather than concentrate on audience response and the reaction of adults and the press, *Jailhouse Rock* instead examines the intricacies of the character, presenting Vince's success as more than his ego can handle. At this point, Elvis Presley's movie career was extremely promising, while his music continued to define popular culture. Elvis was improving with each successive film. However, critics who'd warmed up to the charmingly cynical Elvis in *Loving You* were taken aback by the negative character he played in *Jailhouse Rock*. The *New York Times* stated that "Presley fans may not like the idea of his being the churlish, egotistical wonderboy of TV and screen for a good half of the picture." The *Memphis Press-Scimitar* wrote, "Elvis's advisers might have thought twice before allowing the idol of teenagers to be cast as one who frequents bars, beats a man to death, and remains a pretty unsavory character until a few minutes before the fade out."

Critics had little influence on the moviegoing public, however. A theater owner in Texas reported in *Box Office* magazine: "No use pushing this for it pushes itself. The youngsters like to brag how many times they have seen it.

Judy Tyler, Elvis Presley, Peter Adams

Their enthusiasm is so contagious that the oldsters have to admit it has something special."

Not all of the critical comments were bad. *Motion Picture Exhibitor* stated:

> This is the best vehicle Presley has been given to date. Presley proves a personable performer thanks to the tight direction of Richard Thorpe, what could be a trite story manages to hold interest. There should be plenty of box office power in this one as Presley's phenomenal record sales attest to his draw.

The music in *Jailhouse Rock* is strong and organic to the plot. The highlight is certainly the performance of the title song. Choreographer Alex Romero understood the instinctive nature of Presley's movements and wanted to capture them in a dance sequence. He studied exactly how Elvis moved, seeking the singer's creative input. Presley is always credited with choreographing this sequence, but he did so under supervision. The other musical highlight is a rocking rendition of "(You're So Square) Baby I Don't Care" during an outdoor party scene.

It was around the time of *Jailhouse Rock* that Elvis started gathering an entourage of trusted friends to work for him. The Presley enterprise was growing rapidly and more people were needed to arrange tour flights, road trips, and

Jailhouse Rock newspaper ad shows its immediate success

other such activities. Presley's cousin Billy Smith was one of those people, as he told Alanna Nash in *Elvis Aaron Presley: Revelations from the Memphis Mafia*:

> Elvis wanted friends who were in touch with that Southern world that he came from, not actors and producers from the Hollywood scene. He wanted this little group that talked the same way he did and ate the same kind of food. He needed somebody to do odd jobs, to look after his schedule, and take care of everyday things like getting him to places on time, taking care of his wardrobe, or helping him learn his lines. Eventually we all had specific jobs and titles.

One of Presley's staff that came on board about this time was the late Lamar Fike, who recalled to Nash:

> It was an incredible experience. In '57 everybody wanted to see Elvis because he was a total outright phenomenon. He was even a curiosity in Hollywood. All these big stars were coming around. I'd open the door and people like Robert Mitchum would be standing there with a fifth of scotch asking Elvis to be in his next picture, *Thunder Road*. He wanted him to play his son, a guy who ran moonshine.

Elvis was actually quite interested in doing *Thunder Road*, and Mitchum, who had penned the original story, realized that both had the same sleepy-eyed look that could make them believable as father and son. Colonel Parker, however, demanded more money than the producers were willing to spend. Rather than approach the project as a positive move in Presley's career, Parker looked at it strictly from a financial perspective, foreshadowing the unfortunate direction Elvis's movie career would soon take.

Despite Elvis later recalling the shooting as among the most exciting and positive experience he had making movies, and being proud of what he'd done as an actor, *Jailhouse Rock* was not without problems. While filming the title song's dance sequence, Elvis accidentally loosened a porcelain cap from one of his teeth and it went down his throat. At first he laughed it off, but when he began experiencing chest pain, an x-ray was performed, revealing that he did not swallow the cap, but inhaled it. It had to be removed from his lung.

However, the biggest tragedy connected to *Jailhouse Rock* involved actress Judy Tyler, his costar who played Peggy. Tyler, who was born Judith Hess, had been a beauty contest winner and appeared as a regular on the *Howdy Doody* children's television show before entering movies in 1957. She had appeared in one film, *Bop Girl*, before her role in *Jailhouse Rock*. Shortly after filming ended, Judy Tyler and her husband were killed in an automobile crash. When informed of the crash, Elvis broke down and cried. Judy Tyler never lived to see the release of either movie she made.

Another unfortunate glitch occurred in Presley's recording career shortly after *Jailhouse Rock* filming was completed. Bill Black and Scotty Moore left him. Bill felt that the pay Colonel Parker gave them was a pittance in comparison to Elvis's earnings, and talked Scotty into leaving as well. Elvis had nothing to do with the business aspect of his career, so he was quite upset over the prospect of losing the two men who were in Sun Studio with him recording "That's All Right" only three years earlier, creating the rudiments of what we now know as rock and roll. Parker then put together a new band for Elvis, with Floyd Cramer on piano, Hank Garland on guitar, and Bob Moore on bass (drummer D. J. Fontana had stayed on). They were outstanding musicians and Elvis's music never lost a beat. Scotty Moore would still record with Elvis off and on throughout the sixties, but Bill died in 1965. Upon hearing about it, Elvis met privately with Bill Black's family (he did not attend the funeral, realizing it would become a media circus), and, according to Bill's brother, told them if they needed anything at all to contact him.

Elvis did not attend the Memphis premiere of *Jailhouse Rock*, returning immediately to touring and recording. A concert in Louisiana enforced a "no wiggle" rule, forcing the singer to stand still and deliver his songs. In Los Angeles, the police department filmed an entire Elvis concert in an effort to find a reason to arrest him for indecency (they found nothing). He also recorded a Christmas album, which hit record stores shortly after *Jailhouse Rock* was released in November 1957. His up-tempo take on the song "White Christmas" so offended some radio station owners that some disc jockeys got fired for playing it.[1]

While at this point American adults were gradually accepting Elvis Presley as an actor (theater owners of the time were reporting "curious adults" attending the screenings), his music and method of presentation remained under fire. The enormity of the cultural revolution that Presley had ignited continued to be celebrated by younger people but was still considered a disruptive fad that most adults felt would eventually play out. Still, there were those more open-minded individuals who recognized Presley's talent and understood his music's role in the cultural revolution. They accepted *Jailhouse Rock* as the solid drama it was, but their number was small. Most of those who attended the movie and made it a hit were younger people who made up the demographic for the new rock and roll sound.

By 1957 Elvis Presley's success was coming under fire by African Americans who perceived him as a white man achieving success with music inspired by black artists. In retrospect, we can see how Presley's success paved the way for such brilliant artists as Chuck Berry, Little Richard, and Fats Domino to enjoy their own success on mainstream radio. But while the 1950s were notorious for white artists like Pat Boone, the Crew Cuts, and Georgia Gibbs enjoying chart success with remakes of songs by black artists, Elvis Presley does not fall into this category.

Sepia, a white-owned periodical for black readers, printed an article at the time Elvis was filming *Jailhouse Rock* entitled "How Negroes Feel about Elvis Presley." The article claimed that during a Boston appearance, the singer allegedly stated, "The only thing a nigger can do for me is shine my shoes and buy my records." This prompted Louie Robinson of the black-owned *Jet* magazine to conduct an investigation. The writers of *Sepia* refused to talk to him, but Elvis agreed to an interview on the set of *Jailhouse Rock*. Elvis stated that he had never been in Boston, adding: "I never said anything like that, and people who know me know that I wouldn't have said it. A lot of people seem to think I started this business. But rock n roll was here a long time before I came along. Let's face it: I can't sing like Fats Domino can. I know that."

Robinson interviewed many black musicians and entertainers who knew Elvis, including pianist Dudley Brooks, who said that "he faces everybody as a man. I never heard that remark and can't imagine Elvis ever saying it." One of his black songwriters, Otis Blackwell, confirmed that he was well paid for compositions like "Don't Be Cruel" and "All Shook Up," stating, "I got a good deal. I made money." The *Jet* article cleared Elvis of any claims of racism, and portrayed him as supporting racial equality and integration in the music business; Isaac Hayes stated, "Elvis was due the respect he had. No animosity. No sour grapes. Elvis was the man. The thing was that we didn't get what we deserved. Ignorance is one of the main things. Racism is one of the factors."

For his next movie, Elvis was scheduled to return to his home studio of Paramount for a Hal Wallis production based on the Harold Robbins book, *A Stone for Danny Fisher*. This property had been hanging around for a few years, originally slated for James Dean to play a boxer with filial issues who struggles in life. The project was shelved after Dean was killed in September 1955. When chosen to be the next Elvis Presley movie, the central character was rewritten to be a singer.

Shooting for *King Creole*, which would be the title of the movie based on Robbins's book, was scheduled to begin on January 13, 1958. However, on December 19, 1957, Elvis received a formal notification of induction into the U.S. Army, and was to report on January 20. Paramount Pictures had already spent an initial $350,000 on preproduction for *King Creole*. Therefore the studio got involved, indicating that shutting down the movie would cost several hundred thousand dollars and put a lot of people out of work. The draft board granted Elvis a 60-day extension to complete filming on *King Creole*. Although only his fourth movie, it would remain, in the eyes of many, his greatest role and finest performance.

CHAPTER 5
King Creole
(PARAMOUNT, 1958)

Director: Michael Curtiz
Screenplay: Herbert Baker and Michael V. Gazzo, from the novel *A Stone for Danny Fisher* by Harold Robbins
Producer: Hal Wallis
Cinematographer: Russell Harlan
Editor: Warren Low
Costume designer: Edith Head
Makeup: Wally Westmore
Cast: Elvis Presley, Carolyn Jones, Walter Matthau, Dolores Hart, Dean Jagger, Liliane Montevecchi, Vic Morrow, Paul Stewart, Jan Shepard, Brian G. Hutton, Jack Grinnage, Dick Winslow, Raymond Bailey, Gavin Gordon, Leon Tyler, Ned Glass, Candy Candido, Eugene Jackson, Val Avery, Hazel Boyne, Sam Buffington, Lilyan Chauvin, Charles Evans, Franklyn Farnum, Barbara Gayle, Rita Green, Dorothy Hack, Helene Hatch, Kay Haydn, Trustin Howard, John Indrisano, Jackie Joseph, Alexander Lockwood, Thomas Martin, Walter Merrill, Jacqueline Park, Ziva Rodann, Ric Roman, Tony Russell, Susanne Sidney, Blanche Thomas, Nina Vaughn, Kitty White, Fred Winston, Cliff Gleaves
Songs:
  "Crawfish" (written by Fred Wise and Ben Weisman; performed by Elvis Presley and Kitty White)
  "Steadfast, Loyal and True" (written by Jerry Leiber and Mike Stoller; performed by Elvis Presley)
  "Lover Doll" (written by Sid Wayne and Abner Silver; performed by Elvis Presley)
  "Trouble" (written by Jerry Leiber and Mike Stoller; performed by Elvis Presley)
  "Dixieland Rock" (written by Aaron Schröder and Beverly Ross [as Rachel Frank]; performed by Elvis Presley)
  "Young Dreams" (written by Aaron Schröder and Martin Kalmanoff; performed by Elvis Presley)

"New Orleans" (written by Sid Tepper and Roy C. Bennett; performed by Elvis Presley)
"Hard Headed Woman" (written by Claude Demetri; performed by Elvis Presley)
"King Creole" (written by Jerry Leiber and Mike Stoller; performed by Elvis Presley)
"Don't Ask Me Why" (written by Fred Wise and Ben Weisman; performed by Elvis Presley)
"As Long as I Have You" (written by Fred Wise and Ben Weisman; performed by Elvis Presley)

The *King Creole* soundtrack album spent a week at number two in 1958
"Hard Headed Woman" spent two weeks at number one
"Don't Ask Me Why" went to number 25

Released July 2, 1958
Filmed January 20–March 10, 1958
116 minutes
Black and white
Aspect ratio: 1.85:1
Box office statistics unknown
Released on DVD and Blu-ray by Paramount Home Video. The film was released on VHS by Paramount Pictures in 1986. In 2000, it was re-released on DVD with remastered sound and image, featuring the original theatrical trailer.

Generally considered Elvis Presley's best movie, *King Creole* owes much of its success to Michael Curtiz's direction. The Hungarian-born Curtiz had been a contract director at Warner Brothers during the 1930s and 1940s when Hal Wallis was producing there. As with most contract directors working at major studios during that era, Curtiz was called on to direct films in every genre from low-budget B movies to top-level A pictures. At Warner Brothers, Curtiz directed the horror film *Mystery of the Wax Museum,* the gangster drama *Angels with Dirty Faces*, the musical *Yankee Doodle Dandy*, the colorful *Adventures of Robin Hood*, and the western *Dodge City* among his prolific output at that studio. He remains best known for helming the Oscar-winning enduring classic, *Casablanca*. Curtiz was an expert at advancing a film's story by carefully framing each sequence in a manner that would enhance the dramatic impact. His technique is understated, never flashy, but the intensity his vision adds to the electric chair sequence in *Angels with Dirty Faces* or the airport scene in *Casablanca* is legendary. Curtiz adds the same sensitivity and insight to every scene in *King Creole*. The fact that Elvis continued to improve as an actor and the story uses the best elements that had worked in previous films also help make this an exceptional vehicle for the star.

Elvis was happy to be starring in another solid drama with a strong script, and was also pleased that his director was to be Michael Curtiz. Curtiz initially balked at the assignment, stating he would not direct Elvis, whom he perceived as a flashy diva who was likely to be troublesome. His attitude changed once the two met. Elvis was respectful, praised Curtiz's past work, and gave the veteran filmmaker the accurate impression that he would work hard to do his best in the movie. Curtiz investigated further by arranging a private screening of *Loving You*, Presley's other film for Wallis. Recognizing the inherent ability Presley exhibited as an actor, Curtiz accepted the assignment.

Elvis plays a restless high school student named Danny Fisher who goes against his father's wishes and drops out of school when he gets a job singing at a local nightclub. Danny has issues with his father's general cowardice, seeing him ordered around at his job as a pharmacist. He gets involved in a plan with neighborhood hoodlums to rob his father's employer as the man brings that day's money to the bank, but backs out at the last minute. He does not realize that his father has taken the employer's place for the errand on this night, and is seriously injured when attacked and robbed. Danny's father requires necessary surgery, which is difficult to afford, but suddenly Maxie Fields, the gangster owner of a rival nightclub, arranges for a top surgeon and pays for the procedure, saving the father's life. Danny is now indebted to Maxie and must sing at his establishment or he will reveal to the father Danny's knowledge of the attack. Meanwhile, Danny has struck up a friendship with Maxie's girl, Ronnie, a put-upon prostitute who is staying with the gangster out of sheer desperation. When Maxie does reveal the situation to Danny's father, Danny beats the gangster up and runs away with Ronnie.

Danny Fisher is a victim of his environment in the same manner as Vince Everett had been in *Jailhouse Rock*, but while Vince's personality was shaped by success, Danny's is shaped by failure. He loses his chance to graduate, causing him to drop out of school. He wants to be protective of Ronnie, but realizes the far-reaching power of Maxie Fields. He wants to earn enough to keep his father out of situations where he has to be subservient to his employers, but is limited by his surroundings. His only control is among the area hoods, whose respect he has earned by effectively thwarting their attacks, proving he is tougher than they are.

Many ingredients of *Rebel without a Cause* are evident here. First, Danny has similar issues with his father as Jim Stark had in *Rebel*. In the James Dean movie, the father was powerless against his wife. In the Elvis movie, the father is a widower who jumps at the slightest command by his boss. Danny sees this and remarks how he hates to see his father "crawl."

The difference between the two films is that Danny comes from the seediest area of the New Orleans slums, while Jim Stark was a wealthy suburban kid with no limit on material means (including his own car). Brad Laidman stated in a December 2000 issue of *Film Threat*:

> Presley's potential hoodlum knows exactly what he wants from the world, money and respect. He's not conflicted, he's pissed, reeking of sexual energy and looking for trouble. The kids Presley tangles with here are actual gang-type crooks, not bored suburban punks, and the Presley film's look, tone and feel are considerably darker. Danny Fisher's world has none of the brilliantly colorful possibilities of Stark's. Jim Stark was having a mild identity crisis. Danny Fisher's life is hurtling to almost certain doom.

Presley continued to exhibit remarkable improvement as an actor with each successive film. In fact, each movie is made rather quickly after shooting completes on the previous one. As with his music, Presley is drawing from an innate talent that would certainly have evolved further had he been able to maintain a movie career with strong scripts and solid directors.

The original Harold Robbins book was about a boxer whose fighting prowess helped him rise above his slum surroundings. The screenplay is revamped for Elvis, making the central character a singer. From this basis, Elvis has several dynamics among the supporting characters. Dean Jagger, as his cowardly father, is perfectly understated, exhibiting a discernible shame beneath his filial authoritative facade. Walter Matthau, in only his sixth feature film (he had done a lot of episodic drama for television) exhibits the right amount of bullish swagger as Maxie Fields, projecting a relaxed confidence in the level of his power. As the rival club owner for whom Danny sings initially, Paul Stewart acts as the adult male anchor to the proceedings, displaying measured confidence and no outward fear of Maxie, traits that Danny wishes he could see in his father. Middle-aged Stewart's romance with Presley's twenty-something older sister is presented as a positive element of the story, despite the age difference. The father, who seems only slightly older than Stewart, approves and supports their union.

Carolyn Jones as Ronnie gives what would be the performance of her career in *King Creole*. Best known as Morticia on television's *The Addams Family* in the 1960s, Jones delivers a gamut of conflicting emotions as Ronnie in *King Creole*. Her desperation forcing her union with Maxie Fields is parlayed into an equally desperate yearning to leave him, especially when Danny shows support and understanding. A tragic figure, Jones conveys emotional suffering without going over the top, even in a frightening scene where she is forced to romance a friend of Maxie's as part of her duties. Her revulsion tells us this is not the first time such a service was demanded of her. Danny is perceived as the hero who could deliver her from these clutches, but he is not up to the job. When he runs away with her, Maxie catches up to both of them and Ronnie is shot dead.

Elvis and Carolyn Jones in *King Creole*

Upon completing the shooting of *King Creole*, Presley is reported to have said, "Now I know what a really great director is like." For his part, as reported in *Careless Love*, Curtiz told the press that Elvis could easily develop into one of the finest actors in American film. Curtiz was good at getting the best performances from his actors, even inspiring such seasoned veterans as James Cagney and Humphrey Bogart to turn in their best work. His methods for doing so are legendary. Curtiz was a hard taskmaster on the set and his treatment of actors was demeaning and abrasive. Errol Flynn refused to work with Curtiz, despite the director having helmed some of the actor's best movies. Bette Davis also refused to again work with him after he called her "a sexless no-talent bitch" on the set of a film. Fay Wray recalled that she didn't consider Curtiz a person, but "part of the steel of the camera." However, some actors responded especially well to Curtiz's direction, including Ingrid Bergman, Claude Rains, and Elvis Presley.

Curtiz was as demanding on Elvis as he had been on any other actor. He told Elvis he was too fat and needed to take off ten pounds. Elvis crash dieted and lost the pounds in two weeks. He was told his famous sideburns would have to go. He complied. Curtiz would insist on endless retakes until the other actors were exhausted. Elvis never complained. By this time, Curtiz was referring to Elvis as "a lovely boy" to the press.

Elvis was coached by Curtiz to mentally draw upon his own poor background to understand the many conflicts racing through Danny's head. Where in *Jailhouse Rock* Elvis played the lead role with a defiant swagger appropriate to the character, in *King Creole* the character's toughness is survival, not arrogance. Curtiz carefully frames each shot to bring out the feelings and emotions of the characters, especially spotlighting Presley.

To enhance our understanding of the character, Curtiz uses wide shots at the opening of the film to present Danny's environment. When Danny is in the principal's office, Curtiz uses a medium shot with both actors (the principal is played by Raymond Bailey) framed by inanimate objects. Curtiz's choice to offer a wide enough shot to include such standard office objects as a window (with blinds), a flag in the corner, a coatrack, and a blackboard enhances the insecurity Danny is feeling in the presence of the authoritative figure. Pretending toughness, Danny sits at the edge of his seat, while the principal is relaxed in manner and tone.

As *King Creole* has a decidedly noir feel, Curtiz keeps each scene fairly dark, drawing on his talent for using shadows. The characters are often in the foreground, framed by activity in the background and on either side, while the lighting is sparse. One of the more impressive shots is just prior to Elvis singing "Trouble." He is standing, speaking to a seated Maxie and Ronnie. The activity in the club is all around them but shunted to the background, the band playing onstage in the upper left of the frame. The intensity of the scene taking place is offset by all that surrounds them, and the entire shot is bathed in shadows. It enhances the drama in a manner that draws even greater emotion from the narrative.

While most of the outdoor scenes maintain the noir effect by taking place primarily at night, the lightest scenes are at the end when Ronnie is killed and a struggle between Maxie and Danny causes a gun to go off and end the gangster's

Some ads sold *King Creole* as a drama

life. These sequences show the only time in the movie where someone is killed, and Curtiz chooses to brighten the outdoor atmosphere to the point of looking bleak.

The strong script, great performances, and creative, sensitive direction make *King Creole* the quintessential Elvis Presley movie. It has solid dramatic impact and also showcases his music effectively. While in his first film Elvis only came alive during the musical sequences, seeming tentative and overeager as an actor, in *King Creole* his confidence is palpable throughout the movie. As *King Creole* is set in New Orleans, there is a bit of Dixieland in the compositions written for this film, which include "Dixieland Rock" as well as the title tune. During Elvis's performance of "Trouble," Curtiz chooses to present him in long shot, barely visible within the darkness of the scene despite his white jacket. Curtiz then cuts to a medium shot as the song picks up, switching to occasional close-ups of Presley's face. As the song speeds up toward its conclusion, Curtiz returns to a medium shot so that the singer's gyrations are fully visible in the frame. One song, the brass-backed rocker "Hard Headed Woman," became the biggest hit to come out of the movie yet it is never shown in performance (a portion is used in the background of one scene).

Elvis once again managed to charm his costars as well as his director with his respect, cooperation, and hard work. Walter Matthau stated, "He was an instinctive actor. . . . He was quite bright . . . he was very intelligent. . . . He was not a punk. He was very elegant, sedate, and refined, and sophisticated."

Gradually accepting the fact that Elvis Presley had an innate talent as an actor that was improving with experience, critics were especially impressed with *King Creole*. Howard Thompson in the *New York Times* stated:

> Elvis Presley can act. In Paramount's surprisingly colorful and lively *King Creole*, most of it outright drama, he does a good, convincing walk-through as a downtrodden New Orleans youth who tangles with some gangsters (along with that blasted guitar). It's a sturdy, picturesque job, and so is this Hal Wallis production until it finally lapses into standard gangster shenanigans.
>
> To quote Mr. Presley directly—"I'm a hustler, not a bum, out to make a fast buck." As a surly, befuddled and basically decent musician, bloodied by some tough French Quarter denizens before seeing the light he looks and behaves accordingly. He can also thank his lucky stars for his colleagues. These include Michael Curtiz, a shrewd director; a dandy supporting cast (especially Carolyn Jones) and, in the most curious contribution of all, the two scenarists, Herbert Baker and Michael V. Gazzo. For this is an adaptation of Harold Robbins' *A Stone for Danny Fisher,* that somber story of a northern boy battling upward from the slums. Somehow, these two alert writers and Mr. Curtiz and his players have got it snugly draped around Mr. Presley's shoulders. And there it stays, even with eight or so of those twitching, gyrating musical interludes. (Mr. Presley renders the most persuasive one, "Take My Hand," sitting down.) These also perfectly typify the Bourbon Street honky-tonks that Mr. Curtiz and his fine photographer, Russ Harlan, have beguilingly drenched with atmosphere.

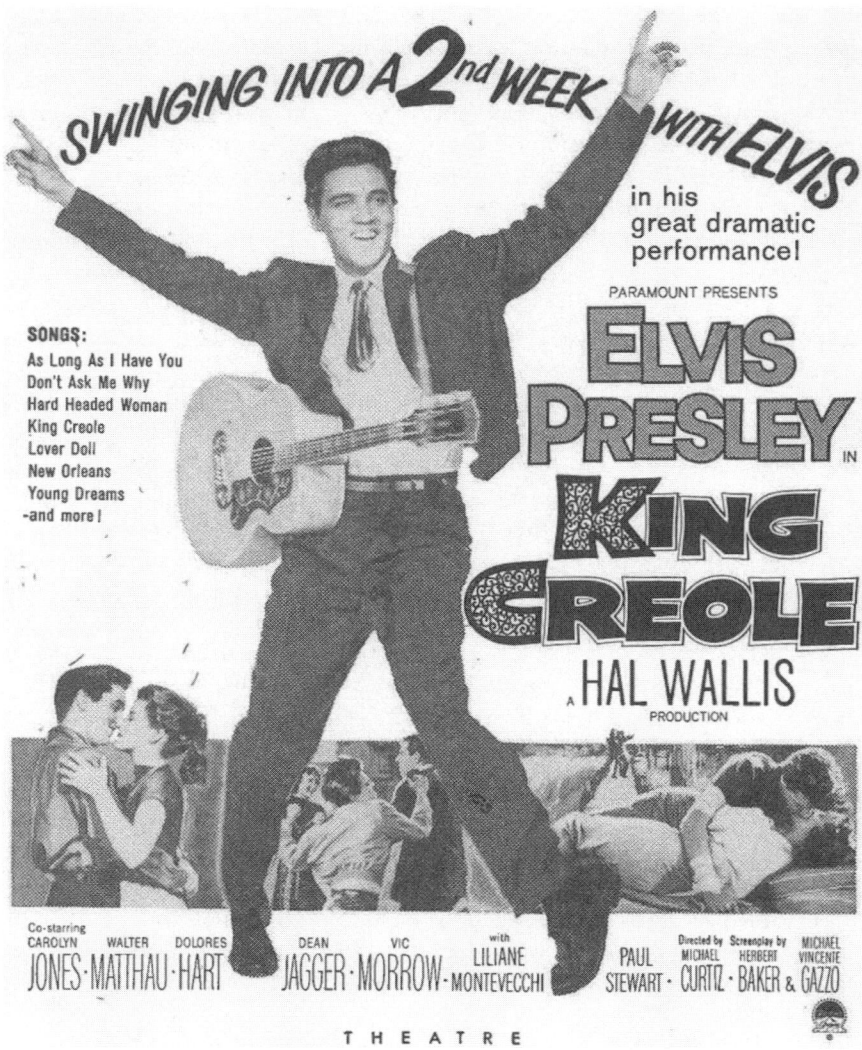

Some ads sold *King Creole* as a musical

As for Mr. Presley, it's a pleasure to find him up to a little more than Bourbon Street shoutin' and wigglin'. Acting is his assignment in this shrewdly upholstered showcase, and he does it.

While this review is quite positive, it is also quite telling. Although Thompson appears to be impressed with Presley's acting, phrases like "that blasted guitar" and "shoutin' and wigglin'" further prove the continued cluelessness regarding rock and roll music. The review in *Variety* pointed out that Elvis "shows himself to be a surprisingly believable and sympathetic actor" but also quickly indicated that he "does some soft and melodic singing," which offsets the rock and roll.

King Creole was a hit movie but met with resistance in Mexico, once again due to accusations of Elvis being racist. Apparently, Elvis (or more likely the Colonel) turned down an invitation to Mexico from a high-ranking official. A rumor was then started that Elvis was racist toward Mexicans. The rumor stated that Elvis said, "I'd rather kiss three niggers than one Mexican." Tijuana tabloids called him a racist, quoting a woman saying, "I'd rather kiss three dogs than one Elvis Presley." Mexican Radio Exitos spearheaded a boycott of the "insolent artist," while the powerful student group Federación Estudiantil Universitaria held public record burnings. When *King Creole* screened in May 1959 at the Américas Cinema in Mexico City, newspapers that had advertised the film under the title *Melodía Siniestra* (Sinister Melody) reported a "riot" occurring.

King Creole was another big hit movie for Elvis, and for Paramount Pictures, but its exact gross (domestic or worldwide) is unknown. It was omitted from *Variety*'s list of top-grossing films of its year, obviously an oversight.

Upon completing *King Creole*, Elvis prepared to enter the armed forces. Two years away from recording, performing live, and making movies could effectively kill the career of any performer, especially one who had ushered in a new sound and style. Elvis spent time in the studio recording several songs other than those he'd done for *King Creole*, so that RCA would have a backlog of singles to release. Not all of these were withheld. One of his best ballads, "Don't," had been released a couple of weeks before shooting on *King Creole* began. Elvis had instructed songwriters Jerry Leiber and Mike Stoller to "write something real pretty." He continued to enjoy singing ballads as much as he did the rock and roll songs. A greatest hits album was prepared, despite Elvis being only two years into his RCA contract. Still, Elvis had so many top hits during this period that an entire album of them was possible. *Elvis' Golden Records* contained "Hound Dog," "Heartbreak Hotel," "Don't Be Cruel," "Jailhouse Rock," "All Shook Up," and other such hits.

While the record company was ready to extend Elvis Presley's song releases throughout the two years he was away, and Colonel Parker would remain active with promotions and merchandising, Elvis would nevertheless remain off television and out of movies. Some older singers whose styles had been rendered archaic by the new rock and roll sound made no attempt to hide their happiness at the prospect of a two-year army hitch causing America to forget what they continued to insist was a passing fad. Elvis himself had his own concerns. He realized how quickly show business could forget a performer, despite the backlog of songs prepared for release over the next two years. He put on a brave face for reporters, indicating he would try to enhance some skills in the army or perhaps arrange for some education. He even hinted at going to college upon his discharge if the music business passed him by. Despite being perhaps the biggest star in the country, Elvis Presley was quite concerned about leaving his career behind when he reported to the Memphis draft board on March 28, 1958, for his induction into the armed forces.

CHAPTER 6
Elvis in the Army
(1958–1960)

When "Heartbreak Hotel" first blasted onto the charts in 1956, it was surrounded by pleasant adult-oriented easy listening fare by Kay Starr, Dean Martin, and Nelson Riddle. By the time Elvis entered the army two years later, the impact of his ensuing hits resulted in the older style being gradually eased out by more rock and roll artists hitting the charts. Chuck Berry had five Top 40 hits in 1956–1958, four of which were Top 10. Little Richard had nine songs reach the Top 40 during the same period. Buddy Holly had seven songs chart before his death in 1959.[1] Jerry Lee Lewis had four before his career took an immediate nosedive after he married his thirteen-year-old cousin. As Elvis entered the army in March of 1958, the radio was playing such Top 40 hits as "Good Golly Miss Molly," "Sweet Little Sixteen," "Maybe Baby," and "Breathless." These rock and roll songs were embraced by younger people, while their elders clung to Perry Como's "Catch a Falling Star" or British youngster Laurie London's monotonous chart fluke "He's Got the Whole World in His Hands," both of which went to number one in 1958.

Elvis Presley's initial report to basic training was a media circus, with photographers and film crews on hand to witness the issuing of his uniform, his weighing in, and his army regulation haircut. They were all left behind once Elvis boarded a bus to Fort Hood in Texas. While the army had suggested a star of Presley's magnitude might consider special forces, Elvis chose to go through basic training as an ordinary soldier, with the same rules, regulations, and chores. During marching drills, the drill instructor would occasionally tease the famous recruit in his platoon by shouting "hup two three wiggle" and other such orders that amused Elvis. Any ribbing he received was said to be good natured, as the army could see he was serious about being a soldier and never put on airs or expected special treatment. When Bob Hope came to entertain the troops he asked Elvis to be part of the show, but Elvis refused, continuing to avoid being singled out.

The idea of Elvis Presley in the army extended into other areas of popular culture, perhaps most famously on an episode of *The Phil Silvers Show* where comedian Silvers played the conniving, scheming Sergeant Ernie Bilko, always looking for a get-rich-quick scheme. A character called Elvin Pelvin (played by Elvis lookalike Tom Gilson)[2] is placed in Bilko's platoon, and the scheming sergeant spends the entire episode trying to get him to sing while he sneakily tape-records it. What is most amusing is the reaction to the singer by the show's characters, including the blustery middle-aged Colonel Hall (Paul Ford) who shivers and stammers like a schoolgirl at the mere mention of Elvin Pelvin's name. While it was a funny parody of what the prevailing culture had become, it now serves to illustrate how quickly Elvis Presley had reached such a lofty status in show business. Silvers liked Elvis, as an entertainer and as a person. There is even footage existing of a 1956 appearance where Elvis announces from the stage that Phil Silvers is in the audience. On another episode of his TV show, a teenage girl is seen wearing an "I Love Elvis" T-shirt.

When Elvis Presley completed his basic training in June, he was allowed to live in a house off base, so he rented a large place in Killeen, Texas, and was joined by his parents, grandmother, and his associate Lamar Fike. During a two-week furlough Elvis went into a Memphis recording studio and cut several tracks for release over the next two years. Some of his best, most rocking tunes were released during this period, including "Wear My Ring around Your Neck," "A Fool Such as I," "I Need Your Love Tonight," "A Big Hunk of Love," "One Night," and "I Got Stung." Each of these songs were huge hits, with "A Big Hunk of Love" going all the way to number one. However, spacing out these songs over two years did not seem to be enough. Thus, a couple of albums were also released: *For LP Fans Only* and *A Date with Elvis*, each containing some old Sun songs along with some previously released RCA tracks, none of which had yet been released on albums.

While the songs are among Presley's best, and were hugely successful, the length of time between releases, even with the LPs, did not allow for the same level of success Elvis enjoyed as a civilian. In 1956 Elvis had 11 songs chart in the Top 40. In 1957 there were nine. The following year there were eight charted hits. But throughout 1959, Presley's second year in the army, only four songs charted. This was due to the material beginning to run out.

Just prior to leaving for Germany, Elvis's mother, Gladys, became ill. Elvis tried to ignore it, believing she would simply get better, but Lamar realized that she was in danger, as her skin started yellowing. Elvis was finally convinced to have a doctor visit the home. The doctor recommended she be taken to a hospital, and it was decided that she be treated in Memphis by doctors she knew. Her husband Vernon accompanied her. Elvis, who was famously very close to his mother, continued to simply blot out any worries and assumed the doctors would treat her and she would recover. In August 1958, Vernon called the house in Killeen and informed Lamar that Gladys was getting worse. Doctors contacted the army's brass asking that Elvis be allowed to return home. The army refused. Doctors persisted.

Lamar Fike recalled for Alanna Nash in *Elvis Aaron Presley*:

> I got in the jeep and went out in the field and got him. We came back in and he went in to request emergency leave. I went in with him. The captain was sitting behind his desk. Elvis said, "I need emergency leave, sir, my mother is dying. And the captain said, "Is she actually dead yet?" Elvis stopped, his jaw tightened up, and he said, "I want you to understand who I am and what I am getting ready to do. My name is Elvis Presley. I sell a lot of records and I am a star. I've played your little army games. I've shot your guns and rolled your tanks. But that's my mother. If I don't get a pass in my hand in the next five minutes I am going AWOL, and it's not going to look good for you when I call a press conference and say the reason I went AWOL is because they wouldn't give me emergency leave to see my mother." It sounded like movie dialog but he actually said it. The captain jumped up from that desk, went to the major's office and was white as a sheet. And that captain came back with a pass in his hand.

Gladys Presley died of a heart attack, brought on by acute hepatitis, on August 14, 1958. Lamar continued:

> Four weeks after Gladys died, Elvis was shipped overseas. He never had time to get over her death. He cried all the time. When we got to Germany he was still reeling, still trying to put it all together. When you chronicle the demise of Elvis Presley, you have to realize the tilt started when Gladys died. That was the most devastating thing that ever happened to him. He would never be the same.

While in the army, Presley's hard work earned him the rank of sergeant. He developed a keen interest in karate while in Germany, continuing to pursue it on his discharge (and achieving the level of black belt). He also met fourteen-year-old Priscilla Beaulieu, daughter of an American army officer, and was immediately smitten with her despite being nine years older. She would eventually come to live with him at Graceland and they would marry in 1967. The army is also where Elvis started experimenting with drugs—uppers and downers to help cope with the various rigors of army life. This unfortunate habit would extend into his personal life once his army hitch was up, in an effort to handle his even more rigorous recording, filming, and touring schedule.

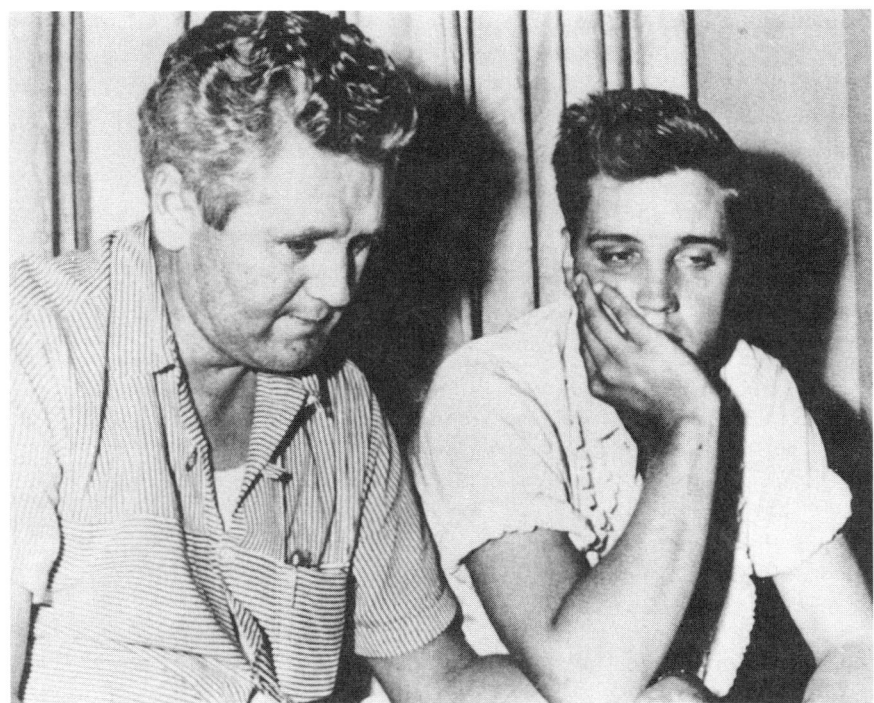

While Elvis (seen here with his father, Vernon Presley) was in the army, his mother passed away

While Elvis was stationed in Germany, Colonel Parker was back in the States continuing to make sure records were released on schedule. Only one month after his induction, the rocking "Wear My Ring around Your Neck" was released, backed by the bluesy "Don'tcha Think It's Time." "Hard Headed Woman," his single from *King Creole*, was released in June 1958, with the movie coming out in July and the soundtrack album in August. One of his finest blues recordings, "One Night," was backed with the rocking "I Got Stung" for a successful two-sided hit in October. His 1959 hits followed suit with the mid-tempo "A Fool Such as I" backed with the up-tempo "I Need Your Love Tonight" and the raucous number-one smash "A Big Hunk of Love" featuring the ballad "My Wish Came True" on its flipside. By the end of 1959, all of these songs were gathered on the album *Elvis Golden Records Volume Two*.

The prerecorded material was getting quite scarce by the time Presley's army hitch was concluding, and he realized the seriousness of his dwindling releases. As the conclusion of Presley's army duty was nearing, Colonel Parker received a bit of a surprise when he was contacted by Frank Sinatra, of all people, who indicated he was preparing a TV special for that May and wanted Elvis as the star attraction. He even suggested it be called *Welcome Home Elvis*. The program would be shot in March, shortly after Elvis returned home from Germany and received his honorable discharge from the army. Sinatra had not let up on his feelings about rock and roll over the past couple of years, even penning an anti-rock article for *Western World* stating:

> My only deep sorrow is the unrelenting insistence of recording and motion picture companies upon purveying the most brutal, ugly, degenerate, vicious form of expression it has been my displeasure to hear and naturally I am referring to the bulk of rock and roll. It smells phony and false. It is sung, played, and written for the most part by cretinous goons.

Colonel Parker realized the exposure would be good for his client, but due to Sinatra's comments about Presley and his work, he charged the crooner $125,000 for a ten-minute appearance, which was an unheard-of amount. Sinatra agreed to pay the fee. Once of the workers on the special was said to have quipped, "I wish I made as much as Sinatra was losing on this show."

Along with the Sinatra show, Elvis Presley also recorded and released a spectacular comeback album, *Elvis Is Back*, containing some of his best work, all new, and none of which was released as a single. Investigating blues, rock, and pop styles, Presley opened the 1960s as if he would remain in complete control for another decade, while fans felt the original rocking rebel would pick up creatively where he'd left off before entering the service. However, it soon became evident that Elvis had indeed changed. Despite the wonderful album that signaled his return, the single he recorded and released for radio play was the rather flaccid pop tune "Stuck on You." What transpired thereafter transformed the rebel rocker into a safe, middle-class entertainer.

The 1960s would become a creatively explosive decade in the culture, especially among young people, and most especially in terms of the music. By mid-decade, the 1960s appeared to be as unfamiliar to Elvis as the 1950s had been familiar. And while his popularity continued, the 1960s was a decade in which Elvis Presley eventually failed to chart hardly any songs in the upper half of the Top 40 for a few years, managing to barely reach the charts at all in 1967 and 1968. He made a triumphant comeback at the end of the decade, but for most of the 1960s, Elvis Presley's movies were more popular and successful than his songs. And as with his music, his film releases after he returned from the army were promising at first, but it was soon evident they would not be carrying on the tradition of *Jailhouse Rock* and *King Creole*.

CHAPTER 7
G.I. Blues
(PARAMOUNT, 1960)

Director: Norman Taurog
Screenplay: Henry Garson and Edmund Beloin
Producer: Hal B. Wallis
Assistant director: Michael D. Moore
Cinematographer: Loyal Griggs
Editor: Warren Low
Costumes: Edith Head
Makeup: Wally Westmore
Hairstylist: Nellie Manley
Vocal accompaniment: The Jordanaires
Technical advisor: Colonel Tom Parker
Cast: Elvis Presley, Juliet Prowse, Robert Ivers, James Douglas, Letícia Román, Sigrid Maier, Arch Johnson, Mickey Knox, John Hudson, Kenneth Becker, Jeremy Slate, Beach Dickerson, Trent Dolan, Carl Crow, Fred Essler, Ron Starr, Erika Peters, Ludwig Stössel, Dick Winslow, Ray Walker, Trude Wyler, Willy Kaufman, Bess Flowers, D. J. Fontana, Marianne Gaba, Edith Angold, Robert Boon, Robert Allison Baker III, Marilyn Gladstone, Joe Gray, Hoyt Hawkins, Edward Coch, Walter Conrad, Michael Sargent, Don Sahlin, Sally Todd, Edson Stroll, Harper Carter, Richard Cowl, Fred Kruger, Willy Kaufmann, Torben Mayer, Scotty Moore, Judith Rawlins, Karen Mann
Songs (in the order performed):
"What's She Really Like" (written by Sid Wayne and Abner Silver; performed by Elvis Presley)
"G.I. Blues" (written by Sid Tepper and Roy C. Bennett; performed by Elvis Presley)
"Doin' the Best I Can" (written by Doc Pomus and Mort Shuman; performed by Elvis Presley)
"Blue Suede Shoes" (written by Carl Perkins; performed by Elvis Presley)
"Frankfort Special" (written by Sid Wayne and Sherman Edwards; performed by Elvis Presley)

"Shoppin' Around" (written by Sid Tepper, Roy C. Bennett, and Aaron Schröder [as Aaron Schroeder]; performed by Elvis Presley)
"Tonight Is So Right for Love" (written by Sid Wayne and Abner Silver; performed by Elvis Presley)
"Wooden Heart" (written by Bert Kaempfert, Kay Twomey, Fred Wise, and Ben Weisman; performed by Elvis Presley)
"Pocketful of Rainbows" (written by Fred Wise and Ben Weisman; performed by Elvis Presley)
"Big Boots" (written by Sid Wayne and Sherman Edwards; performed by Elvis Presley)
"Didja Ever" (written by Sid Wayne and Sherman Edwards; performed by Elvis Presley)

The soundtrack album for *G.I. Blues* spent ten weeks at number one in 1960 No songs from the movie charted as singles, but "Blue Suede Shoes" had been a Top 20 hit for Elvis in 1956 (in a different version than the recording used in this movie)

Released November 23, 1960
Filmed May 2–August 7, 1960
104 minutes
Technicolor
Aspect Ratio: 1.85:1
Budget: $2 million; gross: $4.3 million
Released on DVD by Paramount Home Video

The music world Elvis Presley returned to upon being discharged in 1960 was far different than the one he had left in 1958. Chuck Berry was in prison, Little Richard entered a monastery, Jerry Lee Lewis was banned, Gene Vincent was in Europe, Buddy Holly and Eddie Cochran were dead. Music had become more pop oriented, and less the wild rock and roll that had exhilarated youth in the mid- to late fifties. The Beach Boys, Sam Cooke, the Four Seasons, Dion, Frankie Avalon, Fabian, and the Phil Spector–produced girl groups were among those dotting the Top 40.

Elvis Presley's first post-army single was the rather tame "Stuck on You" backed by the ballad "Fame and Fortune." Despite it not being an all-out rocker in the same class as "Hound Dog," "Stuck on You" sold over a million copies even before its official release on March 21, 1960. It was also his first single released in stereo. The following month saw the release of Presley's post-army album, the appropriately titled *Elvis Is Back* featuring 12 outstanding songs penned by the likes of Otis Blackwell ("Make Me Know It"), the Leiber-Stoller team ("Dirty Dirty Feeling") and bluesman Lowell Fulsom ("Reconsider Baby"). *Elvis Is Back* is a bona fide masterpiece, from rockers like "The Girl Next Door Went a Walkin'" and "Such a Night" to Presley's soulful reading of the Little Willie John classic "Fever," outshining Peggy Lee's sultry hit version.

The month of May saw the telecast of the Frank Sinatra special, *Welcome Home Elvis,* on which Elvis performed "Stuck on You," "Fame and Fortune," and then did a duet with Sinatra where Frank sang Presley's "Love Me Tender" while Elvis crooned his host's hit "Witchcraft." Of course Presley was fully aware of the negative things Sinatra had been saying about rock and roll, as well as about Elvis specifically, but, despite the brief amount of screen time, *Welcome Home Elvis* was centered around the singer's return from the army. According to *Elvis Aaron Presley*, when he finished doing the special, Elvis sarcastically told friends, "To my face they couldn't been nicer. Couldn't do enough for me!" Still, during the broadcast when Elvis and Sinatra were onstage, there was a discernible awkwardness.

While Elvis continued to explore and define rock and roll, as well as the blues and country styles that had been his initial influence, he still wanted to extend past these trappings. Because he had done so well with ballads (citing Dean Martin as an influence), Presley next chose to record an American version of the Italian classic "O Sole Mio." Some have balked at the massive hit "It's Now or Never" as being too blatantly operatic for the singer who had once belted out the bluesy "One Night." In fact, "It's Now or Never" should be applauded for exhibiting Presley's range, showing him as one who could indeed perform hard rockers and tough blues, but also deliver soft ballads and operatic revisions with equal aplomb. The mid-tempo rocker "A Mess of Blues" was the flipside of "It's Now or Never," reminding us that Elvis remained able to exhibit his inimitable prowess with the music that continued to define the era.

While much of his initial music after returning from the army was exciting and versatile, Elvis Presley's first movie release was an unfortunate harbinger of what his film career would soon become. However, it does not appear to be intended to soften the Presley image, as other books have concluded. It seems more likely that Hal Wallis simply felt a light, entertaining military comedy was an appropriate vehicle for the singer after his well-publicized army stint. And while *G.I. Blues* is no more than an average film, it is disarming, engaging, and pleasant. The songs are enjoyable, the story is light, and despite having no real challenge as an actor, Elvis's innate ability is still evident. As this is his first comedy, Elvis displays some amusing nuance to his acting, increasing the humor inherent in each situation.

Elvis plays Tulsa McClean, a singing, fighting G.I. whose platoon bets another on whether he can spend the night with a haughty nightclub dancer (Juliet Prowse). That is the extent of the plot, and the film then deals with Tulsa's various attempts, while stopping to perform a song roughly every ten minutes. As this is essentially a family-oriented comedy, the spending-the-night that Tulsa ultimately accomplishes is babysitting a buddy's infant child with the sympathetic dancer's help. The highlight of *G.I. Blues*, not including the song sequences, is Tulsa's frantic reaction to the crying baby, and his utter helplessness in attempting to quiet the child. Presley seems quite comfortable exhibiting appropriate comic ineptitude as he continually fails to stop the crying. He tries to verbally reason with the baby, attempts to feed it a sandwich, even considers using hand-to-hand combat, muttering, "Oh if you were only my size!" Comedy is difficult, even lighter fare such as this, and Presley handles it very effectively. It is the most amusing scene in the movie.

Throughout *G.I. Blues*, Elvis is a charming, affable, confident soldier who oozes likeability. It is a very different role than any he had previously played, and he conveys all of these qualities effectively. At the time, Elvis was unaware that his career would soon become a series of lightweight musical comedies that steadily decreased in quality and budget. He approached *G.I. Blues* as another job, a role that was different than any he'd played before, and once again offered his best effort. It can be argued that this character was a bit blander and more superficial than those found in his previous movies, but the fact remains that Presley rises to the occasion and conveys what the scenario intends.

While Elvis hardly had the flair for comedy possessed by the likes of Buster Keaton or Groucho Marx, he had a comfortable leading-man presence and an understanding as to how his reactions would enhance the comic effectiveness of the scene. It can be safely assumed that director Norman Taurog, who had directed comedies as far back as the silent era, might have coached Presley to bring out the comic nuance he exhibits in sequences where he is simply reacting to a situation or a piece of dialog. The affability he projects fits comfortably within the niche of the light romantic musical comedy that *G.I. Blues* manages to be.

Presley had requested that Michael Curtiz direct *G.I. Blues*, as he had been pleased with Curtiz's direction of *King Creole*. A contract director for many years, Curtiz was capable of directing in any genre, and had helmed one of the finest musicals in American movies, *Yankee Doodle Dandy* (1942). Curtiz, however, was not available. Elvis did not balk at the prospect of working with Norman Taurog, however, realizing that Taurog had helmed several Jerry Lewis movies, with and without Dean Martin, of which Presley was a big fan. Taurog would become the man who directed the most Elvis Presley movies, and would become one of Presley's favorite directors.

Some of the songs in *G.I. Blues* are good rockers (the title track and "Shoppin' Around" might be the best ones), while others are less interesting (an ersatz "Blue Suede Shoes" knockoff and the part-German "Wooden Heart," which Elvis sings to puppets). And, while they may have had some appeal when the movie was initially released, Juliet Prowse's dance bits are a rather dull distraction. At the time Prowse was dating Frank Sinatra, who would visit the set from time to time, and once stopped in Presley's dressing room to say hello. Still, Elvis and Juliet Prowse were said to have had a fling during filming. According

Newspaper ad for *G.I. Blues*

to *Elvis Aaron Presley*, Lamar Fike would later state, "Elvis was never paranoid about Sinatra, or afraid of him either."

When *G.I. Blues* was released in November 1960, the fact that it was the first Elvis Presley movie to come out since his return to the army made a big difference at the box office, resulting in the film becoming his biggest moneymaker to date. The response from critics was also generally positive, with *Box Office* stating:

> Elvis Presley returns to the screen after two years of military service in a picture which greatly curtails his hip-swinging gyrations and rock 'n' roll renditions. Also missing are his long sideburns. Apparently producer Hal Wallis sought to create a new image of this teenage idol inasmuch as his pre-army fans are now two years older. Co-starred with Juliet Prowse, the pair make a good romantic team. The picture has plenty of lively music, some excellent dancing, and funny comedy moments. All in all, the film is a diverting, rollicking entertainment, and, with Presley's name, should be money in the bank at theaters.

This review appears to believe that producer Hal Wallis was instrumental in reshaping the Elvis Presley image so that it was more palatable for adults and children as well as teenagers. They pointed out the lack of sideburns (obviously a military man would not wear them) and how the movie "greatly curtails his hip-swinging gyrations," believing this blander role was more acceptable entertainment than the challenging parts Elvis had essayed in *Jailhouse Rock* or *King Creole*.

Meanwhile, the stodgy Bosley Crowther of the *New York Times* offered similar praise for *G.I. Blues*, but made certain to include dismissive and often offensive comments about what Elvis represented in pop culture:

> Whatever else the Army has done for Elvis Presley, it has taken that indecent swivel out of his hips and turned him into a good, clean, trustworthy, upstanding American young man. At least, that's the cinematic image projected in the first post-service picture of 1958's most celebrated draftee, the Hal Wallis production, *G.I. Blues*. Honest, you'd hardly know Elvis—the pre-Army Elvis, that is—in the sweet-natured, morally straight young soldier now to be seen on the Victoria's screen. Gone is that rock 'n' roll wriggle, that ludicrously lecherous leer, that precocious country-bumpkin swagger, that unruly mop of oily hair. Almost gone are those droopy eyelids and that hillbilly manner of speech. Elvis has become sophisticated. He's a man of the world—almost. To be sure, he still sings a brand of music that, to many adult ears, is downright Greek, while he whomps a guitar clamped to his pelvis and rhythmically cracks his knees. And

he still gets off solemn aphorisms which are not likely to be attributed to Voltaire, such as, "Ef people got t' know each other better, everthin'll be better all aroun'."

But his hairbrush haircut is trim and tidy, his G.I. uniform is crisp and neat and his attitude is cheerful. Elvis is now a fellow you can almost stand.

As per Crowther's perspective, it is easy to see the marked difference between the teenagers who flocked to Elvis movies and bought his records and the grownups who begrudgingly admitted a fondness for his latest screen offering. Both reviews cited here concentrate on how much Elvis Presley is not like the rebel rocker who exploded onto the scene, applauding the fact that this movie was tame, harmless nonsense. Crowther is especially offensive as he mocks Presley's Southern accent, makes reference to how he "whomps" his guitar, and responds to the music as if it were single-handedly dismantling the prevailing culture.

Perhaps even more useful than critical comments are the theater owners reporting to *Box Office* the successful response *G.I. Blues* received from moviegoers. One stated: "Presley and how! Did he bring them in! Business excellent, picture tops, acting good. In my opinion a family picture from start to finish. Presley has changed a lot for the better!!" Another wrote, "Thanks Elvis! Business was way above average on this. The teenagers came and really ate this up. Elvis really improved on his acting in this. Everyone happy!"

It is certainly worth calling some attention to the claim that "Elvis really improved his acting in this." Since the role he played in *G.I. Blues* was his least challenging to date, it can be assumed the theater owner simply found the character Presley played to be more comfortably likeable than in previous movies.

While much of this film's success was indeed due to it being Presley's comeback movie after returning from the army, perhaps another factor might be involved. Elvis Presley was still considered by many parents, schools, churches, and civic groups as dangerous, and his patriotic service in the armed forces did little to change that manner of thinking in many quarters. Making a simple, light comedy with songs that were energetic but without the suggestiveness in lyric or accosting rhythms of his pre-army hits may likely have won some approval by those who heretofore believed Elvis movies should be restricted. Furthermore, the pleasant, ordinary soundtrack to *G.I. Blues* sold far better than the brilliant, critically acclaimed *Elvis Is Back* album. The fact that rock and roll itself had become less challenging and demanding by the early 1960s also made a difference. The prevailing culture had changed, and Elvis Presley's first movie released in the new decade was a perfect fit.

At about the same time *G.I. Blues* was released in November 1960, Presley's single "Are You Lonesome Tonight" came out. It was a weepy, saccharine ballad

While filming *G.I. Blues*, Elvis went over to the set of *All in a Night's Work* and helped Dean Martin celebrate Shirley MacLaine's birthday

complete with a spoken-word passage, but it was nevertheless a huge hit. The flipside was the mid-tempo rock song "I Gotta Know." Thus, once again Elvis Presley's image was wavering between the conventionally acceptable and the more challenging persona.

Everyone was pleased with the success of *G.I. Blues,* especially Colonel Parker, whose interest was financial rather than creative or artistic. Elvis himself had no interest in continuing this formula, however. He agreed to do the movie because it was unlike anything he'd done yet, and thought he'd have some fun with a musical comedy. But he realized it was fluff, and continued to request more challenging roles in serious movies with good scripts and top directors.

While eventually a formula was set, and an Elvis Presley movie became a recognizable commodity, at this time the producers, and Elvis, were still searching for what worked best. Elvis sought roles, even supporting ones, that would not require music. Producer Wallis and manager Parker were more interested in what made the most money, and took keen interest in the box office reception for *G.I. Blues*.

Elvis Presley's next film would be a western for 20th Century Fox. Eventually called *Flaming Star*, the film had a top director, great screenwriters, and was based on a popular novel. It also had four songs scheduled, but Elvis fought to have two of them removed. While Colonel Parker wanted to use the films to create soundtracks that could be sold as albums and singles, Elvis continued to try to keep his singing and acting careers separate. He had done a musical, and now he wanted to embark on more serious subjects that did not use a lot of music. He also hoped to once again work with Michael Curtiz, having been so impressed with Curtiz's direction of *King Creole* (and despite the director's challenging behavior with actors). Unfortunately, *King Creole* was the only Elvis film that Curtiz would direct. Eager to get started on his next venture, Elvis immediately began studying the script for *Flaming Star*.

Reports in the press began publicizing Elvis Presley's next movie while *G.I. Blues* was still being shot. Colonel Parker wanted two Elvis features in release before 1960 concluded, so while *G.I. Blues* was released in November, *Flaming Star* came out less than a month later, after just four weeks of shooting. This practice would be used again later (the feature *Double Trouble* coming out soon after the release of *Easy Come, Easy Go* in 1967), but at that time, it was due to an anticreative, assembly-line type of production to which the Elvis movies had, by then, descended. However, this was not the case in 1960. *Flaming Star* turned out to be one of Elvis Presley's finest films, and one that some consider his all-time best.

CHAPTER 8
Flaming Star
(20TH CENTURY FOX, 1960)

Director: Don Siegel
Screenplay: Nunnally Johnson and Clair Huffaker, based on Huffaker's book *Flaming Lance*
Producer: David Weisbart
Assistant director: Joseph E. Rickard
Cinematographer: Charles G. Clarke
Editor: Hugh Fowler
Makeup: Ben Nye
Hairstylist: Helen Turpin
Music: Lionel Newman
Vocal accompaniment: The Jordanaires
Technical advisor: Colonel Tom Parker
Cast: Elvis Presley, Barbara Eden, Steve Forrest, Dolores del Rio, John McIntire, Rodolfo Acosta, Karl Swenson, Ford Rainey, Richard Jaeckel, Anne Benton, L. Q. Jones, Douglas Dick, Tom Reese, Marian Goldina, Monte Burkhart, Ted Jacques, Rodd Redwing, Virginia Christine, Roy Jenson, Barbara Beaird, Lon Ballantyne, Larry Chance, Pat Hogan, Foster Hood, Guy Way, Charles Horvath, William Herrin, Griswold Green, Joe Brooks, Tom Fadden, Sharon Bercutt, Ray Beltram, Bob Adler, Henry Margo, Bob Folkerson, Red West
Songs:[1]
 "A Cane and a High Starched Collar" (written by Sid Tepper and Roy C. Bennett; performed by Elvis Presley)
 "Flaming Star" (written by Sherman Edwards and Sid Wayne; performed by Elvis Presley)
The title song "Flaming Star" reached number 14 on the charts in 1961

Released December 20, 1960
Working titles: *Black Heart, Black Star, Flaming Heart, Flaming Lance*
Filmed August 16–September 25, 1960
101 minutes

> Technicolor
> Aspect ratio: 2.35: 1
> Budget: $1.7 million; gross: $2 million (United States and Canada)
> Released to DVD by Fox Home Video

Flaming Star remains one of Elvis Presley's best films, a serious, dramatic western far superior to *Love Me Tender*, his other film in this genre. Veteran screenwriter Nunnally Johnson (who had written the movie version of Steinbeck's *The Grapes of Wrath*) teamed with the original book's author Clair Huffaker to pen a script that addresses the conflict between whites and Native Americans in a manner that is deeper and more complex than most westerns of this time.

The idea to film *Flaming Star* had been around since 1958 when 20th Century Fox purchased the rights to the novel, *Flaming Lance*, which Clair Huffaker had not yet completed. Nunnally Johnson was originally going to write the screenplay and direct the film, which would feature Marlon Brando and Frank Sinatra as brothers. When negotiations broke down with both actors, Elvis Presley was offered the role of Pacer, a young man who was half–Native American and half-white.[2] And while there remained a brother character (played by Steve Forrest), the focal point was now on Pacer, not on both men as it had been when Brando and Sinatra were attached to the project. Nunnally Johnson was relegated to screenwriter only, and Elvis campaigned to get Michael Curtiz to direct, but was unsuccessful.

Perhaps Don Siegel, who ended up directing the film, is a better choice than Curtiz might have been. Siegel's career also crossed over several genres, and by 1960 he had helmed such enduring classics as *Invasion of the Body Snatchers* and *Riot in Cell Block 11*. He had directed a couple of Audie Murphy westerns and would later direct others, including *Two Mules for Sister Sara* with Clint Eastwood (whom Siegel would direct in Eastwood's career-defining *Dirty Harry*) and *The Shootist*, which would be John Wayne's last movie.

In *Flaming Star*, Elvis is the half–Native American Pacer, whose brother, from his father's previous marriage, is white. The father is now married to Pacer's full-blooded Kiowa Indian mother. She is shown as caring, compassionate, and understanding despite the hatred she experiences from others in the area after rampaging Kiowa warriors begin terrorizing white families for settling on their land. Because of Pacer and his mother's heritage, their family is spared from these attacks while friends are massacred. When his mother is killed by a vengeful white man, Pacer's anger causes him to leave his family to live with members of his mother's tribe. When warriors from the tribe engage in a random attack on what turns out to be his white brother, Pacer comes to the rescue and saves his seriously wounded brother's life, but discovers that the Indians have already killed his father. Betrayed, Pacer sets out to battle the Kiowa tribe alone. Pacer returns home mortally wounded just to see that his brother has recovered, then says farewell and rides off to die alone.

Once again rising to the occasion with a solid, effectively understated performance, Elvis found many things in *Flaming Star* to which he could relate. He was actually part Cherokee on his mother's side, so he was intrigued by the depiction of Native Americans. And of course the death of the mother character in the movie was another factor to which he could relate. As with all of his movies, it is evident that Elvis worked very hard at playing his role. There were many scenes in which he had to convey rage, and these moments show how much he had improved as an actor since his debut in *Love Me Tender*. While in the former film his newcomer status made him nervous and caused him to overact, in *Flaming Star* he conveyed similar pent-up rage more subtly and effectively. Much of Pacer's angst stems from his inability to feel comfortable with Indian tribes or white settlers. The earlier scenes show him enduring the prejudicial treatment of his mother from whites, and later ones indicate betrayal from the Kiowa tribe, whose chief had promised Pacer that his brother and father would always be spared. The role of Pacer is a layered character filled with conflicting feelings, and was the sort of acting challenge Elvis welcomed.

The script deals with racism in a far more intelligent and enlightened manner than many other westerns of the time. The anti-Indian bigotry and the anti-white anger are shown as equally misguided. Unlike John Ford's *The Searchers*, where racism is examined as being inherent in a few individuals, in *Flaming Star* it is shown as embedded within the prevailing culture. The Indians attack and kill white families, including children, for coming onto what they believe is their land. The white settlers respond by believing everyone having Native American heritage to be bloodthirsty savages. Confronting this conflict, examining it by offering an interracial relationship that bore children who are now adults, had some basis in contemporary culture when one recognizes the black-white social unrest occurring in the 1950s and 1960s.

Don Siegel's direction is such that this is as much a Siegel movie as an Elvis one. Each scene opens with an establishing shot that uses the widescreen image to show the serene beauty of the landscape over which the Indians and white settlers battle. There are many violent action sequences in *Flaming Star*, and they are bloodier than what can usually be found in westerns of this era. The very first Indian attack comes early in the film and establishes the conflict for the remainder of the movie. While it is only a few minutes long, it is jarring and upsetting, especially because it follows the movie's opening scene, a lighthearted birthday celebration where Elvis sings the only song in the film. As a trio of partygoers returns home in good spirits, they are very suddenly met with violence. A hatchet is buried into a man's skull. Flaming arrows burn the property. Nobody is spared, and the offscreen violence alluded to (one of the white victims is a pretty young woman) is even more terrifying. Siegel uses medium shots, quick edits, and a swirling music score as the attack disrupts the relaxed pace of the opening sequence, causing the film to suddenly have an edge that remains to the end.

Ensuing battles are more intricately staged as whites and Indians weave around each other on horseback, felled by arrows or gunfire. Siegel continues to stage these battles by cutting between close-ups, medium shots, and long shots, while using a fast pace and quick edits. However, not all of the violence occurs during such battles. One of the most stirring, emotional scenes is when Pacer walks in on two trappers who are about to rape his mother. Siegel focuses on the large, pushy trapper slowly creeping toward the diminutive woman backing away fearfully, shooting it all in a tight close-up. Actor Tom Reese, who played the trapper, was a full foot taller than Dolores del Rio, who portrayed Pacer's mother, so the size dynamic between them enhances the effectiveness of the scene. She slaps him away just as Pacer returns to the cabin, seemingly unaware of what almost happened. They leave quickly but Pacer leaves from the back of the cabin and meets them. Swinging the butt of his rifle to hit one man, Pacer then concentrates on the larger one, tossing away his rifle and fighting him man to man. The scene in which Pacer angrily pummels the man, who is now begging for mercy, shows the character releasing the unbridled rage he has continued to harbor.

Flaming Star ends on a sad note when Pacer returns to bid farewell to his brother, now living comfortably among the white settlers. After delivering the message that there would be no more battles, Pacer rides off to die honorably, having heroically ended the struggle between his two heritages. Siegel frames this sequence beautifully, showing a beaten, bloodied Pacer on his horse, addressing his brother in the foreground while the settlers are strategically placed in various areas of the background. Siegel crosscuts between a shot from behind Presley addressing the others, to a frontal close-up that frames him with the colorful scenery.

Flaming Star was the polar opposite of something as light and simple as *G.I. Blues*, and exactly the type of film, and role, that Elvis Presley sought. Westerns had become very popular on early television, with cowboy actors like Roy Rogers, Gene Autry, and William Boyd (Hopalong Cassidy) moving from films to TV production. Other popular series including *The Cisco Kid, The Lone Ranger, Judge Roy Bean, 26 Men, Range Rider,* and *Annie Oakley* permeated the small screen with popular western entertainment. Thus, with such things available at home for free, movie westerns could no longer be merely action dramas. They needed more substance. This led to the sweeping majesty of John Ford films like *Rio Grande* and *The Searchers* as well as the more cerebral approach taken by *Flaming Star*.

Elvis Presley and Barbara Eden in *Flaming Star*

John McIntire, who played Pacer's father, was just taking over the starring role on TV's *Wagon Train* when *Flaming Star* was released. However it was veteran actress Dolores del Rio, whose career dated back to silent movies, who impressed Elvis the most. She had been away from Hollywood for 18 years when she agreed to play Presley's mother in the film. Upon meeting her for the first time, Elvis gave Dolores a bouquet of flowers with a card that indicated how honored he was to be working with "one of the most respected legends of classic Hollywood." He even arranged to wear brown contact lenses in some of the earlier scenes, so that his eyes would match hers, but they made his eyes look too dark, and the idea was dropped.

Barbara Eden, who had the younger female lead, would become a household name as the star of television's *I Dream of Jeannie* a few years after *Flaming Star*. Originally British actress Barbara Steele had been cast in the role, but was replaced during filming. Some sources state it was because her British accent was too pronounced; others indicate that she got into a heated argument with Don Siegel and walked off the project.

Despite the disappointment of not getting Michael Curtiz to direct, Elvis was quite pleased with the support and respect he received from Don Siegel. Siegel recalled years later for *Rolling Stone*:

> I found [Elvis] sensitive and very good, with the exception that he was very unsure of himself. . . . He felt he could have done better things. And his advisors—namely the Colonel—were very much against doing this kind of straight role. They tried to get him to sing throughout the picture. Obviously, they didn't want him to get off the winning horse. But when I was able to calm him down, I thought he gave a beautiful performance.

The studio took out a full-page ad in the November 2, 1960, issue of *Variety*, listing *Flaming Star* as one of their four main offerings for the upcoming Christmas season. Two weeks later they put in a double-page ad for the film. *Variety* reviewed the movie in its December 21 issue, the same day that it was released nationally:

> *Flaming Star* has Indians-on-the-warpath for the youngsters, Elvis Presley for the teenagers and socio-psychological ramifications for adults who prefer a mild dose of sage in their sagebrushers. The plot—half-breed hopelessly involved in war between white man and Redman—is disturbingly familiar and not altogether convincing, but the film, attractively mounted and consistently diverting, will entertain and absorb the audience it is tailored for. There's good business in store for the 20th Century Fox release.

A. H. Weiler's review in the *New York Times* approached *Flaming Star* as a western Elvis happened to be in, rather than an Elvis Presley movie:

> It is surprising, however, that this small, somber view of some of the misunderstanding and bloody strife between settlers and Indians in Texas of the Eighteen Seventies is equally passionate about both. No guitar gala, *Flaming Star* is an unpretentious but sturdy Western that takes the time, the place and the people seriously. Elvis, for the record, is merely one of the principals caught up in the tensions exposed here. Both the author, Clair Huffaker, and Nunnally Johnson, with whom he collaborated on the script, focus as much on his family as they do on the hero. It is a closely knit, loving unit, seemingly integrated with and well liked by the neighbors until some of them are massacred by aroused Kiowas after a birthday party. The Indians are not simply presented as "heavies" but also as beleaguered men being ruthlessly deprived, in their view, of their lands. The hatreds that follow misconceptions are suggested logically.

While most theater owners were pleased with *Flaming Star,* they also indicated that audiences came to hear him sing. And while there are no songs other than during the opening credits and a brief number at the outset of the film,[3] the ads for *Flaming Star* make it appear to have more music than it does. But this is the way Elvis wanted it. He did demand better and more challenging roles.

Unfortunately the business aspect of Elvis Presley's career was run by the anticreative Colonel Parker, who concentrated on dollar signs. *Flaming Star* made only a paltry $300,000 at the box office, which was $2 million less profit than *G.I. Blues* had shown. Part of this may have been the fact that *Flaming Star* came out only weeks after the release of *G.I. Blues*, which was enjoying great success. Another Elvis movie coming out so soon afterward did not seem to hurt the box office of the earlier movie, but may have been a factor in the poor returns for *Flaming Star*.

Unconcerned with the business aspect of his career, Elvis was pleased with *Flaming Star* and happy with his performance. Since the film's release it has lived on as one of director Siegel's most interesting films, and is often cited as the post-army Elvis Presley movie that most clearly displayed how effective he could be as an actor if he had been allowed to build on his innate ability and continued to land good roles.

While all producers are interested in making good movies, their perspective is financial, and the box office returns for *Flaming Star* were comparatively paltry. This did not stop Elvis from insisting on more dramatic roles that did not concentrate on his music. Just as he had been reaching past his immediate trappings as a singer, branching out into different styles, Elvis was also interested in trying different roles and learning how to be a more effective actor. Elvis remained unsure of himself (according to what Siegel later told *Rolling Stone*), but was dedicated, hardworking, and ultimately pleased with the outcome. As a result of his sensitive portrayal in this movie, Native American Wah-Nee-Ota inducted Elvis into the Los Angeles Indian Tribal Council.

As described in *Elvis Aaron Presley*, an amusing incident that occurred during the making of *Flaming Star* involved Presley associate Lamar Fike. Fike was impressed to see writer and poet Carl Sandburg in the 20th Century Fox commissary, having read Sandburg's books on Abraham Lincoln. Fike introduced himself, indicating he worked for Elvis Presley. Sandburg smiled, and said, "How is that young man?" Fike said he was fine, and Sandburg continued, "He's a fine young man, isn't he?" Since Sandburg had an interest in American folk music, his awareness of Elvis and positive reaction was not surprising. As Lamar Fike recalled, however, this was not mutual. When Fike returned to Elvis and excitedly exclaimed, "I just met Carl Sandburg!" Elvis asked, "Who the fuck is Carl Sandburg?"

Although *Flaming Star* was a step forward creatively, the fact that it opened in theaters only four weeks after *G.I. Blues* allowed Paramount executives (as well as Colonel Parker) to compare the box office success of the two movies side by side. *G.I. Blues* reached as high as number two in *Variety*'s weekly list of top-grossing films and finished 14th in the annual poll. *Flaming Star* never made it higher than number 12 and was far below the year's top box office movies. Marketing reports indicated that the success of the *G.I. Blues* soundtrack album resulted in Elvis fans attending the movie multiple times.

Elvis Presley's producer and manager continued to look at the box office returns for *G.I. Blues* and the accompanying soundtrack album's massive sales, and wanted to make another musical. However, Presley's quest for better movies had continued unabated and resulted in the screenplay of his next project being penned by playwright Clifford Odets. While room had to be made for four songs in the movie, Elvis was eager to start work on another well-written drama, especially since he would be playing a troubled young man very similar to the one he'd played in his successful pre-army feature *King Creole,* which he continued to believe was his best performance. In fact, the character in the new film was more layered, more complex, and Elvis turned in another committed performance. The film was already well into production by the time Parker and the Paramount executives were able to assess the box office of Presley's two 1960 films. When the box office receipts indicated how much more successful *G.I. Blues* was over *Flaming Star*, they decided they would wait and see how Presley's next drama would fare at the box office before deciding how to proceed. Unfortunately, *Wild in the Country* became the only Elvis Presley movie to lose money.

CHAPTER 9
Wild in the Country
(20TH CENTURY FOX, 1961)

Director: Philip Dunne
Screenplay: Clifford Odets, based on the novel *The Lost Country* by J. R. Salamanca
Producer: Jerry Wald
Assistant directors: Joseph Rickards, Harry Scott
Original music: Kenyon Hopkins
Cinematographer: William C. Mellor
Editor: Dorothy Spencer
Makeup: Ben Nye
Hairstylist: Helen Turpin
Technical advisor: Colonel Tom Parker
Cast: Elvis Presley, Hope Lange, Tuesday Weld, Millie Perkins, Rafer Johnson, John Ireland, Gary Lockwood, William Mims, Raymond Greenleaf, Christina Crawford, Robin Raymond, Pat Buttram, Doreen Lang, Alan Napier, Jason Robards, Harry Shannon, Charles Arnt, Walter Baldwin, Joe Butham, Jack Orrison, Cosmo Sardo, Frankie Silver, Red West, Will Corry, Sam Harris, Jimmy Horan, Elisha Mott, Hans Moebus, Mike Lally, Kenner G. Kemp

Songs:
"Wild in the Country" (written by Hugo Peretti, Luigi Creatore, and George Weiss; performed by Elvis Presley)
"I Slipped, I Stumbled, and I Fell" (written by Fred Wise and Ben Weisman; performed by Elvis Presley)
"In My Way" (written by Fred Wise and Ben Weisman; performed by Elvis Presley)
"Husky Dusky Day" (sung briefly by Elvis Presley and Hope Lange with no musical accompaniment during a scene while they're traveling in a car)

Another song, "Lonely Man," was recorded for the film but cut before release. A snippet of Elvis performing "Lonely Man" can be seen in the film's original

coming attractions trailer. "Lonely Man" was released as the flipside to the single "Surrender," and rose to number 32 on the charts.
The title song reached number 26 on the charts in 1961

Released June 15, 1961
Filmed November 11, 1960–January 18, 1961
114 minutes
Technicolor
Aspect ratio: 2.35:1
Budget: $2,975,000; gross: $2.5 million
Released to DVD by Fox Home Video

Wild in the Country is often cited as the final time Elvis Presley was given a solid dramatic role to play, and that its lack of box office success resulted in him acting in the more profitable lightweight musical comedies for the remainder of his career, ending any hopes for more substantial roles. It is indeed the only Elvis Presley movie to lose money at the box office, but was only part of the catalyst for his eventual relegation to less serious roles. *G.I. Blues* was already making far more at the box office than *Flaming Star,* and its soundtrack album was climbing the charts as well. Only four musical numbers appear in *Wild in the Country*, out of six originally scheduled. As with *Flaming Star*, Elvis talked his director into removing two of the songs. And while his next film, the musical *Blue Hawaii*, would be his biggest box office success, his following two films—*Follow That Dream* and *Kid Galahad*—would also have a dramatic edge and are not conventional musicals. After *Kid Galahad*, however, Elvis Presley's films adhered more carefully to a formula. Sometimes this would result in a well-crafted use of said formula (*It Happened at the World's Fair, Viva Las Vegas, Roustabout*), but by 1965 and *Girl Happy*, the films stuck more strictly to a lightweight musical structure, began getting progressively worse, and the singer quickly lost interest.

Part of this has some justification. Unlike *Flaming Star* and his pre-army dramas like *Jailhouse Rock* and *King Creole*, *Wild in the Country* is only a fair movie. Elvis clicked with director Philip Dunne, turning in a committed performance that was bolstered by equally solid acting from a strong supporting cast. However the script, by the usually quite reliable Clifford Odets, lets the actors down.

Wild in the Country takes place in a rural South setting. Elvis plays a character who lost his mother at a young age, and who possesses an innate talent that is brought out by a benevolent adult who believes in him. These are all elements to which Elvis could personally relate, and also similar to the traits of his most successful movie character, Danny Fisher in *King Creole*. However, instead of a talent for singing as Danny had, the character of Glen Tyler in *Wild in the Country* has a knack for writing that has been fed by his passion for reading.

Glen is a bitter, sullen man due to his circumstances and surroundings, also similar to the Danny Fisher character in *King Creole*. Danny, however, used his singing talent to earn money and had a supportive family. Glen is a family outcast, forced to live with an accepting, but untrustworthy, uncle. He spends his time reading everything from the Bible to classic literature, and this frame of reference results in drawing out an innate talent for writing fiction. But he does not use his fiction writing for monetary gain the way Danny used his singing. When he first offers a sample of his writing to a friendly social worker, he insists it is for her eyes only.

It is the relationship between Glen and the thirtyish social worker (Hope Lange) that is the axis of the film. Their initial meeting is uncomfortable for both. When first told he likes to read, she responds with "Comic books?" Her innocent inquiry as to his reading matter is wholly repugnant to Glen, who glares at her. When he later starts meeting with her one-on-one, he reveals the contempt he'd felt and how insulted he had been.

The relationship between the two is due to a court appointment made necessary when Glen nearly beats his brother to death in a barn fight supervised by their father. This scene opens *Wild in the Country*, and as Glen is being defeated in the fight there are cutaways to the father looking on with smiling approval. When Glen emerges victorious after his brother is severely beaten, the father's approval turns to scorn and Glen is sent to live with an uncle. There is no pride in Glen's fighting skill, only anger that he hadn't been taught the lesson his father thought the brother could administer.

Danny Fisher in *King Creole* had some superficial filial conflicts, but not quite as deep as those Glen has in *Wild in the Country*. Danny's father is supportive, but cowardly, unable to stand up for himself in the outside world. Glen's father, who is given little footage in the movie and only during the very early scenes, is dismissive, uncaring, and comfortable with the idea of never seeing his son again, especially after Glen seriously injures his brother in a fight.

Along with the father and the social worker, there are several extending characters in the Odets screenplay. The uncle has a daughter (Tuesday Weld) who has an illegitimate child (to save face, the family indicates that the father is overseas in the military). Glen also has a girlfriend (Millie Perkins) whose own father disapproves of their relationship. The script tries to explore these characters, but never gives them a great deal of depth. Even the dynamic between Glen and the social worker, which is explored, has a rather superficial soap opera feel to it, far beneath the talents of a writer like Clifford Odets, whose screenplays include *Sweet Smell of Success* and *None but the Lonely Heart*. *Wild in the Country* was penned years after Odets's productivity declined in reaction to his

Elvis and Hope Lange in *Wild in the Country*

Elvis is an unruly lad in *Wild in the Country*

cooperation with the House Un-American Activities Committee, which made him a pariah in some circles. *Wild in the Country* would be his final screenplay (he died in 1963).

Elvis does his best in the role of Glen, inspired by the character's Southern background, as well as being both motherless and misunderstood. The character's similarities to the role Elvis had played in *King Creole* was likely another inspiring factor, as that continued to be Presley's most satisfying movie experience. But the script lets him down, as it does for the other actors. The focus eventually rests on Glen falling in love with the social worker, who responds with the same feelings. When a local troublemaker spreads a false rumor of a sexual encounter between the two at a hotel, the humiliated social worker attempts to commit suicide, but survives. In the original script the woman dies, but a new ending had to be reshot when test screenings indicated that the audience was too upset by the original idea, which is a good example of this film's shortcomings. In an attempt to please the audience, the movie was revamped to have a more positive ending.

Director Philip Dunne, who was primarily a screenwriter, responded well to Presley, and Elvis responded well to him. Dunne had a good cast to work with, but realized Presley was the star and carefully showcased him by placing him in the foreground even in scenes where he does not happen to be the central figure. Presley draws upon his personal emotional reserve during a fairly long soliloquy in which Glen recounts his family dynamic and the death of his mother when he was nine years old. However, while Elvis seems committed and honest in his performance, the scene and dialog come off as more stilted and maudlin than moving.

Glen is presented as a constant misconception, always stumbling into situations with troublesome results. He is angry and withdrawn, but the narrative justifies this by presenting him as the victim of situations he is unable to control. Falling in love with the social worker disrupts her relationship with a man closer to her own age. It is that man's son who spreads the rumor about Glen's meeting her at a hotel. Glen responds with violence, and the young man dies. He had a weak heart, and it is a heart attack that killed him, but his vengeful father lies in court about his son's condition in an effort to send Glen to prison. During the court proceedings, word comes through that the social worker has attempted suicide, so Glen darts out of court, where he is on trial for his life, and goes to see her. When police try to stop them, the judge states to let him go. She survives, and the man recants his court testimony and admits his son's weak heart was the cause of his death, so Glen is found innocent. Of course this entire sequence of events is completely implausible and another example of the narrative's shortcomings.

Other studies have claimed a certain irony in Elvis Presley playing a writer. Elvis notoriously never composed his own songs, relying on songwriters from the Hill and Range music publishing company. Presley often gets a short shrift for this; his rearrangement of the songs and understanding of production is where his creativity often redefined popular music, so not being a songwriter is of little consequence to his impact, just as a great actor's impact would not rely on whether or not he or she also penned the screenplay.

The central character's writing talent is presented in *Wild in the Country* by having him present his knowledge of biblical verse and scripture during the court's decision. When Glen arrives at his uncle's house, his suitcase is filled with books (the Bible prominent among them). Many of Glen's books are literary fiction that have reached longtime classic status. However Glen's own writing is more suited for children, filled with imagery and an attractive, lilting rhythm. When, with Glen's permission, the social worker has an expert read Glen's prose, the man responds with, "I wish I had written it."

Rather than explore this talent more deeply, Odets only uses Glen's talent as further catalyst for the romantic feelings he develops toward the social worker. She is older, attractive, helpful, warm, and kind. From these qualities, Glen has found his missing mother connection as well as companionship from a level that is much more intellectually based than the one he has with his same-age girlfriend, feeding his literary connection and supporting his talents from a position of authority.

One of the better performed scenes in *Wild in the Country* is an offbeat sequence in which Glen and his cousin get drunk and show up at the home of the social worker, where Glen stumbles about in the front yard and hollers that he wants his story back. The point of the scene is to show Glen wavering between the irresponsibility of his youth and the natural rebellion toward authority. Both Presley and Hope Lange are quite effective in this scene, which is made somewhat more impressive in that Elvis did not drink. In fact, during the filming of *Wild in the Country*, Hope Lange came to visit the singer at the residence he had in California while shooting the movie, and Elvis was embarrassed when she asked for a vodka and he had no liquor in the house (he would thereafter stock it for guests).

Tuesday Weld was only eighteen years old when she appeared in *Wild in the Country* but had already done film and television work, and was currently appearing in a recurring role on TV's *The Many Loves of Dobie Gillis*. She recalled:

> Elvis was just so physically beautiful that even if he didn't have any talent . . . just his face, just his presence. And he was funny, charming, and complicated, but he didn't wear it on his sleeve. You didn't see that he was complicated. You saw great needs.

Wild in the Country received a pretty scathing review from the stodgy Bosley Crowther in the *New York Times,* whose contempt for Elvis was obvious, even to the point of his poking prejudiced fun at the singer's Southern roots. His backhanded complimentary review of *G.I. Blues* was the last Presley film he critiqued (*Flaming Star* had been reviewed by A. H. Weiler). His response to *Wild in the Country* was:

> Apparently the good, clean Elvis Presley who returned from the Army to the screen in *G.I. Blues* was not what the teen-agers wanted the guitar-playing lover-boy to be. And so, in *Wild in the Country*, which came to the Paramount yesterday, Elvis is back as a problem for himself, the parole board and us. In this seamy, sentimental lot of nonsense, which we are requested to believe that Clifford Odets has written, our nemesis plays a kid who has all the education and social presence of an underprivileged resident of Tobacco Road. Nonsense, that's all it is—sheer nonsense—and Mr. Presley, who did appear to be improving as an actor in his last picture, is as callow as ever in this. The few times he sings are painful—at least they are to our ears—and his appearance is waxy and flabby. Elvis has retrogressed. So have Jerry Wald, the producer; Philip Dunne, the director; and, alas, Mr. Odets.

While *Wild in the Country* was not a good movie, its limitations were not as Crowther described. They were not due to Elvis playing an angry character rather than a smiling, affable lightweight. There was a deeper complexity to Glen, but the problem was that the script never explored it with any real intelligence. They relegated the character to trite situations and defined his anger as little more than classically misunderstood. The narrative was cluttered with thematic ideas that were given too little attention to develop, and the somberness had a deadening effect rather than an intriguing one.

Theater owners of the time indicated that *Wild in the Country* drew enough of a crowd, but it was determined that "Elvis made this movie for the older people" rather than for his usual teenage base. However, the fact that *Wild in the Country* was the only Elvis Presley movie to lose money at the box office makes it obvious from a marketing standpoint that this is not the way Presley's fans wanted to see him. *G.I. Blues* had set a standard for success—lightweight romantic musical comedy with enough songs for an album that will also move up the charts. The recording and the movie play off each other, resulting in massive success for both. It was perfect for Colonel Parker or Hal Wallis, but Elvis had other ideas. He continued to want his movie career to be separate from his music. *Wild in the Country* had two song numbers cut because of Presley's insistence and director Philip Dunne's acceptance of the singer's directive. Still, *Wild in the Country* was marketed as if it were a musical, the ads showing a smiling, guitar-wielding Elvis that bears no resemblance to the character he actually plays in the movie.

In an interview, Fike related that Colonel Parker was said to have confronted Elvis, stating that "you wanna do this dramatic stuff we won't make any money." Thus, Elvis agreed to do another musical believing that he could then return to more serious drama. His next film, *Blue Hawaii*, would feature 14 songs, enough for a full album that would be marketed with the movie as had happened so successfully with *G.I. Blues*. Elvis read the script, looked over the songs, and was not impressed with the project. But unlike many superstar performers who would leverage their star power to insist on things their way, Elvis Presley's mind never ventured too far from his dirt-poor roots, and Parker could easily manipulate him by indicating that he could lose all he had earned if success did not continue. He approached movies as a job he was hired to do. And while he may have been able to offer enough creative input to get songs cut from *Flaming Star* and *Wild in the Country*, he was unfortunately limited from choosing his own projects. *Blue Hawaii* would be the next Elvis Presley movie.

The fact that *Wild in the Country* was unsuccessful at the box office had a lot to do with the unfortunate fact that audiences seemed to prefer the lighter fare like *G.I. Blues*, but the general climate for iconic movie stars was not particularly rewarding in any case. Marilyn Monroe's film *Let's Make Love* was fraught with problems and failed to recoup its production costs as well. The box office was being dominated by epics at the level of *West Side Story*, *El Cid*, and *The Guns of Navarone,* which further pushed a film like *Wild in the Country* aside, especially since the film was not directed specifically to the youth market that had initially embraced Elvis.

None of the songs from *Wild in the Country* became a hit. Only the title song was issued as a single, but as the B side. The A side was the non-movie rocker "I Feel So Bad," which is one of his better songs from this period. Continuing to explore different possibilities, Elvis also cut the operatic "Surrender," which was another big success. However the best of the songs that came out between the release of *Wild in the Country* and *Blue Hawaii* was the upbeat rocker "Marie's the Name (His Latest Flame)" which used a Bo Diddley–styled guitar riff and became one of the best Elvis singles of the 1960s. Along with the singles, Elvis also released the album *Something for Everybody*, which characteristically included diverse musical styles.

The rock purists among Presley's fans were becoming more and more chagrined at his steadily moving away from his base rock and roll roots. The achingly pure vocal performance on his Sun and early RCA recordings like "Mystery Train" and "Trying to Get to You" and the unbridled rock and roll of "Hound Dog" and "Jailhouse Rock" seemed to fade into memory as the post-army Elvis explored different avenues. As late as the twenty-first century essays decried the direction Presley's music ended up taking. Elvis, however, was as influenced by pop stylist Dean Martin as he was by the blues, country, and R&B pioneers, and thus, wanted to investigate the depth of his capabilities as a singer.

With his movies, however, Presley continued to hope for serious drama, with no connection to his music. With *Blue Hawaii* in preproduction, Elvis realized his film and music careers could not always be separate entities. He was willing to compromise to some extent if making the occasional musical comedy would net him the opportunity to appear in more serious films. But Elvis was no businessman, and allowed all of the business to be handled by his management. And his manager had other ideas as to how Presley's film career should progress. Elvis would now begin shooting what would become the most financially successful movie of his career.

CHAPTER 10
Blue Hawaii
(PARAMOUNT, 1961)

Director: Norman Taurog
Screenplay: Hal Kanter, from a story by Allan Weiss
Producer: Hal Wallis
Associate producer: Paul Nathan
Assistant director: Michael D. Moore
Cinematographer: Charles Lang Jr.
Editor: Terry Morse
Editorial supervisor: Warren Low
Costumes: Edith Head
Makeup: Wally Westmore
Hairstylist: Nellie Manley
Vocal accompaniment: The Jordanaires
Technical advistor: Colonel Tom Parker
Cast: Elvis Presley, Joan Blackman, Angela Lansbury, Nancy Walters, Roland Winters, John Archer, Howard McNear, Steve Brodie, Christian Kay, Iris Adrian, Hilo Hattie, Jenny Maxwell, Pamela Austin, Darlene Tompkins, Lani Kai, Jose De Vega, Frank Atlenza, George DeNormand, Gregory Gaye, Flora Hayes, Roger Clark, Bobby Barber, Bess Flowers, Pamela Akert, Yolanda Hughes, Thomas Glynn, Pat Fackenthall, George Halas, Sharon Lee Connors, Lillian Culbert, Veronica Ericson
Songs (in the order performed):
  "Blue Hawaii" (written by Leo Robin and Ralph Rainger; performed by Elvis Presley)
  "Almost Always True" (written by Fred Wise and Ben Weisman; performed by Elvis Presley)
  "Aloha Oe" (written by Queen Liliuokalani; performed by Elvis Presley)
  "No More" (written by Don Robertson and Hal Blair; performed by Elvis Presley)
  "Can't Help Falling in Love" (written by George David Weiss, Hugo Peretti, and Luigi Creatore; performed by Elvis Presley)

"Rock-a-Hula Baby" (written by Fred Wise, Ben Weisman, and Dolores Fuller; performed by Elvis Presley)
"Moonlight Swim" (written by Sylvia Dee and Ben Weisman; performed by Elvis Presley)
"Ku-u-i-Po" (written by George David Weiss, Hugo Peretti, and Luigi Creatore; performed by Elvis Presley)
"Ito Eats" (written by Sid Tepper and Roy C. Bennett; performed by Elvis Presley)
"Slicin' Sand" (written by Sid Tepper and Roy C. Bennett; performed by Elvis Presley)
"Hawaiian Sunset" (written by Sid Tepper and Roy C. Bennett; performed by Elvis Presley)
"Beach Boy Blues" (written by Sid Tepper and Roy C. Bennett; performed by Elvis Presley)
"Island of Love (Kauai)" (written by Sid Tepper and Roy C. Bennett; performed by Elvis Presley)
"Hawaiian Wedding Song" (written by Charles E. King, Al Hoffman, and Dick Manning; performed by Elvis Presley)

The *Blue Hawaii* soundtrack album spent 20 weeks at number one in 1961
"Can't Help Falling in Love" reached number two on the charts
"Rock-a-Hula Baby" reached number 23

Released November 22, 1961
Filmed March 27–May 1, 1961
102 minutes
Technicolor
Aspect ratio: 2.35: 1
Budget: $2 million (estimated); domestic gross: $4.7 million
Released to DVD by Paramount Home Video

Blue Hawaii did not set out to be the quintessential Elvis Presley movie, but that is exactly what it turned out to be. Light, breezy comedy, an abundance of musical numbers, lots of color, pretty girls, and a dollop of narrative conflict would eventually become the standard ingredients for any Elvis movie for the balance of his career.

Blue Hawaii is not a bad movie any more than *G.I. Blues* had been. However, Presley's plans to grow as an actor were thwarted by this film's success. Realizing he had a job to do, Elvis moves through *Blue Hawaii* just fine, with a committed, likable performance. He had not yet given up on the idea that he would make the occasional lightweight musical comedy in order to also secure better roles in films that would be separate from his singing. However his producer, Hal Wallis, and his manager, Colonel Tom Parker, approached it as purely a business venture. They had seen the box office receipts for *G.I. Blues* and the success of the accompanying soundtrack album, then measured

Elvis in *Blue Hawaii*

that against the box office disappointment of both *Flaming Star* and *Wild in the Country*, which were made on loan to 20th Century Fox and did not feature enough songs for an album. So when Elvis returned to his home studio of Paramount, producer Hal Wallis chose another musical like *G.I. Blues* in an effort to repeat that success. He also arranged to fill the movie with a whopping 14 musical numbers, the most in any Presley vehicle. He even went so far as to cast Elvis as a returning soldier. The result was the sort of massive success the producer and manager had hoped to achieve, and the sort of fluffy, superficial entertainment that Presley was less interested in doing.

Unlike *G.I. Blues*, which quickly established its rather simple plot, *Blue Hawaii* takes its time in doing so. This film's opening scenes are a rather disjointed pastiche of various events attempting to establish characters and conflicts. The girl waiting for the returning soldier, the old friends on the beach, the conflict with his wealthy parents, and his interest in finding a job are all given some marginal attention in a series of scenes that stumble rather clumsily into each other. Elvis has time to immediately sing a song upon being picked up from the airport, accompanying the instrumentation coming from the car radio. There is also time for an island dance bit as we are waiting for some semblance of a plot. Once this plot is established, the film never grows into a solid narrative, just a series of conflicts and scenes that are accented by musical numbers that range from good to bad. Director Norman Taurog keeps the VistaVision shots wide so that a great deal of the beautiful location scenery dresses up the background, and the resulting package is a free-form, mindless film of unremarkable music and easy comedy that, taken as a package, is successful within its own creative parameters.

Elvis plays Chad Gates, returning from the army to his home in Hawaii where his socialite mother (Angela Lansbury) takes umbrage with his waiting girlfriend Maile (Joan Blackman) who is of a lower social class. Chad's father (Roland Winters) is accepting of his girl, but hopes that Chad will join the family business. Tired of taking orders, Chad wants to relax and have some fun on the beach with his friends, and is satisfied with a job as a tour guide, due to his thorough knowledge of the island. He is given the job of acting as guide for a pretty young teacher and her teen girl charges during their stay in Hawaii, and must not only deal with the jealousy of his girl, but with a bratty student who ends up falling for him.

Despite so many characters, *Blue Hawaii* remains very simple and straightforward, its appeal being the scenery, the songs, and the light, breezy comic situations. Elvis is the central figure in each of these tangential plots, all of which tie together in the end. *Blue Hawaii* features the ballad "Can't Help Falling in Love," which was a big hit, as well as the upbeat "Rock-a-Hula Baby," but most of the other dozen songs are unremarkable. Also, the way the songs are staged are more in line with a standard musical production rather than a rock and roll musical. In most rock and roll musicals, including Presley's own *G.I. Blues*, the musical numbers have an organic connection to the narrative. Whenever a song comes on, it is being performed on a stage in a club, or some such situation. In *Blue Hawaii*, the songs are randomly performed—in a car, or on the beach—with no justification for the orchestra music that backs him up. While this is standard practice for musical films, *Blue Hawaii* is the first Elvis Presley movie that presents them in this manner.

One of the main conflicts is Chad's difficulty with the recalcitrant Ellie (Jenny Maxwell),[1] a seventeen-year-old tourist who is part of a group chaperoned by a pretty teacher. Ellie exhibits haughty boredom at each of Chad's attempts to present interesting tourist attractions, while the others respond favorably to his ideas. It is eventually revealed that she is attracted to Chad, and even goes as far as sneaking into his room at night. Her comeuppance at the end of the movie has Chad turning her over his knee and spanking her. This results in better behavior. However it also further redefined Presley's image. He was no longer the representative of teenaged angst, but a paternal figure who administers parental-type discipline to effectively teach a young girl a lesson.

Of course the attractive teacher and her impressionable students are the catalyst for Maile's jealousy, which is justified in that Chad immediately proves himself to be unfaithful in his first appearance on-screen. As he disembarks from the plane during that scene, he is shown amorously kissing a pretty stewardess goodbye. Maile is quickly forgiving when Chad claims, "She means nothing to me," as she is so pleased to have him home from the army.

The dynamic here is indicative of the era and the gender roles in films such as this. Chad, the virile soldier, is automatically forgiven, and his dalliances end as soon as he steps off the plane and returns to his original surroundings. He is home from the army, Maile is his girl, and he spurns the interested teacher and the crushes of her younger charges. Thus, whatever he might have done in the service, all the way up to and including the plane ride home, is somehow justified. This seems rather outrageous from the perspective of twenty-first-century thinking, but it does depict rather standard gender stereotyping of its era.

For his role, Elvis seems comfortable and effective. His manner is cool, his responses are sound, his facial reactions are amusing, and his delivery is confident. Presley makes Chad an attractive, amusing individual whose confidence while conducting the tour of his homeland turns to confusion and borderline panic when Ellie barges into his room as he answers the door, and plops on his bed. This is where *Blue Hawaii* toys with farce, as another knock on the door forces Chad to hide Ellie from the other young girls who have now pushed their way into his room. Ellie's response to Chad's lack of interest is to run into the ocean and try to drown herself. It is this activity that causes Chad to conclude

Elvis as disciplinarian in *Blue Hawaii* (with Jenny Maxwell)

that she needs "a good old-fashioned spanking," and proceeds to administer just that. No matter how far fetched the scenes may be, Elvis never oversells his role.

The structure of *Blue Hawaii* is initially uneven, with the aforementioned opening scenes taking their time to arrive upon a narrative. The script attempts to justify these scenes as Chad wanting to spend a couple of days back on the island without having to see his demanding parents. Even once a narrative is established, it seems to be just a backdrop for the songs and beautiful scenery. Every few minutes the plot development is interrupted for a musical number. While the songs, as indicated, are not among Presley's best, they maintain the breezy pace that such a film would warrant. The entire package resulted in the sort of massive success that Colonel Parker wanted out of Presley's movie career, while the simple nature of the film was exactly what Elvis did not want. However, the success of the film is undeniable. *Blue Hawaii* was applauded by critics in *Box Office* magazine as "just the type of film Elvis Presley should be doing," while theater owner reports included such comments as "an extra box office attraction in gorgeous color," "a wonderful family picture that played to big crowds for nine shows," and "a jewel."

It appears that the beautiful color scenery and lightweight pop songs were enough for moviegoers, and the Presley character's harmless demeanor was deemed acceptable to critics. *Blue Hawaii* seems far removed from serious dramatic productions like *Jailhouse Rock* and *King Creole*.

One of the positive aspects of the film, other than its box office success, is its use of strong supporting players, which would be another staple of Presley's subsequent movies. Veterans like Roland Winters, Angela Lansbury, John Archer, and Howard McNear are welcome additions to the cast, although Lansbury would later denounce *Blue Hawaii* as the worst movie in which she would appear.[2]

Joan Blackman was the producer's second choice to play Maile. Originally wanting to find yet another ingredient from the success of *G.I. Blues*, that film's leading lady, Juliet Prowse, was offered the role. Prowse accepted only on condition that her makeup stylist from her home studio of 20th Century Fox be hired, and that her secretary be flown to the location shooting at Paramount's expense. Heated discussions resulted in her being taken off the picture by producer Hal Wallis. Her home studio of Fox also suspended her, as her demanding actions resulted in losing valuable loan-out money for that studio.

Despite the soundtrack album containing absolutely no rock and roll other than the aforementioned "Rock-a-Hula Baby," it was a massive success, remaining at number one for 20 weeks and staying on the charts for a year and a half. The single released from this album contained the movie's two hit songs, "Can't Help Falling in Love" and "Rock-a-Hula Baby." Elvis would not release a studio recording until the beginning of 1962, the soundtrack for this movie providing enough revenue. Colonel Parker saw that a light musical with an exotic setting, pretty girls, and a soundtrack album's worth of songs was the most financially successful format for an Elvis Presley movie. He huddled with producer Hal Wallis and they realized they had stumbled upon a formula that would suffice for Presley's subsequent movies.

Elvis was already committed to two pictures for United Artists, *Follow That Dream* and *Kid Galahad*, each of which had the dramatic component that Presley preferred and only a handful of songs. However, after those were produced, Colonel Parker saw to it that Elvis Presley movies would follow at least some aspect of the formula that resulted in greater box office success, much to the singer's chagrin.

Screenwriter Hal Kanter did not originally intend to rely strictly on pretty scenery, girls, and pop songs. He wanted to include at least some dramatic substance to his plot. An entire subplot concentrating more seriously on the conflict between Chad and his parents was jettisoned, as were other isolated dramatic sequences. Associate producer Paul Nathan told Hal Wallis that Kanter was trying to turn Elvis into "another Jimmy Dean," who, ironically, happened to be one of the actors Presley most admired.

At one point during filming, Colonel Tom Parker stood up and yelled, "Cut," which is something only the director is allowed to do. Parker's interruption was due to the fact that Elvis happened to be wearing his own watch in a scene. The Colonel had it stipulated in Presley's contracts that if the singer wore any of his own clothing or jewelry in any movie scene, his fee would increase by $25,000. Director Norman Taurog had Elvis remove his watch and reshot the entire scene.

As with *G.I. Blues*, there is some harmless fun to be had in *Blue Hawaii*. The scene where comedy actor Howard McNear plays the head of the tourist company where Chad is looking for work is one highlight. He cagily quizzes Chad, who answers all the questions correctly; McNear's halting delivery is so amusing that Elvis is noticeably cracking up during the scene. Elvis is quite amusing during the scene where Chad's private room is invaded by the student tourists, his comic reactions showing that he knows exactly how dangerous a situation he is in despite his innocence. And the very ingredients that pleased moviegoers at the time of the film's initial release—the breezy pace, the beautiful scenery, the pretty girls—still hold up as reasons the film remains pleasantly entertaining over a half century later.

The fact is, both critics and moviegoers preferred Elvis in these mindlessly entertaining musicals. His management embraced them for their financial success. And while Elvis attempted to fight for good scripts and top directors, the success of this and *G.I. Blues* caused his management to overrule any of his creative ambition. Parker told Elvis that the dramatic films would lose money, as proven by *Wild in the Country*. And while Presley never lost his creative ambition, he also never forgot that he was a dirt-poor Southerner who was now very wealthy, and he signed contracts in advance for his next several films. He approached movies as a job, and he did what he was hired to do. But he was said to be quite upset when he found out that the financial success of *Blue Hawaii* allowed Paramount to produce the prestigious *Becket* with Richard Burton and Peter O'Toole. Elvis did not like the idea doing lightweight musicals in order to finance the type of prestigious picture for which he would like to be considered.

Dave Marsh in his 1982 book *Elvis* stated:

> In addition to celebrating his victory, fans also demanded, as the price of their loyalty, that he behave according to prevailing standards, that he cease challenging them and begin delivering safe and platitudinous doses of the already known. Elvis' fans caged him much more effectively than the record companies, movie moguls, TV censors, song publishers, or even the military could have hoped to do. Because Elvis had never escaped the employee mentality, he related to the audience as his boss. His own needs and desires were, if not entirely subordinate, beside the point.

Critics who were supportive of *Blue Hawaii* (and of *G.I. Blues*) were not indicating that either was great cinema by any definition. These critics were simply pleased that they were not to take Elvis Presley seriously as they had been forced to do with *Jailhouse Rock, King Creole, Flaming Star*, or even *Wild in the Country*. It was far more convenient to approach Elvis as a lightweight singer cavorting about in a simple musical comedy, than to assess his work at the level of a serious actor in a serious drama.

However it was not the critical reaction that mattered to the likes of Hal Wallis and Colonel Parker. Critics do not buy tickets. The fact that moviegoers, as Marsh indicates, preferred the affable Elvis in lightweight musicals is why these productions would soon become identified with Presley as a series of star vehicles. *Blue Hawaii* is therefore a very important production in the Elvis Presley filmography.

CHAPTER 11
Follow That Dream
(UNITED ARTISTS, 1961)

Director: Gordon Douglas
Screenplay: Charles Lederer, based on the novel **Pioneer Go Home** by Richard Powell and the play by that title by Herman Raucher
Producer: David Weisbart
Editor: William B. Murphy
Makeup: Dan Striepeke
Hairstylist: Madine Danks
Techinical advisor: Colonel Tom Parker
Cast: Elvis Presley, Arthur O'Connell, Anne Helm, Joanna Moore, Jack Kruschen, Simon Oakland, Roland Winters, Alan Hewitt, Howard McNear, Frank DeKova, Herbert Rudley, Gavin Koon, Robin Koon, Robert Carricart, Barry Russo, Pam Ogles, Harry Holcomb, Red West
Songs (in the order performed):
  "What a Wonderful Life" (written by Sid Wayne and Jerry Livingston; performed by Elvis Presley)
  "I'm Not the Marrying Kind" (written by Sherman Edwards and Mack David; performed by Elvis Presley)
  "Sound Advice" (written by Bill Giant and Anna Shaw; performed by Elvis Presley)
  "Follow That Dream" (written by Bernie Weisman and Fred Wise; performed by Elvis Presley)
  "Angel" (written by Sid Tepper and Roy Bennett; performed by Elvis Presley)
The title song reached number 15 on the charts in 1961

Released April 11, 1961
Filmed July 11–August 28, 1961
109 minutes
Technicolor
Aspect ratio: 2.35:1
Domestic gross: $2.8 million
Released to DVD by MGM Home Video

With only four musical numbers (including the song over the opening credits), *Follow That Dream* is not only structured in a manner that pleased Elvis Presley, it remains one of his best films and is one of Presley's most impressive performances as an actor. Charles Lederer, whose work as a screenwriter encompassed everything from the snappy comedy *His Girl Friday* (1939) to the original *Ocean's Eleven* (1960), adapts Richard Powell's folksy book *Pioneer Go Home* and adds an attractive comic element that is most successful. Gordon Douglas, whose directing efforts include work by such comedians as Harry Langdon and Laurel and Hardy, effectively builds upon the comic sensibility in Lederer's script. Never forced or obvious, *Follow That Dream* retains the book's folksy style and is both funny and charming. For his part, Elvis Presley completely absorbs the personality of Toby Kwimper, a simpleminded but sensible young man whose brute strength and trusting ways are central to the narrative's success.

The film opens as the Kwimpers, a makeshift hillbilly family traveling by auto through Florida, run out of gas at a public park near the water and set up housekeeping. Uneducated, but with a simple, folksy knowledge of their rights, they identify themselves as homesteaders to a state supervisor, indicating a right to live on public property. They even confront the governor who is passing by in a motorcade, and the statesman is pleasantly impressed with their zealousness. The state supervisor, however, is chagrined and decides to engage a pretty welfare worker to use her wiles to investigate the situation.

This is the basis of the film's plot, with Elvis as part of an ensemble rather than the absolute focal point of each scene. The makeshift family consists of Elvis as Toby Kwimper and Arthur O'Connell as his father, Pop Kwimper. They are the only two members of this family that are actual blood relatives. The others include Holly, a teenage girl, as well as twin boys and a smaller child, who are orphans the Kwimpers have taken in as their own. The confrontation by the state supervisor, played with gusto by Alan Hewitt, is a nice character contrast. The Kwimpers are simple, friendly, patient, but stubbornly fixed on their understanding of their rights. The supervisor's threatening bluster does not faze them.

From this basic plot structure, Lederer's script introduces other characters in tangential situations that relate directly to the central narrative. An amusing bit where a suit-clad business sort comes by as Toby and Holly are attempting to hook a fish works effectively as an isolated sequence within the film's context, but is actually a setup for a later, more significant scene. The businessman, introducing himself as a banker, is captivated by Toby's attempt to reel in a large stingray, and is delighted when Toby hands the fishing pole over to him. He reels in the fish triumphantly and has a perfectly delightful time doing so. Toby and Holly realize a business opportunity with the good fishing just off the pier of their homestead, and plan to create a business. Starting out small at first, the

Elvis, Anne Helm, Gavin Koon, Robin Koon, and Arthur O'Connell in *Follow That Dream*

business soon grows to the point where providing bait and equipment is not enough. They want to expand to include boats and other high-level accessories. A loan from the bank is necessary.

At this point it is already quite evident how effectively Elvis Presley performs the role of Toby. While he is an uneducated backwoods man, he has the logical sensibility that allows him to draw conclusions in the simplest terms. He is also immediately presented as having amazing physical strength. When their car first runs out of gas, Toby lifts it off the ground and pushes it off the road.

When Toby and Holly prepare to go to the bank, they find a parking meter with a bit of time left on it, believing the fifteen minutes remaining on the meter will be enough time to secure a loan. However Toby's vacant stare and controlled manner seems intimidating, and he is mistaken for a burglar. Alarms go off, the bank is locked, the customers crouch to the floor, and armed guards confront Toby. Confused, he hits a guard, takes away his gun, and then tries to revive the man he just hit. The bank president comes out of his office. It is the man who'd enjoyed fishing with Toby in an earlier scene. He realizes there is no danger, while Toby still does not understand that he has been mistaken for a criminal.

The earlier fishing scene sets up the fishing business Toby and Holly start, which in turn sets up the scene at the bank where they attempt to secure a loan. That the character who acted as catalyst for the development of their fishing business becomes the man from whom they must secure a loan is a nice tie-in that extends the characters and makes each scene more amusing.

It is worth noting that the loan officer who mistakes Toby for a bank robber is played by Howard McNear, who had also done an amusing comic turn in *Blue Hawaii*. At the time *Follow That Dream* was being filmed, McNear had a recurring role on television's *Andy Griffith Show*, which had some similarities in character presentation as this film. Andy Griffith played a small-town sheriff in North Carolina, whose folksy sensibility outsmarted visiting lawmen from the big city on more than one episode. While this was an extension of Griffith's standup comedy character (and the sheriff role would be modified over the TV show's eight seasons), there are some similarities to the role Elvis plays in *Follow That Dream*.

Another extension of the plot features a nearby trailer that houses a gambling operation run by mobsters. As the Kwimpers have set up a homestead, Toby has himself legally promoted to sheriff by getting the small community who live in the area to support him (including the mobster, who believes Toby will be of no consequence to their operation). Toby does, however, attempt to thwart the gambling, not for the illegality of the practice but simply because the late-night noise has been disturbing others who live nearby. When two thugs attempt to attack Toby, he assumes they are simply demonstrating a technique of attack he must watch out for as a lawman, and counters, accidentally knocking them both out. The mobsters then realize they have to hire hit men to take care of the problem rather than rely on their own resources.

The scenes in the bank and with the mobsters are good examples of Elvis finding the humor inherent in his role. He plays it straight, projecting a bewildered innocence to which the viewer responds favorably. Toby never realizes he is in danger in either situation; he just accepts the behavior of those around him without any attempt to analyze it. When he subdues the two thugs, his reaction is "Gosh, I didn't mean to hurt you," but his reaction is not one of surprise, indicating this might have happened before. When he sees that the bank patrons have crouched to the floor and two armed guards have drawn weapons on him, he forcibly takes the guns and scolds each, indicating they could hurt someone that way. His naïveté is never frustrating to the viewer. It is endearingly amusing, and Elvis plays it with his usual commitment. He never wavers from the character.

This persona extends to the sequence where hired hit men from Detroit seek out Toby for elimination. Interestingly, this is played purely for comedy. Toby is walking down a woodsy path with Holly when a car swerves and nearly hits them. He orders Holly to go home while he assumes his sheriff duties and deals with what he believes are drunk drivers. Even when the men shoot at him, Toby continues to believe that they are so intoxicated, they don't realize what they are doing. With his knowledge of the woods, he easily ditches them, throwing rocks in different areas to distract the criminals from where he is. He finally manages to sneak up on the head crook and take his gun, soon getting the others as well.

Throughout this scene Toby is confident and in control despite his uneducated simple manner. He is now within his niche, in familiar surroundings, whereas the city-bred criminals are completely out of sorts. The crooks play this entire sequence as comic heavies, exhibiting comical frustration. They never appear scary or menacing as hit men from a big city might be in a more serious drama. When Elvis sneaks up on the leader and takes his gun, the hit man runs away and finds the others. "Boss, where's your gun?" one of the others asks. "Never mind, just get him!" is the reply. This boisterously comic scene does not seem out of place in what is otherwise a more subtly amusing film. The inherent humor in the proceedings allows this sequence to stand out as a comic highlight rather than a distraction from the movie's prevailing structure.

Follow That Dream takes a somewhat more serious turn when a welfare worker hired by the state supervisor comes to the Kwimper homestead and talks to Toby in a purring, flirtatious manner in an attempt to entice him into revealing information that could help the supervisor to make a case against their intrusive homestead. Toby does not fall victim to her wiles; his innocence puts up an emotional shield. Undaunted, she makes a case for the twins and younger child to be put in foster care, and the family ends up in court. Toby acts as the family's attorney and, with his folksy sensibility, makes his case.

Presley plays this scene beautifully, looking bewildered once his family recruits him, and exhibiting a tentative approach to the bench ("I ain't so good at talkin', Judge, but Pop has faith in me and he's usually right"). Toby first exhibits his usual logical philosophy: "If I was a judge deciding who should bring up three nice kids, I'd just want to know if Pop is a good man and if Holly was a good woman. You can ask the twins about Holly. Kids know who they love. Holly's just a kid too, but they don't come no better."

The welfare worker points out that Toby's answers on a word association test are cause for concern. It is decided that Pop should take the same test, being that he would be the children's guardian. Toby whispers something to the judge, and the test begins. The welfare rep very negatively analyzes the answers the judge reads, including the response of "shine" to the word "moon." She states that it displays Pop's fondness for illegal liquor. The judge seems offended: "What about 'Shine on Harvest Moon'?" It is then that the judge reveals the answers are not Pop's but his own. That was Toby's whispered suggestion. The judge tells Pop from the bench, "You were right about not needing a lawyer. You couldn't have had a better one." So the family set up a homestead, fought back criminals and governmental intrusion, emerged victorious and successful, and did it all with simple folksy common sense.

Producer David Weisbart, who had worked on Presley's film debut *Love Me Tender,* remained sympathetic to the singer's interest in stronger roles with more acting and less singing. Elvis was on loan to United Artists at that time, and those behind the production seemed to believe that his fans were as interested in seeing him act as they were in hearing him sing. Elvis always rose to the occasion with each movie role, even those he found less challenging. But his role in *Follow That Dream* is the most unusual one he would play in his career (even more so than his roles in *Flaming Star* and the much later western *Charro!*). Presley must convey both Toby's slow wit and genuine intuition. Elvis plays the role with lumbering movement and a vacant stare. The sly, all-knowing twinkle in Presley's eye during a film like *G.I. Blues* is gone. The sullen anger that comes out in *Jailhouse Rock* or *King Creole* is also missing. Toby is a completely different character, and one that Elvis plays as perfectly as any of his movie roles.

The relaxed subtlety of the pacing blends nicely with the backwoods innocence and inherent honesty of the characters. They do not live the fast-paced life of the banker, with his myriad of responsibilities. Thus, while the banker sees the fishing opportunity as a means to escape, Toby and Holly see it as a possible way of life—a means for their survival.

Richard Powell, writer of the original novel *Pioneer Go Home* on which *Follow That Dream* is based, was initially displeased about Elvis Presley being cast in the role of Toby, but changed his mind after seeing the movie. He thought Elvis captured the character perfectly.

Throughout the film's running time there is always an element of humor embellishing the folksy charm. There are two running gags. One has Toby reciting the multiplication tables every time a girl becomes flirtatious toward him (including the welfare worker and the pretty Holly). Toby even discusses this method for distracting him from his base instincts, recalling that "one girl once had me all the way up to the twelves." Another running gag features Pop Kwimper's attempts to install a fully functioning outhouse, but the plumbing keeps backing up and drenching him with water.

Presley associate Lamar Fike recalled in *Elvis Aaron Presley* at least one amusing incident that occured during the filming of *Follow That Dream.* Fike was asked to drive a car onto the scene, but the auto got stuck in the sand "all the way up to the axles." It had to be removed with machinery, causing a delay in filming. The director, Gordon Douglas, and the camera crew all started cussing out Fike. Usually very well behaved and polite on the sets of his movies, Elvis became quite agitated to see the director and crew yell at one of his associates. According to Fike, the singer said, "Any of you motherfuckers think you can pop off to one of my people, you're mistaken. If this happens again, I am walking off the set!" According to Fike, "Everyone was really nice after that."

Another interesting event that occurred during the filming of *Follow That Dream*. Tom Petty, eleven years old at the time, was visiting his uncle who was involved in the production of the movie. He got the chance to meet Elvis, whose charismatic friendliness and kindness had an enormous impact on the youngster. Shortly thereafter, Petty recalls trading his slingshot for a collection of Elvis records. They inspired him to become a musician. Two years later he saw the Beatles on Ed Sullivan, and proceeded to form his own band.

Rural comedy and folksy sensibilities seemed to be rather popular in American culture during this period. The Ma and Pa Kettle movie series, about a rustic couple with several children attempting to adjust to a more modern lifestyle, had been very popular with audiences during the 1950s. Television's *The Real McCoys* and the aforementioned *Andy Griffith Show* were currently on the air, and *The Beverly Hillbillies* would premiere in the fall of 1962 (this pattern would continue with other rural-based sitcoms like *Green Acres* and *Petticoat Junction* throughout the decade). *Follow That Dream* fits this niche.

There are fewer songs in *Follow That Dream* than would be found in the musicals. While that would change soon, *Follow That Dream* was completed, and Presley's next film, *Kid Galahad*, was already in production before *Blue Hawaii* was released. It would be during the filming of *Kid Galahad* that *Blue Hawaii*'s profits would convince his manager and producer that musicals were the way to stronger profits. And it was profits, not critics, that someone like Colonel Parker heeded, as *Follow That Dream* enjoyed good reviews as something different. *Variety* even went so far as to state that the song numbers were a distraction from the story and should not have been used at all. Such a review pleased Elvis, who was proud of his performance in the movie. He was reminded by the Colonel that critics do not buy tickets. Or soundtrack albums.

Variety further stated:

> Scenarist Charles Lederer has constructed several highly amusing scenes in tailoring Richard Powell's novel, *Pioneer, Go Home*, to fit the specifications of the screen. And director Gordon Douglas has made capital of the screenplay's better moments, translating the comedy of the typewriter into amusing and fast-paced visual terms.
>
> Presley buffs figure to take very kindly to the David Weisbart production, which displays their hero in good form in the kind of vehicle

in which the record shows him to be salable . . . Presley conveys the right blend of horse sense and naiveté in his characterization.

The stodgy Bosley Crowther of the *New York Times* sniffed:

> Fan us with a palm frond—and a ragged one, at that. Elvis Presley, who was seen in *Blue Hawaii* now appears on the Florida coast as a combination Sir Galahad and Li'l Abner in *Follow That Dream*. Judging by this laboriously homespun and simple-minded exercise about just plain folks, somebody must have decided that the Presley films have been getting a little too glossy lately. In any case, compared to yesterday's serving of cornmeal mush, *Blue Hawaii* was caviar.

As there is nothing in his review that could not be garnered from the film's coming attractions trailer, it is possible Crowther did not bother watching the movie at all. Crowther was always particularly dismissive of the Presley movies, clearly representing the old guard's dislike for the rock and roll cultural revolution. It is notable that the *New York Times* hadn't even bothered to review *Blue Hawaii*, which was among the top ten biggest grossing films of 1961.

Follow that Dream did not reach near the success of *Blue Hawaii* at the box office. It only ranked among the top grossing films for a couple of weeks, peaking at number five, while *Blue Hawaii* remained at number one for some weeks and ranked eighth among all the films released that same year. *Follow That Dream* ranked a respectable 30th for the year 1962, but that is a far cry from the top ten. The songs from *Follow That Dream* were released on an extended play record (EP) but only the title track and the ballad "Angel" were particularly good.[1] And while Elvis released the outstanding double-sided non-movie hit "Little Sister" and "(Marie's the Name) His Latest Flame," the soundtrack for *Blue Hawaii* was the most profitable record at the time *Follow That Dream* was being filmed.

Theater owners reported the reduced box office for *Follow That Dream*, often indicating a good opening night led to weaker business over the next few days. Word of mouth got around that this was not the Elvis Presley who projected affable confidence and a plethora of musical numbers. This was Elvis the actor, essaying a more defined role. That the character allowed Presley to tap into the extent of his acting ability meant nothing to his fans. The box office response to *Follow That Dream* versus the one for *Blue Hawaii* made it quite clear that moviegoers wanted songs flooding a light romantic comedy.

Upon completion of *Follow That Dream*, Elvis started work on the next film he'd been contracted to do for United Artists. *Kid Galahad* was a remake of a stirring 1937 Warner Brothers drama that had starred Edward G. Robinson, Bette Davis, and Humphrey Bogart. Elvis had reportedly seen and enjoyed the

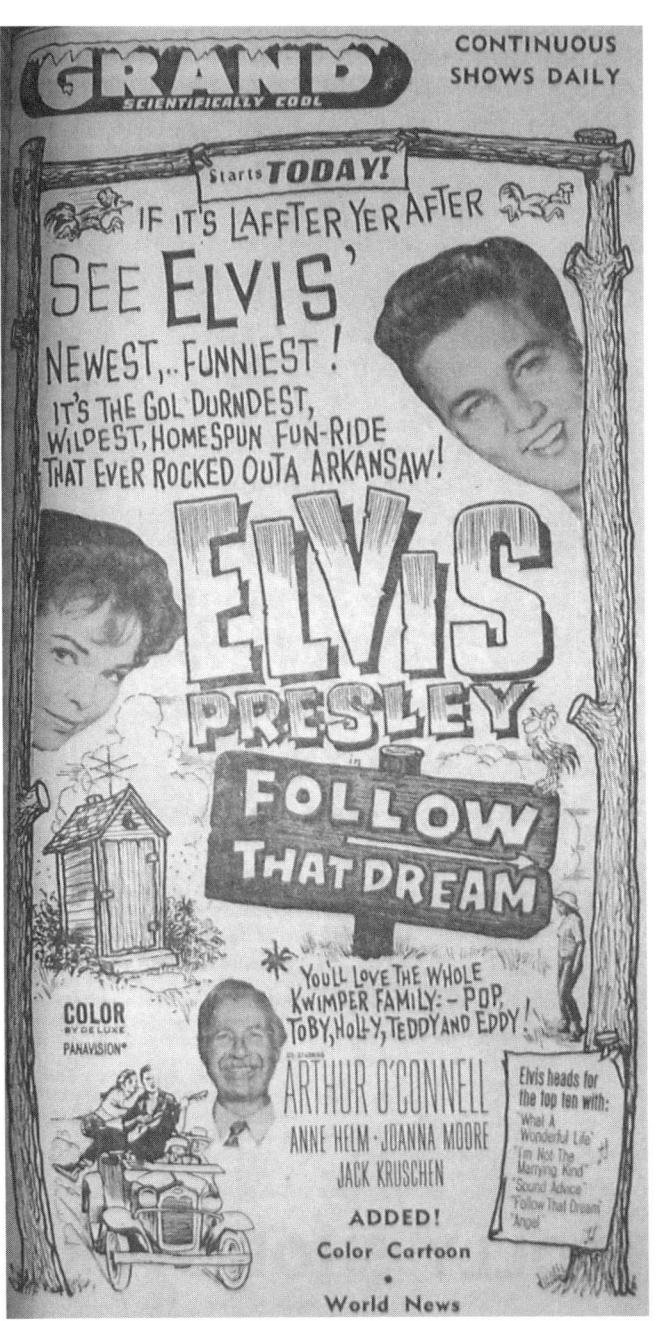

Newspaper ad for *Follow That Dream*

98   CHAPTER 11

Crowded premiere for *Follow That Dream*

original film, and was excited to be starring in a reworking of the story. Another strong point from Presley's perspective was that the 1937 version had been directed by Michael Curtiz, who remained the singer's favorite director. Elvis inquired as to the possibility of having Curtiz direct this remake. He was saddened when told that the director had been in poor health since completing directorial work on the John Wayne western *The Commancheros* (1961), suffering from the cancer that would take his life in April 1962.

Once production began on *Kid Galahad*, Elvis became aware of the massive success *Blue Hawaii* was enjoying at the box office. Elvis realized that meant he would be doing more musicals. However, the fact that he was currently filming another serious drama with fewer songs gave him the impression that agreeing to do the occasional musical would allow him to continue pursuing better movies that contained fewer song numbers. Presley remained optimistic about his movie career and was willing to compromise when it came to doing the musicals about which he would privately complain to his associates. Meanwhile, Colonel Parker told the press that Elvis chose all of his own movie roles from scripts that were sent directly to his home, when in fact it was Parker who recognized that the formula utilized in *Blue Hawaii*—a plethora of mediocre songs, a simple comic plot, and lots of pretty girls—is what made the most money. While Elvis had creative aspirations as an actor, wanting to grow and achieve greater things, the Colonel remained strictly motivated by money. Even when *Time* magazine wanted to put Presley's picture on their cover, the Colonel told them it would cost $25,000. Thus, it didn't happen.

According to Marty Lacker in *Elvis Aaron Presley*, "All of these big time agents and managers and producers would dress really nice. But what would Colonel wear? A big smock that said 'Elvis Elvis Elvis.' He looked like a clown, but he didn't care. If somebody asked him about it, he'd say 'You remember whose name is on there, don't you?'"

Because of Parker's concentration on box office over creative achievement, *Kid Galahad* would be the last Elvis Presley movie that had the dramatic edge and limited number of songs that Elvis favored.

CHAPTER 12
Kid Galahad
(UNITED ARTISTS, 1962)

Director: Phil Karlson
Screenplay: William Fay, from a story by Francis Wallace
Producer: David Weisbart
Assistant director: Jerome Siegel
Cinematographer: Burnett Guffey
Editor: Stuart Gilmore
Makeup: Lynn Reynolds
Hairstylist: Alice Monte
Boxing stuntmen: Dick Dial, Joe Gray
Technical advisor: Colonel Tom Parker
Cast: Elvis Presley, Gig Young, Lola Albright, Joan Blackman, Charles Bronson, David Lewis, Robert Emhardt, Liam Redmond, Judson Pratt, Ned Glass, George Mitchell, Roy Roberts, Michael Dante, Richard Devon, Jeffrey Morris, Chris Alcade, Jimmy Lennon Jr., Mike Lally, Tommy Hart, Ralph Moody, Orlando De La Fuente, Frank Gerstle, Mushy Callahan, Bert Remsen, Jeffrey Sayre, Paul Sorensen, Sara Taft, Ed Asner,[1] David Caliente, Nick Dimitri, Louie Elias, Joe Esposito, Sonny West, Joe Gray, Kip King, Gil Perkins, Al Silvani, Hal Taggart, Sailor Vincent, Harry Wilson, Bill Zuckert, Red West, Ralph Vokie, Charles Sherlock
Songs (in order performed):
  "King of the Whole Wide World" (written by Ruth Batchelor and Bob Roberts; performed by Elvis Presley)
  "This Is Living" (written by Fred Wise and Ben Weisman; performed by Elvis Presley)
  "Riding the Rainbow" (written by Fred Wise and Ben Weisman; performed by Elvis Presley)
  "Home Is Where the Heart Is" (written by Sherman Edwards and Hal David; performed by Elvis Presley)
  "I Got Lucky" (written by Dolores Fuller [as Dee Fuller], Fred Wise, and Ben Weisman; performed by Elvis Presley)

> "A Whistling Tune" (written by Sherman Edwards and Hal David; performed by Elvis Presley)
>
> The song "King of the Whole Wild World" reached number 30 on the charts in 1962
>
> Released August 29, 1962
> Filmed November 6, 1961–January 5, 1962
> 95 minutes
> Technicolor
> Aspect ratio: 1.85:1
> Domestic gross: $2.5 million
> Released on DVD by MGM Home Video

While this film is said to be a remake of the 1937 Warner Brothers drama *Kid Galahad*,[2] it only has a few marginal similarities to the earlier movie. In this one Elvis is yet again a returning G.I., this time traveling back to the city where he was born. He had been orphaned and subsequently adopted, so this is a return to his roots. He ends up in the fight game after getting a job as a sparring partner and knocking out an up-and-coming boxer during a training session.

Boxing dramas had become fairly clichéd even as early as the 1937 movie, all of them utilizing the same narrative arc of a young, fresh-faced kid who packs a good punch being trained to achieve a championship title. There are invariably conflicts along the way, usually allowing the various characters to develop. For instance, in both this and the 1937 film a distraction is the fight manager's pretty sister. In the 1937 film, Edward G. Robinson's fight manager is fiercely protective, and angrily thwarts any romance. In the remake, Gig Young's fight manager is annoyed but eventually accepting. It is a focal point in the earlier movie, but merely a tangential plot element in this version.

Otherwise, the similarity between the two films is quite standard. Elvis plays Walter Gulick, whose fighting skills are eventually honed, but who dreams of owning his own garage and working as a mechanic. In the earlier film Wayne Morris portrays a fighter whose dream is to own a farm. Both versions of the character have a homespun quality, but Morris plays it with far more innocence and naiveté. The Elvis character is returning from the army. He has seen the world. He understands people and is not easily duped.

There is a gangster element to both films, more predominant in the earlier one as mobster movies were quite popular during the 1930s. It was the era in which John Dillinger and Bonnie and Clyde became folk heroes for robbing banks, as these institutions invariably held the mortgage on homes during Depression America. They were the bad-guy capitalists who profited from the

Elvis as Kid Galahad

struggling working class. Therefore, the gangsters who stole from them became antiheroes, as did the movie tough guys who played fictionalized representations of them. By 1962, the time of this film, the gangsters depicted were not the rugged Depression-era types as played by Humphrey Bogart or Edward G. Robinson. They are more business oriented, and their violence is less impulsive. This is another tangential element in the 1962 version that had been much more central to the plot of the original.

Director Phil Karlson was a seasoned veteran by the time he directed this Presley picture, having helmed everything from classic film noir like *The Phenix City Story* and *Kansas City Confidential* to movies featuring the Three Stooges and the Bowery Boys. While he has none of the stylistic grace that Michael Curtiz gave to the original, Karlson has a journeyman quality that allows the story to be effectively told. His filming of the final fight sequence is one of the movie's highlights. However, he seems more out of place when helming the musical numbers, most of which seem out of place within the context of a boxing drama. Elvis would have preferred there be no music at all, but stops are made for a handful of song sequences. The best is "King of the Whole Wide World," which Elvis sings over the credits while hitching a ride on the back of a truck. Karlson shoots it in a medium shot, with Elvis singing and drumming his palms on his thighs, obviously enjoying his freedom from the service and looking forward to his hometown journey. A few of the other songs—"I Got Lucky," "This Is Living" and "A Whistling Tune"—are good, but seem out of context and distracting from the story.

A tried-and-true subject, a good director, a committed performance by Elvis, and a strong supporting cast, and yet *Kid Galahad* is a disappointment. The story is a bit too clichéd, too predictable, and the characters aren't absorbing enough. *Kid Galahad* is just another average boxing drama with a few songs. Not a bad movie, but not a particularly good one either.

One of the more effective character elements is the relationship between Walter and his trainer Lew, played by Charles Bronson. For all the chemistry Elvis and Bronson shared on-screen, this apparently did not extend to real life. Bronson was a loner, and said little to others on the set. He appeared to be suspicious of Presley, while Elvis respected Bronson's acting background and his talent. Elvis also liked to practice his karate between takes, and would sometimes put on demonstrations for the other cast members during breaks. Bronson seemed to dismiss these events as showing off. While some references indicate that Bronson kept his distance from Elvis throughout the filming and would not speak to him except during a scene, those who were on the set disagree. According to Presley associate Lamar Fike in *Elvis Aaron Presley*, "Charlie was real quiet, but real strong. He and Elvis sort of circled each other for a while. After they got to know each other they got along real well." Their relationship on-screen is one of the purest and most natural things in *Kid Galahad*.

Charles Bronson also has one of the most stirring scenes in the film. When Lew refuses to comply with the gangsters, they get even by breaking both of his hands. While the actual violence is not shown, Bronson's reaction is most effective. He plays it with stoicism despite his body trembling in pain and his hands now immobile. When Walter comes to the rescue and starts battling the thugs, Lew stands up and helps with kicks and blocks, despite being unable to use his fists. Not only one of the more inspiring scenes in the movie, it is significant for not centering specifically on Elvis. Presley preferred to not have to single-handedly carry a picture, and *Kid Galahad* allows the veteran acting heavyweights to work in scenes that do not always involve his character.

The film builds up to a climax where the gangsters want to put Elvis against an opponent he cannot beat and then bet against him for a big payday. They choose a rough veteran fighter from Puerto Rico. Naturally Elvis ends up winning the fight despite the gangsters' various attempts to manipulate the outcome, from the breaking of Bronson's hands to putting their own cut man in Elvis's corner to make sure his bleeding doesn't stop (the man is knocked out in the locker room by the fight manager before he can enter the ring).

Because it is the concluding scene, the final fight is one of the movie's highlights. Karlson films it quite brilliantly, switching from overhead shots, to medium shots, to close-ups, to lower-level shots. Quick edits and fast movement by each fighter, along with peripheral movement among the audience in the background, makes this sequence fast and exciting.

When the 1937 *Kid Galahad* concluded, the gangsters were quite unhappy that the outcome went differently, and the fight manager is gunned down. In this version, the gangsters who had been so menacing in the scenes leading up to the fight are not seen at all once the fight concludes. Their reaction is not even presented on camera. The film ends with a celebration in the locker room, as Elvis and the manager's sister kiss for the fade-out. The mobster dynamic that had been so predominant is dropped and forgotten.

That is the chief problem with *Kid Galahad*. It never focuses long enough on any of the narrative's elements. It does not concentrate on the boxing aspect, and when it does present fight scenes, it shows Elvis being pummeled in the ring until a culminating punch knocks out his opponent. Such a strategy seems ineffective, but it somehow works in context. By the final fight, he has altered this style. The romance between Presley's character and the fight manager's sister (Joan Blackman from *Blue Hawaii*) presents Elvis as a veritable role model rather than the angry, rebellious character he had played in previous dramas. He suggests marriage, and is offended when the manager insinuates that premarital sexual relations are going on.

Even the gangster element seems like just another subplot and never feels integral to the narrative, especially when it is dropped as a loose end at the movie's conclusion.

Award-winning actor Gig Young, who plays the fight manager, turns in his usual strong performance despite the rather tepid material. Presley associates recall Elvis being quite taken with Young's wife at the time, actress Elizabeth Montgomery, who would visit the set on occasion. Montgomery would become a household name in another two years when her TV show *Bewitched* would hit the airwaves. Elvis was distracted by his attraction to Montgomery while former boxer Mushy Callahan would be trying to train him to look believable in the boxing scenes.³

Kid Galahad enjoyed some success at the box office, but once again did not achieve anywhere near the numbers of either *G.I. Blues* or *Blue Hawaii*. One theater owner was particularly pleased with the success of the movie, stating in *Box Office* magazine, "Despite blizzard conditions, this was a smash at the box office as King Elvis came up with another bigger, better-than-ever, grosser. More total admissions on Sunday than attended *King of Kings* in four days. Move over Rock Hudson, Elvis is king here!"

Critics were generally satisfied with this as a prototypical boxing picture, except for the Elvis-hating Bosley Crowther, who continued to represent the archaic old guard unable to comprehend that the culture had long since changed. He stated:

> The last thing you might think Elvis Presley is qualified to do is act a diffident amateur boxer who turns out to be a tiger in the professional ring. And you might well persist in that opinion after seeing him in "Kid Galahad," a sportive remake of an old Wayne Morris picture, which came to the Astor yesterday.
>
> Mr. Presley is certainly no model for a statue of Hercules, and his skill at projecting an illusion of ferocity is of very low degree. The expanses of flesh that he exposes when he gets into boxing togs are a fair indication that most of his muscles have come from punching a guitar, and his pout when he clouts a rival bears no resemblance to a killer's slit-mouthed sneer. Furthermore, the proclivity assigned him by his genius and William Fay's script of expressing himself at odd moments in conspicuously un-pugnacious songs, brought up from what seems a ruptured larynx, does not endow him with a gladiatorial air. No, we'll have to agree that Mr. Presley does not make a very convincing pug. But somehow this clique-ridden [*sic*] picture, which has its origin in an ancient novel by Francis Wallace that has been drawn upon (or snitched from) for any number of Golden Boy films, makes a moderately genial entertainment. It's not explosive, but it has the cheerful top of a lightly romantic contrivance that ranges between comedy and spoof.
>
> For this we can thank the other actors who played their roles ardently and Phil Karlson, who has directed at a brisk and deceptive pace.

Even when he gives the film a backhanded good review, Crowther is unable to resist a personal attack on Elvis Presley. His reviews are interesting reading now because of how wrongheaded he was about the prevailing culture, and how his close-minded approach to that culture appears more dated than any of the movies he covered.

Kid Galahad would be Elvis Presley's last film with a more solid story and a dramatic edge for several years. And while not a particularly great movie, *Kid Galahad* is once again another example of Elvis being able to act in the lead role of a serious drama with long stretches of dialog. He is committed and convincing as usual. Elvis yearned for more creative challenges as an actor, just as he continued to explore other avenues for his music. He did not limit himself to the rock and roll that put him on the map, but also explored the limits of his vocal range with more operatic pop fare. While the music of the early sixties was not as daring or immediate as the songs of the fifties had been, Elvis continued to dominate the charts for the first half of the decade.

Kid Galahad is also notable for something that Presley associate Marty Lacker recalled in *Elvis Aaron Presley*:

> We were doing *Kid Galahad* when I first noticed what Elvis called his makeup case. It was a professional Hollywood makeup case with little drawers in it. He carried it with him wherever he went or had one of us carry it. It wasn't for makeup. He used it to carry pills.

The drug taking that Elvis had begun while in the army continued afterward. While he would not do marijuana, cocaine, LSD, or any of the drugs that became more popular with rock musicians as the 1960s continued, he would abuse prescription and over-the-counter drugs quite regularly.

Lacker continued:

> The whole top layer of that kit was nothing but prescription bottles. All legal. Uppers and downers. Pain pills. You name it: Emperin with codeine number 3, the strongest there is. Demerol. Percodan. Tuinal. Placidyl. He had a pharmacy in that box.

The explanation usually given regarding Elvis Presley's drug habit is that he was forced to live a nocturnal existence in order to function at all. His stardom was so enormous, he was very much a prisoner of his own fame. He would rent out theaters after closing time to see the latest movies with an entourage of friends, family, and associates. He would almost never visit clubs, and would leave quickly when recognized. And while he would agree to sign autographs, he would soon be mobbed and despite being with associates, the situations would sometimes become dangerous. Rings, watches, and other personal items would be pulled right off of him. In order to cope with this offbeat way of living, Elvis used pills to stay awake, pills to fall asleep, pills for pain, pills for mood. This situation would later have tragic results, as it would become the undoing of Elvis.

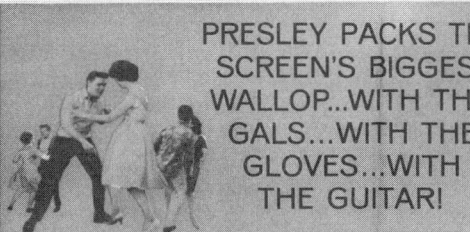

Poster for *Kid Galahad*

Kid Galahad would make a modest profit at the box office, about at the same level as *Follow That Dream*. Based on theater owner reports of the era, *Kid Galahad* was well received by moviegoers, some of them indicating that the audience was no longer limited to teenagers when an Elvis movie was playing. Grownups had gotten over their initial shock in 1956 when "Heartbreak Hotel" crashed on the radio waves, interrupting the likes of Perry Como and Kay Starr. They had moved past the rugged, rebellious upstart who exhibited counterculture attitude in *Jailhouse Rock* or *King Creole*. Elvis had served in the military, sung opera-influenced pop songs, made quaint, amusing musicals. He was now a pleasant, affable performer with no danger about him. Purists continue to point to this as a veritable dismembering of the entire rock and roll myth. In fact, Presley's evolution resulted in continued success and greater versatility with his music, and guaranteed box office success for his movies.

Elvis would next return to Paramount and Hal Wallis, who was set to produce another big-budget musical that would be carefully tailored to Presley's style in the same manner as *G.I. Blues* and *Blue Hawaii*. Elvis continued to be less interested in musical productions and sought dramatic films without a lot of music (as *Kid Galahad* and *Follow That Dream* had been), but also continued to reason that the occasional musical would continue to allow him the opportunity to pursue roles more akin to his interest. He wanted to grow as an actor, but realized that since he did indeed have to work in the occasional lightweight musical comedy, he tried to do his best to also develop as a musical comedy performer. Elvis would often cite Frank Sinatra, who did musical comedies but also played in dramas, even winning an Oscar for his supporting role in *From Here to Eternity* (1953).

Elvis Presley's next movie at Paramount for Hal Wallis was entitled *Girls! Girls! Girls!* and would be another huge box office hit.

CHAPTER 13

Girls! Girls! Girls!
(PARAMOUNT, 1962)

Director: Norman Taurog
Screenplay: Edward Anhalt and Allan Weiss, from a story by Weiss
Producer: Hal Wallis
Cinematographer: Loyal Griggs
Editor: Stanley Johnson
Makeup: Wally Westmore, Jackie Bone, Gary Morris
Hairstylist: Nellie Manley
Vocal accompaniment: The Jordanaires
Technical advisor: Colonel Tom Parker
Cast: Elvis Presley, Stella Stevens, Jeremy Slate, Laurel Goodwin, Benson Fong, Robert Strauss, Guy Lee, Frank Puglia, Lili Valenty, Beulah Quo, Ginny Tiu, Elizabeth Tiu, Alexander Tiu, Nestor Paiva, Mary Treen, Barbara Beal, Betty Beal, Gavin Gordon, Richard Fairservice, Richard Collier, Marjorie Bennett, Kenneth Becker, Pamela Duncan, Ann McCrea, Anna Wai Hong Lin, Lance LeGault, Robert Kupihea, June Jocelyn, Alexander Didio, Hal Blaine, Stanley White, Masako Yoshimoto, Jack Nitzsche, Linda Rand, Wilfred Watanabe, Edward Sheehan, Red West
Songs (in the order performed):
   "Girls! Girls! Girls!" (written by Jerry Leiber and Mike Stoller; performed by Elvis Presley)
   "I Don't Wanna Be Tied" (written by Bill Giant, Bernie Baum, and Florence Kaye; performed by Elvis Presley)
   "We'll Be Together" (written by Charles O'Curran and Dudley Brooks; performed by Elvis Presley)
   "A Boy Like Me, a Girl Like You" (written by Sid Tepper and Roy C. Bennett; performed by Elvis Presley)
   "Earth Boy" (written by Sid Tepper and Roy C. Bennett; performed by Elvis Presley, Ginny Tiu, and Elizabeth Tiu)
   "Return to Sender" (written by Otis Blackwell and Scotty Moore; performed by Elvis Presley)

> "Because of Love" (written by Ruth Batchelor and Bob Roberts; performed by Elvis Presley)
> "Thanks to the Rolling Sea" (written by Ruth Batchelor and Bob Roberts; performed by Elvis Presley)
> "Song of the Shrimp" (written by Sid Tepper and Roy C. Bennett; performed by Elvis Presley)
> "The Walls Have Ears" (written by Sid Tepper and Roy C. Bennett; performed by Elvis Presley)
> "We're Coming in Loaded" (written by Otis Blackwell and Scotty Moore; performed by Elvis Presley)
> "Dainty Little Moonbeams" (written by Jerry Leiber and Mike Stoller ;performed by Elvis Presley)
> "I Don't Want To" (written by Janice Torre and Fred Spielman; performed by Elvis Presley)
> "Never Let Me Go" (written by Jay Livingston and Ray Evans; performed by Stella Stevens)
> "The Nearness of You" (written by Ned Washington and Hoagy Carmichael; performed by Stella Stevens)
> "Baby, Baby, Baby" (performed by Stella Stevens)
> "Mama" (written by Charles O'Curran and Dudley Brooks; performed by the Four Amigos)
> "Where Do You Come From" (written by Ruth Batchelor and Bob Roberts; performed by Elvis Presley)
>
> The *Girls! Girls! Girls!* soundtrack album reached number three on the charts
> "Return to Sender" was number two on the charts for five weeks
>
> Released November 21, 1962
> Filmed April 9–May 16, 1962
> 106 minutes
> Technicolor
> Aspect ratio: 1.85:1
> Domestic gross: $2.6 million
> Released to DVD by Paramount Home Video

Back at his home studio of Paramount, Elvis was once again singing and sunning in Hawaii, surrounded by beautiful, colorful scenery, and being plagued by his relationship with the title characters.

Star vehicles are not unusual. There were films tailor made for John Wayne, Bob Hope, Doris Day, and many other stars during this same period. Sometimes there would be a deviation. Bob Hope would make the biographical drama *Beau James*. Doris Day would appear in the suspense film *Midnight Lace*. John Wayne would portray Genghis Khan in *The Conqueror*. But for the most part, Hope stuck with breezy comedies, Doris Day with romantic comedies, John Wayne with western action dramas. Elvis Presley had deviated with his more dramatic films. But he was a singer. And singers made musicals.

Poster for *Girls! Girls! Girls!*

While many discussions of Presley's movies are dismissive of the musicals, and Elvis himself was unhappy with the unchallenging nature of such light fare, the formula was successful. The earlier films of this nature were popular, well liked, crossed over several demographics, made money, and were reasonably entertaining in an insubstantial way. They were not great cinema, but Elvis himself never sought to make great cinema. He just wanted solid dramas with no music where he could hone an area of skill that he would like to have pursued. He did not expect to be as innovative in film as he had been in music. He made no creative contribution beyond acting (and singing) in his movies. But Elvis liked movies, and wanted to make good ones that did not rely on his music career.

Girls! Girls! Girls! is the same sort of disarming entertainment that *G.I. Blues* and *Blue Hawaii* had been. The movie opens by introducing Elvis as Ross Carpenter, a handsome, virile fisherman who works and lives on a boat that he and his father had built. He wants to someday save enough to buy the boat from the current owners, a kindly older couple. However they must move to a dryer climate for health reasons, so Elvis suddenly loses his job and a place to live.

This introductory scene takes very little time to set up Ross Carpenter's plight, which forces him to be pragmatic and resourceful. In a matter of minutes, he goes from comfortably singing the title song over the opening credits, to having to readjust his entire life. He goes to the nightclub where Robin, a girlfriend (Stella Stevens), works as a singer. She argues with Ross about his continued need to own the boat, stating, "Your father is gone and so is that part of your life." When she refuses to go onstage for her next song, Ross is asked by the club owner (Robert Strauss) to take her place for one song. He wows the audience. The club owner indicates Ross can make money at the establishment anytime he'd like to appear regularly as a singer. Ross dismisses the opportunity, stating, "I'm just a fisherman."

This first song in the movie (other than the title track over the opening credits) has an organic connection to the narrative. It takes place with Elvis onstage, backed by a band, and even the number itself ("I Don't Wanna Be Tied") relates directly to the conversation he just had with his girl. The song is good, upbeat, and leads directly into a conflict that introduces another character integral to the plot. An obnoxious drunk becomes loud and abrasive toward Ross, who asks the man's attractive companion about the situation. The woman is Laurel (Laurel Goodwin), who explains that she is on an unhappy blind date. The drunk is easily removed from the establishment and Ross brings Laurel home.

At this point all of the conflicts and central characters have been introduced. Robin is conflicted, angry, still interested but unable to appreciate Ross's dream. Laurel is new, interesting, amusing. When Ross takes her home and says, "Aren't you going to ask me upstairs?" she quickly replies, "They double the rent for that!" It is, therefore, quickly established that a transition is being made from Robin to Laurel. It is not frivolous. Ross needs support at this time, and Robin simply is not offering it.

From this point the movie continues with a series of scenes that are light and breezy, much like the structure of *Blue Hawaii*. The narrative is always lurking, as are the various conflicts that define its structure, but they are often subliminal to the action. A new conflict is introduced when Ross gets a job working for the new owner (Jeremy Slate) of the boat he wants to buy. He is allowed to live on the boat, and must also maintain it. However when he takes it for a fishing expedition as instructed, the owner pays him a smaller percentage than had been promised. There is little Ross can do except throw a couple of punches, but that does not allow for much success in his ultimate quest to own the boat.

There are isolated sequences that are enjoyable in *Girls! Girls! Girls!* just as there had been in *Blue Hawaii*. One of them has Ross coming over to dinner at Laurel's place. Her attempt to cook dinner results in a roast burning in the oven, so Ross has her relax while he uses immediately available resources and cooks dinner himself. The romantic nature of this scene is augmented by what is perhaps the most comedy *Girls! Girls! Girls!* boasts. Ross arrives at the door just as everything is going haywire. He greets her with a cheerful "Hello!" but is pulled into the apartment by his arm and asked to help put out a fire.

There are some one-liners sprinkled through the frantic putting out of fires. "Do you have any salt?" Ross asks, realizing enough of it could smother the blaze. Laurel is not sure. Ross opens the doors under the sink. "Are you looking for salt there?" Laurel asks. "No, a place to hide!" Ross answers. As he looks around for something to salvage their dinner plans, Ross opens the loudy, creaky refrigerator door and looks inside. "Do you have any oil?" he asks. "Oh I don't mind that the door squeaks," Laurel replies. "Cooking oil!" Ross loudly clarifies, exhibiting comic frustration.

What is most interesting about the film's occasional attempt to be funny is Presley trying to make each scene more amusing with nuanced expressions. When he is pulled into the apartment, he does not simply express the macho confidence that had been established with his character, but offers a confused wide-eyed comic expression. He frequently displays subtle comic reactions such as this throughout the movie, even when his character is a peripheral part of the action. Laurel works in a hat shop. In one scene she must deal with a haughty customer while Ross waits for her. The customer loftily announces, "I am Mrs. Figgett!" The comical sound of her name, especially in context of her announcing it to command greater attention and respect, causes Ross to roll his eyes in a most amusing manner. This appears to be a nuanced reaction from Presley's own instincts as an actor. It is small, understated, but evident as he stands in the foreground of the scene. It is not a double take so much as it is a light comic reaction that simply makes the already amusing context that much funnier. These reactions are good examples of Elvis attempting to bolster the material.

The songs in *Girls! Girls! Girls!* are a mixed bag. The aforementioned "I Don't Wanna Be Tied" is a highlight, as is the title track, penned by one of the singer's favorite songwriting teams, Jerry Leiber and Mike Stoller (who composed "Hound Dog" and "Jailhouse Rock," among others). When Ross finally agrees to sing at the club, becoming more desperate for the money to buy the boat, his opening night performance includes "Return to Sender," one of Presley's greatest songs (penned by Otis Blackwell who also wrote "Don't Be Cruel" and "All Shook Up," among others). However the film is also filled with dull tunes like "Song of the Shrimp" and "Earth Boy," the latter done with two little Chinese girls, adding to its cuteness factor. With the exception of the highlights, most of the dozen songs in *Girls! Girls! Girls!* seem to be hastily composed to fill up a soundtrack album. Some songs, including "I Don't Want To," "Mama," "Plantation Rock," and "Where Do You Come From," were recorded for the movie but not used. A brief bit of Elvis performing "I Don't Want To" can be found in the film's coming attraction trailer.

However, the movie's biggest flaw is its conclusion. Laurel turns out to be from a very wealthy family, but kept the information from Ross in order to make sure he wasn't after her for her money. Once it is established that the romance is genuine, she quietly buys his coveted boat and plans to give it to him as a gift. When Ross finds out, he is offended, spouting a soliloquy about having grown up poor and needing to rely on handouts and announcing that he is too proud to do so now. She sells the boat back to its owner, and Ross decides he is "over it," no longer wanting the boat he'd coveted for the entire movie.

The film's conclusion, where Laurel ends up out on the ocean with the boat's owner, who attempts to have his way with her despite her objections, offers a nice exciting climax as Ross comes to the rescue. He rushes out in a speedboat that leaps over waves, jumps onto the ship, and subdues the villain. The crosscut between location footage and studio back-projection shots is capably handled by director Norman Taurog.

Despite its many flaws, *Girls! Girls! Girls!* is the type of movie Elvis fans wanted. While it did not have the same box office numbers as *Blue Hawaii* (no other Presley film would), it was extremely popular, with theater owners announcing to *Box Office*: "Thanks Elvis for giving me one of the best Saturdays since school started. Beautiful color, songs, and a sprinkling of comedy made this very enjoyable movie fare. Laurel Goodwin has the makings of another Debbie Reynolds," and "Elvis is our most consistent money maker. He never lets us down and as a general rule brings out more of the older people than any other screen personality."

Lobby card for *Girls! Girls! Girls!*

Other exhibitors echoed these sentiments, even mentioning that many moviegoers were coming back to see *Girls! Girls! Girls!* for the second and third time during its run. The fact that this breezy musical resulted in Elvis bringing out "more of the older people than any other screen personality" is more proof of how his image had changed since returning from the army. Compare this with the fact that MGM decided to re-release the 1957 *Jailhouse Rock* to theaters around this same time, causing a theater owner to write, according to *Box Office*, "Time sure has changed our Elvis—his acting and carrying on in this '57 release sure was not our Elvis of today. Not a bad picture, though. The teens enjoyed it—and wondered." So, five years after its triumphant release, a solid Elvis Presley drama with a top director and strong script left even his teenage audience baffled, while the theater owner appears to indicate that "our Elvis" has become far more acceptable now that he was shrugging off his ability in fluffy product.

Elvis Presley's image redefinition continues to be pointed out as detrimental to his career and to his entire mystique as the king of rock and roll. To some extent this is understandable, and his formulaic movies of the 1960s, isolated from the cultural and political events of the entire decade, is a broad way of looking at the development of his movie career. Another equally vast assessment is that the direction taken was beneficial to Elvis, despite the singer's own misgivings. Perhaps the campy, breezy musicals better define the lighter aspects of an otherwise tumultuous decade, a means of escapism from the often unsettling social and political climate; hence, their continued popularity.

It is the smaller and more specific areas of the situation that seem more unnerving in regard to the Presley image and its redefinition. One of the most brilliant aspects of Presley's musical performances was the unbridled movements that overtook him while singing. In *Girls! Girls! Girls!* the rock numbers, even the brilliant "Return to Sender," show him doing the twist—a hugely popular dance in 1962 that makes the screen performance of this great song seem more dated than the choreography Elvis himself inspired in *Jailhouse Rock*. Even the film's title is not so accurate—Elvis is dealing chiefly with just two girls during the course of the film (and the talents of Stella Stevens are wasted in a small role).

Variety stated:

> Hal Wallis' production, directed by Norman Taurog, puts the entertainer back into the non-dramatic, purely escapist light musical vein. The thin plot . . . has him the romantic interest of two girls. Hackneyed tale is of poor boy fisherman who meets rich girl who doesn't tell him she is rich but who, naturally, falls in love with him. Presley, on the other hand, is far more interested in recovering a sleek sailboat originally built by his father but then forced into other hands. All the usual elements, including a dastardly villain who turns out to be a wolf, but not in disguise, are present.

The New York Times did not bother reviewing the film at all, just as they had skipped reviewing *Blue Hawaii*.

Unlike his previous movies, Elvis is not surrounded by top supporting players. The only real veteran actors in the cast—Stella Stevens, Robert Strauss, Benson Fong, even Mary Treen—have little to do. Ms. Stevens was initially pleased to be working in an Elvis movie as his romantic lead, but when she read the script and discovered Robin is the woman he discards early, giving her little screen time, she refused to take the role. This got her into big trouble with Paramount, and she took the part only after being threatened with suspension. To this day she refuses to watch the movie. This lack of strong support among the other actors (Laurel Goodwin, making her movie debut, couldn't have been more inexperienced) forced Elvis to carry the movie alone, which is something he never wanted to do. Elvis was also dissatisfied with this type of movie, and since this is the only style of film he would be doing now that a proven formula for financial success had been established, his interest started to wane with each new project. At one point in *Girls! Girls! Girls!* Ross proclaims, "I am the world's biggest jackass!" Sometimes that is how Elvis felt, despite each movie's popularity and genuine sense of fun. The blueprint for Elvis Presley movies was now set.

Perhaps it is the box office success that most defined the success of *Girls! Girls! Girls!*, as it was nominated for a Golden Globe Award for Best Musical. It lost to *The Music Man*, but remained the only Elvis Presley movie to receive such an honor. Furthermore, Elvis came in second as Best Actor of the Year at the Exhibitor Laurel Awards, losing to Rock Hudson. It is really no wonder that studio executives found no reason to change the formula in the future.

At this checkpoint in our study we must approach the Elvis Presley movies as star vehicles with similar traits in their structure, and assess them on how successfully they utilize said formula for maximum impact. Their status as pure and simple entertainment vehicles would still result in some real success within those parameters, especially during those times when Elvis himself was inspired by the material—be it the script, the songs, or a bit of both—to exhibit a greater level of enthusiasm. There are definite highs and lows for the remainder of his movie career, but Presley's creative aspirations were shunted aside and he often felt as trapped as he did by his fame.

CHAPTER 14
It Happened at the World's Fair
(MGM, 1963)

Director: Norman Taurog
Screenplay: Si Rose, Seaman Jacobs
Producer: Ted Richmond
Cinematographer: Joseph Ruttenberg
Editor: Fredric Steinkamp
Makeup: William Tuttle
Hairstylists: Sydney Guilaroff, Shirley Althouse
Vocal accompaniment: The Jordanaires
Cast: Elvis Presley, Joan O'Brien, Gary Lockwood, Vicky Tiu, H. M. Wynant, Edith Atwater, Guy Raymond, Dorothy Green, Kam Tong, Yvonne Craig, Jacqueline DeWitt, Tom Greenway, Evelyn Dutton, Kurt Russell, Henry Johnson, Red West, Robert Williams, Wilson Wood, Hal Riddle, Max Smith, Erna Tanler, Russell Thorson, Patrick Waltz, David Tyrell, Charles Victor, J. Lewis Smith, John Hart, Paul Gross, John Francis, George Cisar, Don Brodie, Joe Esposito, Bill Cole, John Daheim, Max Cutler, Bill Quinn, Joe Quinn, Bill Lee, Jong Ook Kim, Sid Kane, Linda Humble, John Indrisano, Mike Mahoney, George Milan, Troy Meton
Songs (in the order performed):
"Beyond the Bend" (written by Ben Weisman, Fred Wise, and Dolores Fuller; performed by Elvis Presley)
"Relax" (written by Sid Tepper and Roy C. Bennett; performed by Elvis Presley)
"Take Me to the Fair" (written by Sid Tepper and Roy C. Bennett; performed by Elvis Presley)
"They Remind Me Too Much of You" (written by Don Robertson; performed by Elvis Presley)
"One Broken Heart for Sale" (written by Otis Blackwell and Winfield Scott; performed by Elvis Presley)
"I'm Falling in Love Tonight" (written by Don Robertson; performed by Elvis Presley)

> "Cotton Candy Land" (written by Ruth Batchelor and Bob Roberts; performed by Elvis Presley)
> "A World of Our Own" (written by Bill Giant, Bernie Baum, and Florence Kaye; performed by Elvis Presley)
> "How Would You Like to Be" (performed by Elvis Presley)
> "Happy Ending" (written by Ben Weisman and Sid Wayne; performed by Elvis Presley)
>
> The soundtrack album went to number four on the charts
> The single "One Broken Heart for Sale" went to number 11 in 1963
>
> Released April 3, 1963
> Filmed August 27–September 25, 1962
> 105 minutes
> Technicolor
> Aspect ratio: 2.35:1
> Domestic gross: $2,250,000
> Released to DVD by Warner Home Video

What is most striking about *It Happened at the World's Fair* is how carefully it follows what has already become a pattern for an Elvis Presley movie: music, pretty girls, nice scenery, and a few comedic moments. This marks the third musical comedy Norman Taurog directed. Elvis liked working with Taurog, even while disdaining the films on which they collaborated. The director was sympathetic to the singer's aspirations, but also had a job to do.

As with most of the Elvis Presley musicals, *It Happened at the World's Fair* is not so much a bad movie; it just wasn't what Elvis wanted out of his film career. Those close to Presley stated that Elvis was prone to signing contracts ahead of time, being paid large fees arranged by Colonel Parker, and thus was committed to so many films over a certain period of time. These films were at the discretion of the producer. At other studios, there had been some attempt to explore Presley's talents as an actor, while at his home studio of Paramount it was quickly discovered that musicals were the biggest moneymakers. By the time Elvis made *It Happened at the World's Fair* for MGM, it was fully realized that this should be the vehicle for him. Even critical comments were more favorable for these lesser movies, perhaps because of the more rebellious image Elvis had projected in his better films. And theatergoers would state that Elvis Presley's acting was improving with each picture, despite the fact that his ensuing films were less and less challenging in that area. *It Happened at the World's Fair* follows the pattern of song, comic scene, and fight scene during its opening (a fight against card sharks earlier in the film is interesting in that Elvis uses some karate moves, likely incorporating that himself into the choreography).

The musical subculture of the 1960s had not blossomed by 1963. This was the era of the Beach Boys, the Four Seasons, Lesley Gore, and the various Phil Spector–produced girl groups who offered innocent pop songs rather than the more challenging efforts by past pioneers like Jerry Lee Lewis, Little Richard, or the pre-army Elvis Presley. So when Elvis sings to a little girl in *It Happened at the World's Fair*, accompanied by windup toys as his background music, it is a good example of where his movie career was heading. The unfortunate result is that Elvis relied on the soundtracks for his movies, which eventually became the only music he produced. The only really good song in *It Happened at the World's Fair* is "One Broken Heart for Sale," penned by Otis Blackwell, one of Presley's best songwriters. And for every strong number like "Return to Sender" from *Girls! Girls! Girls!*, there are plenty of total misfires like "Song of the Shrimp" from that same film, or "Cotton Candy Land" from this one.

There are two things that help *It Happened at the World's Fair*. First, it was shot at the actual Seattle World's Fair, director Taurog using enough overhead shots and long shots to allow the excitement of the fair to surround the action in the foreground, offering quite a spectacle for the viewer, while there never appears to be too much going on in the frame to create a distraction. Second, Elvis amps up his participation as indicated in the chapter on *Girls! Girls! Girls!*, adding a comedic nuance to his reactions that bolster the sequences. Otherwise this story of a freelance pilot entrusted with the care of a little girl is the sort of mild sitcom fodder that might have entertained moviegoers, but had trouble sustaining the interest of its star.

Elvis plays Mike Edwards, a freelance pilot who has a partner that gambles away most of their earnings. Their plane is impounded by the sheriff, so they hitch a ride to Seattle and try to find work there. Mike's partner gets them a place to stay in a trailer court due to his poker skills, sustaining them financially by engaging the older men who live in the court in regular card games. Meanwhile, Mike finds himself taking care of a seven-year-old Chinese girl whom he met while hitchhiking (she and her uncle had picked Mike and his partner up as they headed for the World's Fair). Her uncle appears to have abandoned her, and Mike decides to search for him while taking care of her.

From these narrative points, the film is able to include a pretty nurse, mobsters, welfare workers, lots of footage taking place at the World's Fair, and a dozen fairly forgettable songs (excluding the aforementioned Otis Blackwell composition). The chief romantic dynamic involves Mike trying to get the attention of a pretty nurse, and this is also where we find most of the comedy. However there is an opening scene that establishes Mike's success with women. While making a stop after doing some crop dusting with their plane, Mike and his partner split up and take care of their own personal business. Mike visits a girl with whom he is obviously acquainted (Yvonne Craig) when her parents arrive home unexpectedly. The father goes for his gun and chases Mike away.

This not only establishes an element of Mike's character; it sets up the humorous situations in which he will hereafter be involved. Mike sings the song "Relax" to the girl, starts to make his move, and the parents come bursting in the door. Mike tries to maintain his cool ("Hi mom, hi dad") even when the father runs upstairs to get his shotgun. Mike walks quietly and at an even pace out of the yard and down the block, as the father comes bursting out of the house, his daughter and wife trying to pull the gun from his hands. The gun goes off in the air, and Mike is shown running down the block.

Elvis plays the scene for as much comedy as he can garner from the material. His reaction to the parents' arrival is a comical expression of surprise. His coolness is by no means the sort of brash confidence the Elvis of *Jailhouse Rock* might have shown. He tries to retain composure amidst the angry tumult of the parents, and as he leaves the house, director Taurog allows for him to slowly and quietly walk down the path outside the picket fence that encloses the yard, and down the sidewalk. It is several seconds long, silent, and bracketed by two sudden bursts: Elvis walks through the screen of the storm door as he departs, and the family bursts out of the house after him. It is a nicely played scene, well directed, and a good portent to the innate humor that would exist in every Elvis Presley musical.

The little girl, Sue-Lin, is the catalyst for Mike's interest in the pretty nurse. While at the fair, Mike spends all of his remaining funds showing the child a good time. His lack of experience as a parent results in her enjoying all of the various treats available, as well as all the rides. Eventually, Mike must take her to the fair's medical facilities due to a stomachache. There he meets Diane, the pretty nurse (Joan O'Brien). However Mike's amorous intentions are clearly rebuffed as attention is given to Sue-Lin's plight.

The scenes at the World's Fair that lead up to this sequence do not enhance the narrative or even develop the characters to any extent. It is just an excuse to present the fair, and Taurog does so quite effectively. With a career dating back to silents, Taurog was very competent at getting a great deal of action within the frame while not distracting from the central figures. As Mike and Sue-Lin walk through the fairgrounds in a combination of long and medium shots, they are surrounded by the action of rides, vendors, and passersby. Keeping them at the center of the frame, Taurog maintains their significance to the scene while neatly framing them with the fair festivities. There are cutaways for brief comic sequences, such as Mike's futile attempt to win a prize for Sue-Lin at a coin toss game. When the child simply tosses a coin over her shoulder looking away from the game, she wins the grand prize. Elvis once again adds an eye-rolling comic

CHAPTER 14

Vicki Tiu and Elvis in *It Happened at the World's Fair*

nuance to his reaction as the child is awarded a stuffed animal that is nearly as big as she is.

Vicki Tiu, the Philippine-born actress who played Sue-Lin, later married Ben Cayetano, governor of Hawaii. She recalled Elvis Presley's kindness while filming the World's Fair sequences. Nervous and lonesome without her family, Tiu recalls a scene having as many as 30 takes because she kept flubbing her lines. Elvis sensed her uneasiness and announced that she and he were going to take their dinner break. Tiu recalled in *Honolulu Star Bulletin*, "That shows you the kind of man Elvis Presley was. He showed a lot of compassion. I will never forget his kindness and patience."

In one of the more amusing sequences, Mike concocts a scheme to see the pretty nurse again. He pays a random child 25 cents to kick him in the shin. The boy does so, and Mike limps painfully to see the nurse, who notices the nasty bruise. "I must have tripped on something," says Mike, and Diane agrees to give him a lift home. He talks her into first having dinner at a nearby restaurant.

It is notable that the young boy who kicks Elvis in the shin is actor Kurt Russell making his movie debut. Russell would go on to a long, successful career in movies, well into adulthood. In 1979, he portrayed Elvis Presley in the TV movie *Elvis*, and in *3000 Miles To Graceland* (2001) he is disguised as Elvis when a boy runs up and kicks him in the shin. Years later, Russell would recall his reluctance to kick the singer, but Elvis finally talked him into doing it by giving him five dollars.

While the connection between Mike and Diane is significant to the movie, the scene in which they connect is among the least interesting in the movie. It is amusing when Diane is about to put Mike in a cab for home, and he starts moaning in pain, indicating he is blacking out and needs food, prompting her to suggest going to a restaurant together. But once they are in the restaurant, the movie slows down, the ballad Elvis sings is perfunctory at best, and the film does not pick up until they leave the establishment and the young boy approaches asking if he'd like another kick in the shin because "I could use another quarter." Mike gives the boy 50 cents to go away, and the boy misunderstands and kicks him again. Diane figures out the ruse and storms off.

Presley's nuanced comedic reactions are again evident during the two instances where he is kicked. He does not simply get hurt, he gives a wide-eyed comic reaction and starts limping heavily. His expressions as the boy later approaches, trying to cover up any possibility of Diane getting wise to his ruse, are also subtly amusing, much more so than the blatant howling he emits in order to trick Diane into having dinner with him. It appears that Elvis tried to find anything in the script that he could latch onto and enhance with his own creativity.

Sue-Lin again acts as catalyst to get Mike and the nurse together. She leans close to a space heater so that her face and head feels hot. She insists on seeing the nurse from the World's Fair ("because doctors are all men!") so Mike calls her. In the line of duty, she comes over. Sue-Lin continues her ruse, which effectively brings Mike and Diane back together again. A conflict occurs when a welfare agent, stating she was summoned by Diane, comes to take a tearful Sue-Lin from Mike.

The basis for this plot development has its roots in Charlie Chaplin's *The Kid* (1921), although it is uncertain if that specific film inspired the situation in *It Happened at the World's Fair*. Mike feels betrayed by Diane, later discovering it was not she who turned in the child, but his partner using the nurse's name (he felt the child was getting in the way). Sue-Lin runs away, Mike finds her, the welfare workers locate the uncle (the explanation is that he was injured in a truck accident), and Mike and Diane end up together, working at NASA, him with his flight experience, her in the medical field, as the films wraps up its loose ends. As with many Elvis movies, the wrap-ups are convenient, but that did little to detract from its immediate entertainment value. It is the process that entertains the viewer, not the conclusion. But such a structure does not result in a technically good movie.

There is one curious scene in *It Happened at the World's Fair* that is worth discussing, as it is unlike anything Elvis had done in previous movies. During the ballad "They Remind Me Too Much of You," the song plays in the background while Mike rides the monorail back home with a sleeping Sue-Lin by his side. For the entire duration of the song, Elvis sits and thinks pensively about his situation—with the child, with the nurse, with his quest for employment as a pilot, and so on—and never acknowledges the song, which remains just background for the scene. It is a very effective dramatic scene, and one of the more impressive and unusual moments in the film.

Theater owners were quite pleased with the box office success of *It Happened at the World's Fair,* based on their comments to *Box Office*: "This is a very good picture. I hope the film companies continue to make big productions out of the Presleys. He is my top star and there is nothing else that comes close to him. And, too, I hope he stays away from TV!" Another exhibitor stated, "Elvis is always box office for me and he did it in this one too. The shots of the World's Fair were good. . . . My people are always satisfied with a Presley picture." Others pointed out that despite its success, it was not as good as *Blue Hawaii*, which continued to be the example that had been set for success, not a better film like *Jailhouse Rock, King Creole*, or even *Follow That Dream.*

Variety was more accurate when it reviewed the film:

> This is apt to be tedious going for all but the most confirmed of Presley's young admirers. The 10—count 'em—10 tunes [staged by Jack Baker] he sings may be cause for rejoicing among his more ardent followers but, stacked up proportionately against the skinny story in between, it seems at least three too many. Admitting the slim scenario, so many warbling interruptions upset the tempo of the yarn and prevent plot and picture from gathering momentum.
>
> Screenplay springs off to a fairly bright start, thrusting "bush pilot" Presley and sidekick Gary Lockwood into several situations, airborne and earthbound, that have a fair humor content. Most of the action takes place at the 1962 Seattle Fair and vicinity, the yarn implicating Elvis with a temporarily abandoned type (Vicky Tiu) and a nifty nurse (Joan O'Brien).

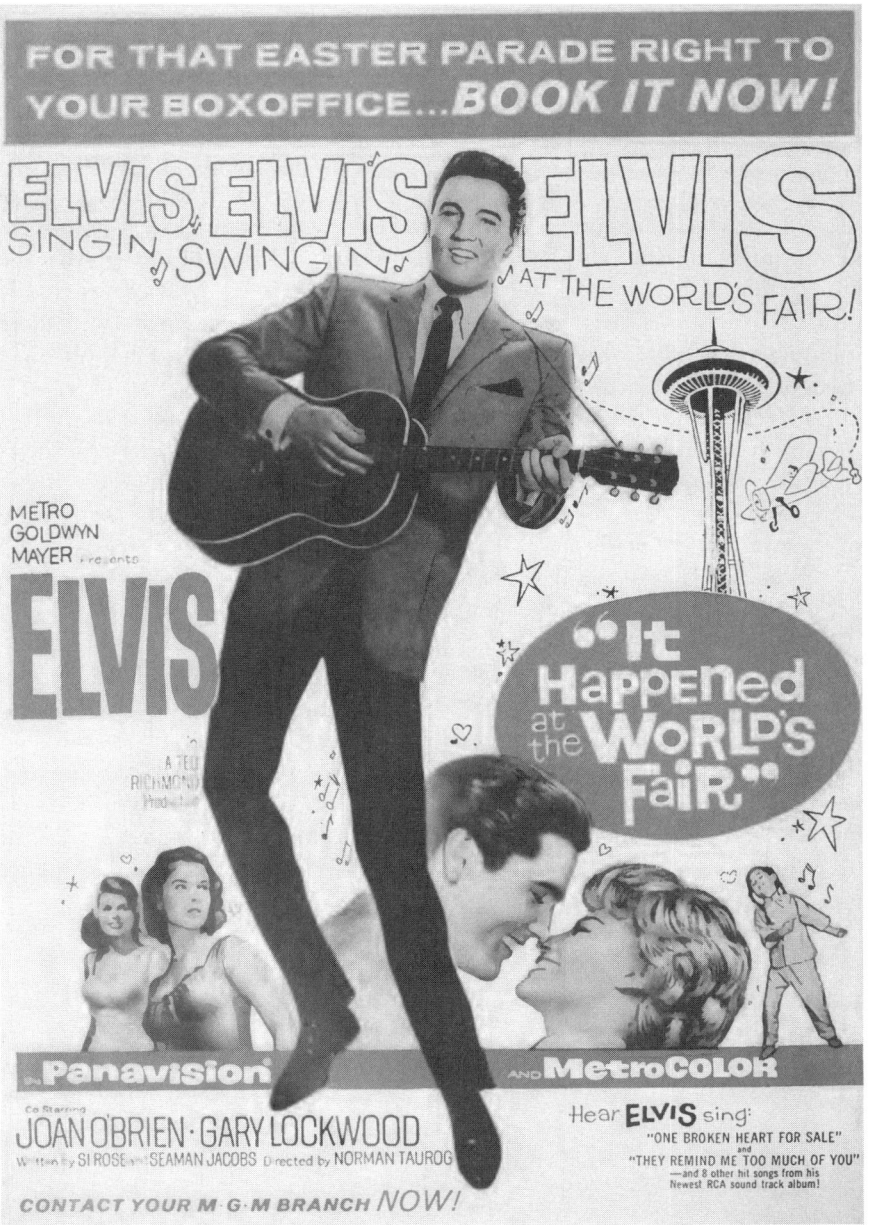

Magazine ad promoting the release of It Happened at the World's Fair

> Presley effortlessly executes his customary character—red-blooded wolf on the crust, clean-cut nice guy at the core. Lockwood, as his gambling chum, makes a good impression. O'Brien is easy to look at. Little Miss Tiu is tiu precious for words.

It is interesting that the review points out that the songs interrupt the tempo of the action, especially in that this is not the first time *Variety* made such a statement. Elvis was likely quite pleased if he ever became aware of such reviews, as he continued to want to explore other avenues for his acting. However, what the critics said was not as impactful as how audiences reacted. Moviegoers giddily proclaiming that the Elvis Presley vehicles were surefire box office hits were more important than critics who wished that there were fewer songs and that Elvis had more of a chance to act.

It Happened at the World's Fair was certainly not the box office smash that *Blue Hawaii* had been. But it was a hit, it pleased moviegoers, and its formula was in the manner that caused the Elvis Presley movies to extend past his immediate fan base and become more mainstream. Many say that was at the expense of his integrity as a performer. Elvis would eventually agree.

As the Elvis Presley movies had now settled into a formula, his next film, back at Paramount, was another musical comedy. It did, however, reunite him with Richard Thorpe, who had directed Presley in *Jailhouse Rock*, one of his better pre-army movies, so Elvis hoped for some level of creative challenge. *Fun in Acapulco* was not filmed on location, relying instead on stock shots of Mexico, but it did feature the colorful production and pretty girls that defined the Elvis movies produced by Hal Wallis. Even theater owners recognized that the most popular Presley movies were Wallis productions for Paramount Pictures. Elvis, however competent and willing he was to do his best in such movies, still had his sights on roles that better suited his perspective and his personality. Another musical did not allow the growth that Elvis sought.

CHAPTER 15

Fun in Acapulco
(PARAMOUNT, 1963)

Director: Richard Thorpe
Screenplay: Allan Weiss
Producer: Hal Wallis
Assistant Director: Michael D. Moore
Cinematography: Daniel L. Fapp
Editor: Stanley E. Johnson
Costumes: Edith Head
Makeup: Wally Westmore
Hairstylist: Nellie Manley
Vocal accompaniment: The Jordanairres
Technical advisor: Colonel Tom Parker
Cast: Elvis Presley, Ursula Andress, Elsa Cárdenas, Paul Lukas, Larry Domasin, Alejandro Rey, Robert Carricart, Teri Hope, Mariachi Los Vaqueros, Mariachi Aquila, Salvador Baguez, Charles Evans, Howard McNear, Mary Treen, Darlene Tomkins, Teri Garr, Martin Garralaga, Roberto Iglesias, Rachel Parra, Adele Palacios, Alex Giannini, Genaro Gomez, Tom Hernandez, John Indrisano, Marco Lopez, Stuart Grey, Ralph Hanalei, Francisco Ortega, Alberto Morin, Alberto Monte, Bob Harvey, Ron Veto, Gene Simmons, Richard Reeves, Linda Riviera, Linda Rand
Songs:
  "Fun in Acapulco" (written by Sid Wayne and Ben Weisman; performed by Elvis Presley)
  "Vino, Dinero y Amor" (written by Sid Tepper and Roy C. Bennett; performed by Elvis Presley and the Four Amigos)
  "I Think I'm Gonna Like It Here" (written by Don Robertson and Hal Blair; performed by Elvis Presley and the Four Amigos)
  "Mexico" (written by Sid Tepper and Roy C. Bennett; performed by Elvis Presley and Larry Domasin)
  "El Toro" (written by Bill Giant, Bernie Baum, and Florence Kaye; performed by Elvis Presley)
  "Marguerita" (written by Don Robertson; performed by Elvis Presley)

"The Bullfighter Was a Lady" (written by Sid Tepper and Roy C. Bennett; performed by Elvis Presley)
"(There's) No Room to Rhumba in a Sports Car" (written by Fred Wise and Dick Manning; performed by Elvis Presley)
"Bossa Nova Baby" (written by Jerry Leiber and Mike Stoller; performed by Elvis Presley)
"You Can't Say No in Acapulco" (written by Dorothy Fuller and Lee Morris; performed by Elvis Presley)
"Guadalajara" (written by Pépé Guizar; performed by Elvis Presley)

The soundtrack album went to number three on the charts
"Bossa Nova Baby" went to number eight on the charts

Released November 27, 1963
Filmed January 28, 1963–March 16, 1963
97 minutes
Technicolor
Aspect ratio: 1.85:1
United States and Canada gross: $3.1 million
Released to DVD by Paramount Home Video

Fun in Acapulco is an Elvis Presley movie that has great potential, but none of it is explored. The film offered the opportunity to shoot on location in Mexico. Much of the beauty of *Blue Hawaii* had been the scenic backgrounds obtained by the location shooting. However, as a cost-cutting measure *Fun in Acapulco* was shot on the Paramount backlot with stock footage and phony-looking process screen backgrounds representing Mexico. There is also a Latin flavor to all of the songs, which could have enhanced interest, but other than the hit "Bossa Nova Baby," the soundtrack features little of interest. Perhaps the low point is the song "No Room to Rhumba in a Sports Car," which is as ridiculous as its title.

Perhaps the most egregious flaw is that the film's narrative features a dramatic element that allows Elvis to do some actual emoting, but this is relegated to subplot status while the typical romantic conflict is at the forefront. Elvis doing a dramatic role while being reunited with director Richard Thorpe, who had helmed *Jailhouse Rock*, would have pleased the singer immensely. But little attention is given to the story of a trapeze artist who is plagued by a fear of heights after bad timing causes his partner to be killed. This is shown in flashback and is referenced during the film as a problem he has to solve, but this problem remains peripheral until the end of the movie when Presley's character performs a high dive off a cliff. Every so often Elvis's character will witness a high dive or sit near a high place, and react with subtle trepidation. Otherwise *Fun in Acapulco* is standard romantic fluff.

Elvis plays Mike Windgren, a lifeguard at an upscale Acapulco hotel who sings in nearby clubs in the evening. His buddy and confidant is an enterprising young boy who finds him singing gigs. He is caught between two women, a female bullfighter named Dolores (Elsa Cárdenas) and Marguerita (Ursula Andress), a girl who works at the hotel. A third element is a champion high diver, Moreno (Alejandro Rey), also a lifeguard at the same hotel who has designs on Marguerita. The situations are basic and superficial, with both girls showing up at the club to hear Mike sing, forcing him to leave by climbing out the back way, and one girl showing up while Mike is entertaining the other. He never fully romances either girl, each relationship seeming far more casual. But jealousies abound as Marguerita likes Mike and he likes her, but his friendship with the lady bullfighter is a problem.

Elvis has surprisingly little chemistry with either actress. When the sexually aggressive Dolores makes herself available, he backs off, enjoying the pursuit more than the conquest. The more conservative Marguerita is more interesting to Mike but in the one scene where they move in for a kiss, the picture fades and cuts to another scene before their lips touch.

Both Cárdenas and Andress were veteran performers by this time, both having started in the 1950s. Here Cárdenas plays the sexually aggressive woman,

Elvis and Ursula Andress in *Fun in Acapulco*

shunning traditions like marriage, while Andress establishes her character as sexually conservative (despite both women being sex symbols at the time). Standing 5 feet, 5 inches, Andress was not particularly tall, but also not petite. Elvis joked that he was afraid to remove his shirt in front of her, because she had broader shoulders. She had already established herself as the first James Bond girl in *Dr. No* (1962) opposite Sean Connery as Bond.

Perhaps it is young Larry Domasin with whom Elvis has the most chemistry. It is similar to the connection he had with young Vicky Tiu in *It Happened at the World's Fair*, each representing the few times Elvis worked closely with children. His relaxed confidence enhance the scenes with young Domasin, who even gets to sing a duet with Elvis.

The dramatic element is the most interesting, and least used, aspect of *Fun in Acapulco*, a film so titled in order to bring in the legion of moviegoers who wanted the sort of fluffy lightweight musical the movie turns out to be. During scenes in which Mike confronts heights or witnesses activities involving high places, Elvis projects a nervous tension that informs the viewer of the character's anxiety. Conveying emotion without dialog is often tricky for an actor with no training, but Presley's natural ability makes these scenes most effective. His rival Moreno discovers Mike's past after a bit of investigating, and points out his cowardice. To save face, Mike must perform a high dive at the conclusion of the movie, after the obligatory fight scene between him and Moreno.

The conflict between Mike and Moreno initially appears to stem from Mike's insecurity about his brother's fatality. Moreno is a champion high diver with the confidence and virility Mike can no longer find within himself. Had the film concentrated more on the dramatic elements of the narrative, this conflict would have been explored. Instead, Moreno appears chiefly as a rival for Marguerite's affections.

Elvis once again looked for ways to improve his scenes with nuance, even reacting with eye-rolling surprise when the horns blare loudly during a song number. Perhaps in an effort to simply make his job more interesting, Elvis also insisted on doing his own stunts in the fight scenes and the trapeze flashback. Producer Hal Wallis never liked actors to perform stunts that might be dangerous, but Presley insisted. All necessary precautions were taken for the singer's safety, while the trapeze scenes were filmed after principal photography was finished, so that if Elvis was injured, it would not suspend production. Presley performed all of the stunts without incident.

Theater owners were pleased when *Fun in Acapulco* showed up on their screens, with one stating to *Box Office*: "Paramount seems to have the best results with the Elvis attempts. A fast-moving pleasant little picture. It does not measure up to *Blue Hawaii* but teenagers will tromp to it."

At least some of the critics were noticing a pattern with the Elvis musicals and how they were becoming more and more formulaic. *Variety* stated:

> Elvis Presley fans won't be disappointed—he sings serviceable songs and wiggles a bit to boot. However, Presley is deserving of better material than has been provided in this screenplay in which he portrays an ex-trapeze catcher who has lost his nerve after a fatal mishap. Richard Thorpe's direction keeps the routine story on the move, a strong asset since opportunity for developing characterization is virtually nil.

The *New York Times*, usually dismissive of every Elvis movie especially when reviewed by Bosley Crowther, offered a veritable rave via critic Howard Thompson, who called the film

> a pleasant, idyllic movie that never takes itself seriously and moves briskly under Richard Thorpe's direction. The excellent color photography and the balmy atmosphere of the resort—the luxury hotels, the beaches and the quaint byways—were positively eye-popping. . . . The songs, in native rhythm, come thick and fast. The melodies and staging are generally bright and imaginative. And Mr. Presley has never seemed so relaxed and personable.

The fact that Elvis comes off "relaxed and personable" in this cheaply made, formulaic musical is a real testament to his acting ability. Still hoping to make the occasional drama without songs, Presley was continually reminded by his management that those films made less money. Even this film's best song, "Bossa Nova Baby," which climbed to number eight on the charts, was not original. Songwriters Mike Leiber and Jerry Stoller, who penned the classic "Jailhouse Rock," had grown weary of the silly musicals to which they were asked to contribute. Thus, they offered "Bossa Nova Baby," an old song they had composed for rhythm and blues group the Clovers, who had released it a year earlier (but with no chart success).

It is unfortunate that as Elvis became a better and more experienced actor, his films became more formulaic. The fact that he was relying on the soundtracks to these movies as his record releases made the necessity of doing musicals even greater. Elvis had wanted to be another Marlon Brando or James Dean, but according to Hal Wallis's autobiography, "We didn't sign Elvis to be another Jimmy Dean, we signed him to be Elvis Presley," and thereafter the films shaped his image. The James Dean connection was at least tangentially present in *Fun in Acapulco* in that Elsa Cárdenas had appeared in Dean's final film, *Giant* (1956), while Ursula Andress had a torrid love affair with the actor that was so beset by troubles. Dean once quipped he was learning her native

Elvis celebrated costar Larry Domasin's birthday on the set of *Fun in Acapulco*

German so they could argue in another language. Dean had invited Andress to travel to San Francisco in his Porsche 550 Spyder on September 30, 1955, but left without her on realizing she was in love with actor John Derek (whom she would later marry). Dean was killed in a car crash en route.

Fun in Acapulco was released five days after the assassination of President John F. Kennedy, another cultural event that altered the course of American culture and indirectly affected the film, television, and music industry as well. As Bob Dylan sang, the times were a-changing. Presley associate Marty Lacker recalled Elvis Presley's reaction to the JFK murder for Alanna Nash in *Elvis Aaron Presley: Revelations from the Memphis Mafia*:

> I went in the hallway and knocked on his door. I said, "Elvis you need to get up, President Kennedy was just assassinated and it's on TV." I thought he would turn on the TV in his room, instead he yelled, "Have them bring some coffee in the den." And he got up, put on his robe, and came downstairs. Most of us were silent, but Elvis was hollering. "What kind of no good motherfucker would do that? Kennedy was a good man!" He slammed the coffee cup onto the marble table and cut his hand. Pieces of the cup shot everywhere. Elvis stayed glued to the TV for two days.

Lacker believed that Presley's fondness for keeping firearms probably increased at that time, believing that if someone could kill the president, they could do the same to Elvis. Presley had frequently received death threats, as do many famous people. On more than one occasion his karate came in handy when dangerous fans got a bit too close. His entourage of associates also acted as bodyguards, including childhood friends Red and Sonny West, two brothers whose size and strength were effective in keeping unruly people away. However, the assassination of the president had a far-reaching effect on most Americans, including Elvis, who increased his collection of firearms, according to Lacker.

Fun in Acapulco was very well received, even by critics, and its success further proved producer Wallis and manager Parker's point that the lightweight musicals were better because they were more profitable. Elvis was pleased to have at least some moments in this movie to offer some depth to his character beyond the superficial limitations of most of his musical comedy roles, but continued to complain privately to close associates that he wanted to grow as an actor and hoped to pursue more roles in nonmusicals to do so.

Fun in Acapulco was also the last Elvis Presley movie released before the Beatles came to America and ignited the noted British Invasion, which would change the direction of popular music with as much force and impact as Elvis had a decade earlier. The Beatles themselves attended a screening of *Fun in Acapulco* while on their first American tour.

CHAPTER 16
Kissin' Cousins
(MGM, 1964)

Director: Gene Nelson
Screenplay: Gene Nelson and Gerald Drayson Adams, from a story by Adams
Producer: Sam Katzman
Cinematographer: Ellis W. Carter
Editor: Ben Lewis
Makeup: William Tuttle
Hairstylists: Sydney Guilaroff and Mary Westmoreland
Vocal accompaniment: The Jordanaires
Techical advisor: Colonel Tom Parker
Cast: Elvis Presley, Arthur O'Connell, Glenda Farrell, Jack Albertson, Pamela Austin, Cynthia Pepper, Yvonne Craig, Donald Woods, Tommy Farrell, Beverly Powers, Hortense Petra, Robert Stone, Robert Carson, Lonni Lees, Maureen Reagan, Joan Staley, Joe Esposito, Sailor Vincent, Dallas Johann, Teri Garr, Gail Ganley, Lynn Fields, Kent McCord
Songs (in the order performed):
   "Kissin' Cousins" (written by Fred Wise and Randy Starr; performed by Elvis Presley and the Jordanaires over the opening credits)
   "Smokey Mountain Boy" (written by Lenore Rosenblatt and Victor Millrose; performed by Elvis Presley)
   "One Boy, Two Little Girls" (written by Bill Giant, Bernie Baum, and Florence Kaye; performed by Elvis Presley)
   "Catchin' On Fast" (written by Bill Giant, Bernie Baum, and Florence Kaye; performed by Elvis Presley)
   "Tender Feeling" (written by Bill Giant, Bernie Baum, and Florence Kaye; performed by Elvis Presley)
   "Barefoot Ballad" (written by Dolores Fuller and Lee Morris; performed by Elvis Presley)
   "Once Is Enough" (written by Sid Tepper and Roy C. Bennett; performed by Elvis Presley)
   "Kissin' Cousins (No. 2)" (written by Bill Giant, Bernie Baum, and Florence Kaye; performed by Elvis Presley)

> "Pappy, Won't You Please Come Home" (written by Sid Tepper and Roy C. Bennett; performed by Glenda Farrell)
> "There's Gold in the Mountains" (written by Bill Giant, Bernie Baum, and Florence Kaye; performed by Elvis Presley, Pam Austin, and Yvonne Craig)
> "Anyone (Could Fall in Love with You)" (written by Bennie Benjamin, Sol Marcus, and Louis A. DeJesus; performed by Elvis Presley, but cut from film)
> "Echoes of Love" (written by Bob Roberts and Paddy McMains; performed by Elvis Presley, but cut from film)
> "(It's a) Long Lonely Highway" (written by Doc Pomus and Mort Shuman; performed by Elvis Presley, but cut from film)
>
> The *Kissin' Cousins* soundtrack album made it to number six on the charts
> The title song made it to number 12 on the charts
>
> Released March 6, 1964
> Filmed October–November, 1963 (exact dates unknown)
> 96 minutes
> Metrocolor
> Aspect Ratio: 2.35:1
> Released budget: $800,000; Gross: $2.8 million.
> Released to DVD by Warner Home Video

Kissin' Cousins is another rural comedy, but not like *Follow That Dream,* despite casting Arthur O'Connell from the former movie in the patriarch role once again. Where *Follow That Dream* was quieter and more subtle, *Kissin' Cousins* is noisy and broad. Elvis plays two parts in *Kissin' Cousins,* which he welcomed as something different. But the fact that he played lookalike cousins gave him some pause in that he himself was a twin (his brother, Jesse Garon, was stillborn). He also was unhappy with the strawberry blonde wig he had to wear while portraying one of the characters. Finally, he did not care for the script, or the songs he was expected to sing.

The plot deals with the army needing land in the Smoky Mountains for a missile site. The land belongs to a rustic hillbilly family that suspiciously shoots at any strangers approaching the property. Elvis plays Josh Morgan, an educated soldier with a Southern hills background. He is enlisted as the most effective liaison, and a troop of soldiers head to the property. Immediately upon their arrival, they are met by gunfire.

The idea of building a nuclear missile site in rustic territory resonates more clearly when taking into consideration the context of the movie's era. The Gaither Report of 1957, from the Office of Defense Mobilization, warned that the Russians were becoming a stronger force in nuclear power, estimating that "by the early 1960s," a security threat could be critical. Thus the concept was

Elvis played a dual role in *Kissin' Cousins*

quite topical back in 1964, despite being used as a mere plot convenience for an Elvis Presley comedy. Josh Morgan is instructed to carry a white flag up the hill and meet with those firing on the soldiers. Having already received permission to wear civilian clothes, Morgan would therefore not represent the government (of whom mountain moonshiners suspected were revenuers).

A comic trajectory takes place immediately. Josh has been ordered to be the liaison, and is now being ordered to confront opposing fire. The only white flag available is a nylon stocking from a wayward soldier's exploits tied to a walkie-talkie antenna. Josh ventures up the hill with trepidation, Elvis comically stammering to his commander, "Th-th-those people are shooting live ammo, sir!" When he makes it up the hill, he is met by two pretty young women armed with shotguns. They react with surprise, confusing Josh, until their brother Jody (also played by Elvis) comes walking out of the brush. Josh and Jody react to looking identical, with Josh asking, "Hey, what are you doing with my face?" and maintaining the comic trajectory throughout this transitional scene.

The difference between the two characters Elvis plays is immediately established. Josh is the antithesis of what the rock and roll rebel had been. Josh is educated, accomplished, and conservative, despite his poor Southern beginnings. Jody is still raw, untamed, and remains a man of the hills, inviting the newcomer to "rassle." Elvis Presley himself, despite wealth and stardom, changed very little of his personal dynamic. By all accounts he remained the Southern-bred poor boy who accepted the jobs he was offered, trusted his management when signing contracts, but still longed to do great movies and great music. So with the two characters in *Kissin' Cousins*, we see the experienced, settled Elvis who continues to follow orders despite his misgivings, and the rustic Elvis of his roots, who smiled little and exhibited closer to the persona found in pre-army movies like *Jailhouse Rock* and *King Creole*. Jody is the tough, suspicious, uncompromising adolescent representative. Josh is the reasonable, responsible parental figure. It is the successful Elvis re-entering his past world and meeting the hillbilly Elvis.

However, the film does little more than use this dynamic as another plot contrivance. It is established that Josh is part of the Tatum bloodline, and is therefore accepted as "kin." This allows him to succeed as liaison between the family and the army, who spend the rest of the film trying to secure the land for a missile site. From this basis we get a series of comic situations and obligatory song numbers, all with a rural hillbilly theme, an idea that remained popular in mainstream entertainment. The rural-themed shows that were mentioned as television ratings successes in chapter 11 remained so two years later, along with an even bigger hit, *The Beverly Hillbillies*, which had premiered only months after *Follow That Dream* was released. By the release of *Kissin' Cousins*, rural comedy was enjoying a level of popularity that was so strong, it spawned even more such TV shows throughout the decade, like *Green Acres* (premiering in 1965) and *Hee Haw* (premiering in 1969).

Another aspect of the character dynamic in *Kissin' Cousins* is its structural similarity to Al Capp's classic comic strip *Li'l Abner*. Glenda Farrell, who plays matriarch Ma Tatum, bears great similarity to the tough, pipe-smoking Mammy

Yokum from Capp's strip, while the Jody character effectively represents Abner himself.

However, these various influences have elements that *Kissin' Cousins* lacks. The *Li'l Abner* comic made political and sociocultural statements through its humor, garnering the interest of such comic luminaries as Charlie Chaplin and Harpo Marx. There was a Broadway musical and two film versions. The 1940 film featured silent comedy veterans like Al St. John, Edgar Kennedy, and Buster Keaton in supporting roles. Elvis himself was considered for the title role in the 1959 version, but Colonel Parker did not want the singer to appear on a musical where other actors could also sing, thus taking some of the spotlight from his client.

Kissin' Cousins has none of the satirical cleverness of *Li'l Abner*, despite some general similarities. And it also lacks the comic bite of the television shows whose popularity were likely inspirational to its creation. Theater owners frequently complained about films being released to television too quickly, dismissing television comedy as vastly inferior to movies. A film like *Kissin' Cousins* uses elements of popular rural TV comedy but with less effect. Even the idea of "twin cousins" is lifted from the then-popular television program *The Patty Duke Show*.

There are a few tangential elements that try to add a veiled sexual element to the proceedings. First, a group of man-crazy hillbilly girls known as the Kittyhawks descends on the soldiers in an effort to "make boy babies" because there are too few males in their area of the mountain community. They appear occasionally as a running gag. Then there is the bizarre idea that the attractive cousins are quite taken by Josh, who looks identical to their brother. Elvis pauses to sing several times, each of them disrupting the flow of the action. And while the up-tempo title cut[1] and the jaunty "Smokey Mountain Boy," sung while traveling by jeep to the mountains, are passable, songs like "One Boy, Two Little Girls" and "Barefoot Ballad" are immediately forgettable. Even veteran character actress Glenda Farrell gets to warble "Pappy, Won't You Please Come Home."

Perhaps the most amusing sequence is when the army offers the Tatum family a charge account in order to entice them into turning over their land. The family takes advantage of the situation as Ma Tatum goes about her chores wearing a fur coat while the girls are clad in bikinis. Other sequences feature Jody falling for a military woman who out-wrestles him (so that the "other" Elvis gets some footage) and Josh trying to evoke sympathy from the Tatums by claiming his commander (Jack Albertson) was shot in the head in Korea and "ain't quite right." However, these highlights would be mere throwaways in a better picture.

Kissin' Cousins was produced by Sam Katzman, who had a long-standing veteran status in Hollywood for being one of the most efficient B-movie producers in the business. He enjoyed great success with East Side Kids programmers, B westerns, and science-fiction films like *It Came from Beneath the Sea* and *Earth vs. the Flying Saucers,* before producing the musicals *Rock Around the Clock, Don't Knock the Twist,* and *Hootenanny Hoot,* all of which popular with teenagers, Presley's chief demographic. Colonel Parker became friendly with Katzman, who indicated that he could shoot a Presley picture in a mere 15 days at a fraction of the budget. This delighted Parker, who realized it meant a greater profit.

Katzman hired Gene Nelson, the director of *Hootenanny Hoot,* to helm *Kissin' Cousins* with a 15-day shooting schedule and a budget of only $800,000 (compare that to the $4 million spent on *Blue Hawaii,* which remained Presley's biggest box office success). Elvis knew nothing of the business negotiations behind his movies; he just looked at the script and music. He was displeased with both, but pleased that Gene Nelson would be directing. Nelson had been an actor in musicals himself, and Elvis was impressed with a rather challenging dance bit the director had done in *She's Working Her Way through College* years earlier.

Nelson was flattered by Presley's compliments and tried to keep the singer comfortable during the shoot, which was done far more quickly than his previous movies. Despite the tension of the rushed schedule and the challenge of having to essay two roles and several songs during the 15-day schedule, Nelson recalled Elvis as always being fully cooperative, eager to please, and easy to direct. Despite his professionalism, Elvis confided in costar Yvonne Craig that he was embarrassed by the film and the songs he performed.

Nelson did his best with the material, even offering Colonel Parker a look at the script ahead of time. Parker was not interested, stating, "We don't know about movies, we have you for that, we just need enough songs for an album. If you want me to read the script, that will cost you a $25,000 consulting fee." Nelson wanted to believe the Colonel was joking; as with all of Presley's directors, he saw the acting potential in his star, even in a movie like *Kissin' Cousins.* But by this time, with the cost-cutting measures coupled with the formulaic approach, Elvis was no longer offered much of a challenge and instead was instructed to coast on his personality.

Presley's stand-in, Lance LeGault, had more to do on this movie with Elvis playing two roles. He saw *Kissin' Cousins* as something of a turning point, telling author Peter Guralnick for his 2000 book, *Careless Love: The Unmaking of Elvis Presley*:

> Up until that time, certain standards had been maintained, but it seems to me from *Kissin' Cousins* on, we were always on a short schedule. It was like, "It's good enough because it's Elvis, and it's in color, and we're gonna make two and a half times negative cost plus another two and a half times." Sometimes Elvis might comment about this that or the other—but he'd go ahead and do it. Very seldom he might go over and say something to the director—but very seldom: he just kind of went along with it. I don't remember how

long we were on *Viva Las Vegas*, but it seems like it was ten or eleven weeks. We weren't off a few weeks when, boom, we jumped back into *Kissin' Cousins*, which was shot in seventeen days. When they realized they could take this guy and do a film that quickly with him, from then on we were on quick pictures.

Viva Las Vegas had already been shot before *Kissin' Cousins,* but the latter film was released first, having been completed before the more elaborate movie was out of post-production. In fact, Katzman was reportedly angry at Gene Nelson for going two days over the shooting schedule.

Colonel Parker spent a lot of extra time and effort promoting *Kissin' Cousins*, realizing the more publicity, the greater the box office, which would be especially lucrative due to the movie's low budget. The film was not only a big hit, but, according to *Box Office* at least one theater owner mentioned Nelson's other directorial effort *Hootenanny Hoot*, stating: "Next to *Hootenanny Hoot*, *Kissin' Cousins* was the very best yet." Other exhibitors gleefully reported packed houses with delighted patrons enjoying the cornball comedy and silly songs. The success of rural comedies on television may have been part of the reason, which is somewhat ironic, while the moviegoers' satisfaction with the movie clearly indicates they expected little more from an Elvis picture. Inexplicably, screenwriters Gene Nelson and Gerald Drayson Adams were nominated by the Writers Guild of America in the best musical category for their screenplay.

Eighteen-year-old Priscilla Beaulieu was now living at Graceland and recalled how much Elvis loved classic movies, including such films as *Wuthering Heights, Miracle on 34th Street, It's a Wonderful Life, Mr. Skeffington, Letter from an Unknown Woman,* and *The Way of All Flesh*. Priscilla claimed in her autobiography, *Elvis and Me*, that Elvis toyed with the idea of producing a remake of *The Way of All Flesh* with his father in the title role. Certainly the gods of cinema are pleased he never went ahead with this idea.

But Presley's appreciation of good cinema, like his respect for great music, fueled his own interests enough so that he recognized when he was working on a bad movie with weak songs. However, Presley never exerted his power in such matters. He would ask for better pictures, but would be reminded that those made less money. Having been taken from a dirt-poor background and placed in a multimillion-dollar industry as its biggest star, Presley's sense of loyalty was such that he believed it was his duty to follow orders. While others stars would exert their authority and insist on more challenging material, Presley did as he was told. He still had some hit records. One of his better songs of this period, "Devil in Disguise," was a success in the summer of 1963, while songs from the upcoming movie *Viva Las Vegas* were beginning to chart as well. But in terms of both film and music, a throwaway like *Kissin' Cousins* was an artistic failure even if it was a financial success.

Howard Thompson of *The New York Times* was more sympathetic to Elvis Presley movies than Bosley Crowther had been, but even he pegged *Kissin' Cousins* as an artistic failure, stating:

> With the flavor of "Fun in Acapulco"—and that it was—fairly fresh, Elvis Presley's movie status takes a nosedive in his latest, "Kissin' Cousins." Yesterday's new arrival, heading a circuit double bill, is a broad, meandering rehash of "Li'l Abner." For Pete's sake, El! This time, shades of Bette Davis, he's twins. Elvis One is a G.I. scout, sent to Tennessee to talk his hillbilly relatives into leasing a mountain for missile-launching. Elvis Two is a surly blond who hates his city-reared cousin. The boys tangle, they toss off songs and they magnetize swarms of scantily clad young beauties roamin them hills wild, and we mean wild. Gene Nelson, who directed, has limbered things up slightly with a couple of group dances. On the whole, though, Sam Katzman's production is tired, strained and familiar stuff, even with double-barreled Presley. Come on, lad—at least one of you. Spruce up or leg it back to Acapulco.

Variety was equally unimpressed:

> This Elvis Presley concoction is a pretty dreary effort. Gerald Drayson Adams came up with a ripe story premise, but he and Gene Nelson appear to have run dry of creative inspiration in trying to develop it. Yarn is concerned with the problem faced by the US government in attempting to establish an ICBM base on land owned by an obstinate hillbilly clan. To solve the problem, the air force sends in a lieutenant (Presley) who is kin to the stubborn critters, among whom is his lookalike cousin (Elvis in a blond wig, no less). Histrionically, Presley does as well as possible under the circumstances. He also sings eight songs. Arthur O'Connell is excellent as the patriarch of the mountain clan, but what a mountainous waste of talent.

It is significant that while Thompson in the *New York Times* places the blame on Elvis, *Variety* believes his palpable talent is wasted in an inferior vehicle. Perhaps Thompson concluded a star of Presley's magnitude could choose his own projects. That should have been the case.

Kissin' Cousins was shot in late 1963, and by the time it was released in March 1964, the British Invasion and, especially, Beatlemania was in full force. Presley associate Lamar Fike recalled to Alanna Nash in *Elvis Aaron Presley*:

> I went over to England in 1963 with Brenda Lee. The Beatles were her opening act. I took one look at them and went, "Jesus Christ! The only time I've seen anything like this was with Elvis!" They just blew me away. Right after that, Elvis came to Nashville. I said,

"Elvis, there's a group coming out of England that's going to be so hot. They're getting ready to break wide open." He couldn't have cared less.

Elvis had trouble dealing with the financial success of what he considered artistic failures. A film like *Kissin' Cousins* enjoying box office success and the reported approval of moviegoers added to the conflict, especially when critics like Howard Thompson placed the blame squarely on Presley's shoulders. He understood his responsibility, but remained under the guidance of his management, who couched things under the terms of which movies made the most money. And while Elvis was dismissive of a new group coming out of England during the making of *Kissin' Cousins*, by the time it was released and Beatlemania was in full swing, he realized his comfortable perch at the top could be challenged. As noted in *Elvis Aaron Presley*, associates stated he would play the first Beatles hits and say, "Yeah, this is the sound I want. I want to get back to doing rock and roll like this again." When the Beatles made their triumphant appearance on television's *Ed Sullivan Show* in 1964, Elvis sent a welcoming telegram, which was read on the air by the show's host.

Elvis Presley's popularity remained strong, however, and despite their dip in quality, his movies were still hits. His next released film, which had been filmed prior to *Kissin' Cousins*, was a far more elaborate production. It had better costars, a better script, and one of the strongest soundtracks of any Elvis Presley movie. *Viva Las Vegas* would remain the best Elvis Presley musical comedy to be released in the 1960s.

CHAPTER 17
Viva Las Vegas
(MGM, 1964)

Director: George Sidney
Screenplay: Sally Benson
Producers: Jack Cummings and George Sidney
Cinematography: Joseph F. Biroc
Editor: John McSweeny
Assistant director: Milton Feldman
Makeup: William Tuttle
Hairstylist: Sydney Guilaroff
Vocals: The Jordanaires
Cast: Elvis Presley, Ann-Margret, Cesare Danova, William Demarest, Nicky Blair, Jack Carter, Eddie Quillan, Roy Engel, George Cisar, John Hart, Pete Kellett, Teri Garr, Ruth Carlson, Christopher Riordan, Ruth Carlson, Howard Curtis, Harry Fleer, Bambi Hamilton, Regina Carroll, Taggar Casey, Alan Fordney, Barnaby Hale, Claude Hall, Connie Hermida, Brad Logan, Beverly Powers, Reb Sawitz, Kay Sutton, Red West, Francis Ravel, Beverly Powers, Robert Nash, Kent McCord, George Klein, Lance LeGault, Ingeborg Kjeldsen, Larry Kent, the Jubilee Four
Songs (in the order performed):
"The Yellow Rose of Texas/The Eyes of Texas" (written by Don George; adapted by Randy Starr and Fred Wise/John Lang Sinclair; performed by Elvis Presley)
"The Lady Loves Me" (written by Sid Tepper and Roy C. Bennett; performed by Elvis Presley and Ann-Margret)
"What'd I Say" (written by Ray Charles; performed by Elvis Presley)
"Viva Las Vegas" (written by Doc Pomus and Mort Shuman; performed by Elvis Presley)
"I Need Somebody to Lean On" (performed by Elvis Presley)
"Come On, Everybody" (aka "C'mon Everybody") (written by Stanley Chianese; performed by Elvis Presley)
"Today, Tomorrow and Forever" (written by Bill Giant, Bernie Baum, and Florence Kaye; performed by Elvis Presley)

"Santa Lucia" (performed by Elvis Presley)
"If You Think I Don't Need You" (written by Red West [as Bob "Red" West]; performed by Elvis Presley)
"Appreciation" (written by Marvin More and Bernie Wayne; performed by Ann-Margret)
"My Rival" (written by Marvin More and Bernie Wayne; performed by Ann-Margret)
"The Climb" (written by Dan Anthony and John Case Schaeffer II; performed by the Forté Four)
"Do the Vega" (performed by Elvis Presley; recorded for the film but not used)
"Night Life" (performed by Elvis Presley; recorded for the film but not used)
"You're the Boss" (performed by Elvis Presley and Ann-Margret; recorded for the film but not used)

The title song made it to number 29 on the charts
That song's flipside, "What'd I Say," made it to number 21

Released May 20, 1964
Filmed July 15–September 16, 1963
85 minutes
Metrocolor
Aspect ratio: 2.35:1
Released budget: $1 million; gross: $5,125,000
Released to DVD and Blu-ray by Warner Home Video

Viva Las Vegas is, on the surface, another Elvis Presley musical following the basic formula, with Elvis as a macho race car driver dealing with a sophisticated rival and a pretty girl. However there are several factors that set it apart, allowing it to emerge as the best of his musical comedies. He would never again top it. *Viva Las Vegas* has a great soundtrack, featuring songs penned by the likes of Leiber and Stoller, Ray Charles, and Doc Pomus. Director George Sidney directs the musical numbers with an understanding and sensitivity that none of Presley's other directors exhibited at this level. The choreography by David Winters belies the fact that *Viva Las Vegas* was his first feature production (he had been Ann-Margret's dance instructor and got the job through her).

The characters are also different in this movie. While Elvis is the usual manly presence with a comical sidekick, Elvis's rival in *Viva Las Vegas* is played by Cesare Danova. He is not the usual frustrated insecure type, but is a sophisticated classy sort who acknowledges a respect for his adversary.

But the biggest factor in this film's success is Ann-Margret playing a character called Rusty. She is not merely support as actresses in past films had been, but an equal costar with billing immediately under the title. Her charisma matches his, she shares in most of his song numbers, has solo songs of her own,

Sparks flew when Elvis costarred with Ann-Margret in *Viva Las Vegas*

and ultimately, she could very well be the best costar of Elvis Presley's movie career.

Elvis was now fully entrenched in an adult role, not the snarly youth of *King Creole* and *Jailhouse Rock*. His rival on the racetrack, Count Mancini, is a witty European sophisticate while Elvis, as Lucky Jackson, is clearly working class. Mancini acknowledges Lucky's greatness on the racetrack, and rather than frantically try to make a move on Rusty, he approaches her with the same sort of relaxed confidence as Lucky. But while the count is wealthy, Lucky is forced to take a job as a waiter to earn enough money for an engine to put in his race car. The count would like Lucky to leave the race and work in his pit crew, would like him to drive his car, or would like to arrange that he block other cars in the race to ensure a win. Lucky turns down each of these nefarious offers, while the count remains relaxed and unfazed by his unsuccessful attempts at getting his rival to work for him. The climactic race adds excitement, while Lucky's ultimate Vegas wedding to Rusty ties up all loose ends effectively as the suit-clad count stands among the wedding's invitees, shaking Lucky's hand in congratulations.

After a decidedly conservative take on the traditional "Yellow Rose of Texas," the first big song number is "The Lady Loves Me," a duet between Elvis and Ann-Margret that establishes director George Sidney's understanding of how to most effectively film the musical numbers. As they sing, Ann-Margret is walking around the hotel pool area while he follows her with a guitar. His lyrics confidently exclaim that she cannot resist him, while her answer lyrics dismiss his confidence and insists she is not interested at all. Sidney follows them with tracking shots, framing both of them in the action that continues up the high diving board. As the song concludes, Rusty pushes the fully clothed Lucky into the pool. Sidney edits from a close-up to a long shot as a double does the fall into the pool, then edits back to show a sopping wet Lucky emerge from the water.

After this, it appears director Sidney is more creatively inspired by the rockers in this movie than the ballads. While a beautiful slower tempo song like "Today, Tomorrow and Forever" is shown in a darkly lit scene with Elvis at the piano and Ann-Margret standing nearby, the rockers "C'mon Everybody" and "What'd I Say" are presented as full-fledged dance numbers with backup dancers and quick edits that go from long shots to medium shots to close-ups, alternating between framing all of the dancers, to just Elvis and Ann-Margret, to cross-cut editing between full shots of their faces. Sidney understands the rhythm and pace of each song, the energy of rock and roll, and proceeds accordingly. They are the best filmed musical sequences in any Elvis Presley vehicle.

"What'd I Say" is especially impressive. George Sidney uses a long shot that incorporates all movement, with Elvis and Ann-Margret surrounded by dancers, and then rises up to an overhead shot, cuts back to a medium shot, and then pans back, all within the context of the song's rhythm. The movement of the dancers fill the frame, and during the "ahhh-oooh" portion of the song Sidney edits back and forth between alternate close-ups of Presley's and Ann-Margret's faces.

Viva Las Vegas also uses an interesting montage to examine the Lucky-Rusty dynamic. They engage in a series of activities including skeet shooting and motorcycle riding, and she overtakes him each time. Some studies have argued that the Rusty character has elements of the burgeoning women's movement in the 1960s, but a later scene where Rusty attempts to help prepare for the race and simply gets in the way is stereotypical of how women were presented in movies at this time. She brings lunch in a picnic basket as the men are trying to work, unplugs important power tools to plug in an electric coffeemaker, accidentally shoots everyone with an oil gun, and becomes frustrated by stamping her foot and going, "Ooh!" when told to stay out of the way. In one of her solo musical numbers, Rusty sings about her rival. Her rival is Lucky's race car.

The comic highlight of *Viva Las Vegas* is when the count invites Rusty to a private dinner party, and Lucky arranges to be their waiter. He tries to disrupt the romantic flow, ultimately popping open a champagne bottle and spraying its contents all over the count. His replacement waiter is tripped as he enters the room, while Lucky returns with a guitar and sings the pleading rocker "If You Think I Don't Need You."[1]

As with most of Presley's movies, *Viva Las Vegas* offers some level of dramatic tension within the context of a light musical comedy. The race car scene is riddled with danger for both Lucky and the count, their maneuvering appearing at times to be attempts to kill one another. That each appears to matter-of-factly accept this as part of the game is reinforced when a gracious count is in attendance at Rusty and Lucky's wedding at the movie's conclusion. What is odd, however, is that the count crashes his car at the end of the race, so the fact that he appears perfectly healthy and without injury at the wedding is a bit disconcerting.

Along with Cesare Danova and Ann-Margret, *Viva Las Vegas* benefits from the presence of veteran character actor William Demarest, who would soon take over the role of Uncle Charlie on TV's popular *My Three Sons*. Demarest, who played Rusty's father, had a career that dated back to the silent era and appeared in the milestone first talkie feature, *The Jazz Singer* with Al Jolson. Elvis was intrigued by Jolson and asked Demarest about this experience. Demarest disliked Jolson intensely and told him in no uncertain terms what he thought of the legendary singer. Elvis thought it hilarious and remained fond of Demarest as a result.

As the obligatory best friend/sidekick, veteran bit player Nicky Blair turns in what may be the performance of his career. As with other Presley films in which a comic sidekick is part of the dynamic, Blair provides a comic energy that is pleasant and enjoyable.

Screenwriter Sally Benson was another Hollywood veteran, having penned the script for Alfred Hitchcock's brilliant *Shadow of a Doubt* (1943), but was now relaxing with lighter fare such as *Summer Magic*, a 1963 Walt Disney effort featuring Disney stalwart Hayley Mills.

Critics were guardedly impressed without taking seriously the film or the Presley impact. Howard Thompson, always among the most sympathetic to Elvis movies among *New York Times* film critics, reviewed *Viva Las Vegas*:

> *Viva Las Vegas,* the new Elvis Presley vehicle, is about as pleasant and unimportant as a banana split. And as fetching to look at, it might be added. By now, after some rocky beginnings, the Presley movie

formula has leveled off to a series of musical romps that are extremely easy to take.

And where our boy Elvis once stumbled, he now ambles along personably. Not only does he sing better—at least more audibly—but the tunes also continue to improve.

This time Metro-Goldwyn-Mayer happily teams him with Ann-Margaret [sic], a perfect musical foil with her galvanized dancing. The story sets up a breezy romantic triangle involving Mr. Presley, as a speed-racing bellhop, Ann-Margaret, as a pool manager, and Cesare Danova, as an Italian racing champion. With the trio trailed by William Demarest and Nicky Blair, the picture as directed by George Sidney, tools along rosily.

The tunes are nice, especially one poolside duet by the hero and heroine, and Ann-Margret rattles the rafters in several rhythm numbers. And the picture winds up with a wing-ding of an auto race across the countryside. Whatever it isn't, *Viva Las Vegas* remains friendly, wholesome and pretty as all get-out.

Variety was a bit less enthusiastic, but the review is a good example of how dismissive critics had become of Elvis movies:

> The sizzling combination of Elvis Presley and Ann-Margret is enough to carry *Viva Las Vegas* over the top. The picture is fortunate in having two such commodities for bait, because beyond several flashy musical numbers, a glamorous locale and one electrifying auto race sequence, the production is a pretty trite and heavy-handed affair, puny in story development and distortedly preoccupied with anatomical oomph. The film is designed to dazzle the eye, assault the ear and ignore the brain. Hackneyed yarn provides the skeletal excuse for about 10 musical interludes, a quick tour of the US gambling capital and that one slam-bang climactic sequence that lifts the film up by its bootstraps just when it is sorely in need of a lift.

Viva Las Vegas was a major box office sensation, and a big-budget MGM musical. Immediately after filming, Elvis began work on the very low-budget *Kissin' Cousins,* which was released earlier and was heavily promoted by Colonel Parker, hoping to eke out as much box office money as possible. *Viva Las Vegas* stood on its own merit and emerged as one of Presley's most successful films and remains among his most beloved. Theater owners reported to *Box Office* full houses every day the film played, and one stated, "Put Elvis and Ann together in another picture." But, sadly, it was not to be.

Along with the success of the movie, what went on behind the scenes extended beyond the usual. Ann-Margret and Elvis did not simply have a casual affair during the filming of the movie—they actually fell in love. They were similar in many

Ann-Margret received as much attention as Elvis

ways, and understood each other as a result. Ann-Margret was not bothered nor did she feel crowded by Presley's gaggle of bodyguards and hangers-on who always seemed to be hovering about. Even when they would tease her with sexual comments, she would laugh and take it in stride. Because she had that attitude, Elvis was not as fiercely protective (that is, they would not have dared to make the same jokes around Priscilla). According to *Elvis Aaron Presley*, Presley associate Alan Fortas once asked Ann-Margret to "run around the block four times and let me have your pants." Elvis and Ann-Margret reportedly fell down laughing. Presley associate Lamar Fike remembered: "Ann-Margret took everything with a laugh. She didn't give Elvis any problems. And she was never threatened by another woman."

The problem with this situation was that their romance was hitting the newspaper gossip columns. And Priscilla was reading them back in Memphis. She recalled in her autobiography, *Elvis and Me*:

> Elvis casually dismissed her as a "typical Hollywood starlet." I knew that his attitude toward actresses was unfavorable. "They're into their careers and their man comes second. I don't want to be second to anything or anyone. That's why you don't have to worry about my falling in love with my so-called leading ladies." I wanted to believe him, but I couldn't help noticing the headlines about their torrid love affair.

It really became difficult when Ann-Margret announced to the press that she and Elvis were engaged. At this point Priscilla became extremely upset and Elvis realized the situation with Ann-Margret had gotten out of hand. He and Priscilla reconciled, and he broke off his relationship with Ann-Margret. Priscilla saw a telegram from Ann indicating unhappiness over Elvis ending things, and she was satisfied. Elvis and Ann-Margret remained friends from afar. For the rest of his life, Elvis would send flowers to Ann-Margret whenever she opened in a new show. Meanwhile, Priscilla would later speak of this entire incident with forgiveness and understanding. When Ann-Margret showed up at Elvis Presley's funeral in 1977, Priscilla recalled, "I felt a genuine bond with her."

The songs in *Viva Las Vegas* enjoyed some chart success, but despite this being one of the stronger Presley movie soundtracks, an album was never released. It was instead represented by singles and a couple of EPs. Some of the songs in the movie did not see release until years later on variously compiled LPs.

Colonel Parker does not receive technical advisor credit on this movie, as he had on the others. Parker clashed frequently with director George Sidney, whom he felt gave too much attention to Ann-Margret at the expense of Elvis. While Parker was protecting his protege, he also had to realize the chemistry between Presley and Ann-Margret was explosive. What he balked at was the film's budget, due somewhat to Sidney's shooting Ann-Margret's dance numbers from several different angles using multiple cameras. *Viva Las Vegas* grossed over $9 million worldwide, $5 million of that from the United States alone. This resulted in a profit, but not as large as Parker wanted. Thus, he insisted on a very low budget for *Kissin' Cousins*, which was filmed afterward but released ahead of *Viva Las Vegas*. Due to the Colonel's heavy promotion, *Kissin' Cousins* grossed strongly at the box office and turned a substantial profit. The budgets would be slashed on all subsequent Elvis movies as a result.

Along with no soundtrack album for *Viva Las Vegas*, there was no summer record release for RCA, Elvis now exclusively relying on his soundtracks to represent his recordings. RCA dusted off the rocking "Such a Night" from the 1960 *Elvis Is Back* album and released it in the summer of 1964. The competition was too strong by that time due to the noted British Invasion that began with the Beatles' triumphant arrival in the United States in February 1964. Of course while *Viva Las Vegas* was released in May 1964, it was filmed in 1963. As a result, no one knew or realized during filming the level of excitement the British groups would inspire. Even the subsequently filmed *Kissin' Cousins* had wrapped production by the end of 1963.

Elvis Presley returned to Paramount for his next vehicle, *Roustabout*, which offered a stronger dramatic narrative and a costar who was one of the true veterans of Hollywood cinema.

CHAPTER 18

Roustabout
(PARAMOUNT, 1964)

Director: John Rich
Screenplay: Anthony Lawrence and Allan Weiss, from a story by Weiss
Producer: Hal Wallis
Cinematography: Lucien Ballard
Editor: Warren Low
Assistant director: Michael D. Moore
Makeup: Wally Westmore
Hairstylists: Nellie Manley and Larry Geller
Music: Joseph J. Lilley
Vocals: The Jordanaires
Technical advisor: Colonel Tom Parker
Cast: Elvis Presley, Barbara Stanwyck, Joan Freeman, Leif Erickson, Sue Ane Langdon, Pat Buttram, Joan Staley, Dabbs Greer, Steve Brodie, Norman Grabowski, Jack Albertson, Jane Dulo, Joel Fluellen, Wilda Taylor, Billy Barty, Lester Miller, Raquel Welch, Lynn Borden, Teri Garr, Joy Harmon, Bevery Adams, Connie Ducharme, Mercedes Ford, Joseph Forte, Carey Foster, Linda Foster, Kenneth Baker, Owen Bush, Roger Creed, Richard Di Paolo, Maugene Gannon, Steve Condit, Jimmy Gaines, Arthur Levy, Chester Hayes, Marianna Hill, Richard Kiel, Buddy Lewis, Mike Mahoney, Barbara Hemingway, Teri Hope, Ray Kellogg, Lance LeGault, Arthur Levy, Buddy Lewis, Max Manning, Diane Libby, Jerry James, Howard Joslin, Kenner Kemp, Theodore Lehman, Sailor Vincent, Red West, Dean Moray, Linda Rand, Kent McCord, Christopher Riordan, Dianne Simpson, Katie Sweet, Jesse Wayne, Glenn Wilder, K. L. Smith, Jack Whalen
Songs (in the order performed):
"Roustabout" (written by Bill Giant, Bernie Baum, and Florence Kaye; performed by Elvis Presley)
"Poison Ivy League" (written by Bill Giant, Bernie Baum, and Florence Kaye; performed by Elvis Presley)
"One Track Heart" (written by Bill Giant, Bernie Baum, and Florence Kaye; performed by Elvis Presley)

> "Wheels on My Heels" (written by Sid Tepper and Roy C. Bennett; performed by Elvis Presley)
> "It's a Wonderful World" (written by Sid Tepper and Roy C. Bennett; performed by Elvis Presley)
> "It's Carnival Time" (written by Ben Weisman and Sid Wayne; performed by Elvis Presley)
> "Carny Town" (written by Fred Wise and Randy Starr; performed by Elvis Presley)
> "Hard Knocks" (written by Joy Byers; performed by Elvis Presley)
> "There's a Brand New Day on the Horizon" (written by Joy Byers; performed by Elvis Presley)
> "Big Love, Big Heartache" (written by Dolores Fuller, Lee Morris, and Sonny Hendrix; performed by Elvis Presley)
> "Little Egypt" (written by Jerry Leiber and Mike Stoller; performed by Elvis Presley)
>
> The soundtrack album made it to number one on the charts, the last Elvis Presley album to do so for nine years.
>
> Released November 11, 1964
> Filmed March 9–April 20, 1964
> 101 minutes
> Technicolor
> Aspect ratio: 2.35:1
> Gross: $3 million
> Released to DVD by Paramount Home Video

Roustabout was made after *Kissin' Cousins,* although *Viva Las Vegas* was released between them. So, at the theaters, this movie followed *Viva Las Vegas*, which had been one of the better Elvis Presley formula movies. While not at the same level, *Roustabout* is good for allowing Presley to play the sort of tough, unsmiling character he liked, one that recalled the style of favorite actors like Marlon Brando, James Dean, and Humphrey Bogart. He was pleased to have Hollywood veteran Barbara Stanwyck in a strong supporting role (it was to be her last theatrical feature film). As the title character, a worker in a carnival, Elvis sings several songs while maintaining the working-class demeanor that the part calls for.

Elvis plays Charlie Rogers, a drifter who performs music to sustain himself. He travels from town to town, venue to venue, because he constantly gets into trouble with the law. This backstory is established when a group of privileged college students come to see him perform. He uses his music to insult them (the song "Poison Ivy League" calls attention to their spoiled, protected status) and they confront him outside afterward. Using karate, he beats up all three men, breaking the arm of one. Realizing their status would result in a likely jail sentence for him, Charlie leaves town.

154 CHAPTER 18

Elvis in *Roustabout*

Elvis plays Charlie as a tough guy, but not in the same manner as the characters in *Jailhouse Rock* or *King Creole*. Charlie is closer to the character in *Loving You*—uncompromising, defiant, but with a work ethic despite having no solid ties to a family or any other such connection. When Charlie comes onstage and notices the privileged college students, he smiles and responds to their heckling in a comic manner, telling the girls to "get rid of the guys and I'll meet you later on," delighting in their building anger as his comebacks overpower their heckles. The song, with lyrics talking about students who get a free ride from their parents and a guaranteed job from the same source, is the final insult to the college boys.

These students represent the upper class and Charlie represents the working class in the same manner as Elvis himself represented, especially during the 1950s. The students wear top fashions and letter sweaters, in contrast to the jeans and modest attire of Charlie, not unlike the rugged appearance Elvis projected in his initial 1956 TV appearances in contrast to the tuxedo-clad singers who otherwise appeared on the program. Beating up the confrontational rich boys, despite being outnumbered, and being jailed for it (until an enamored waitress friend bails him out the next morning) shows how the privileged students who started the fight are given greater respect than the working-class Charlie, who simply defends himself. His response to the girl who bails him out is to hop on his motorcycle and ride off to another town, refusing her request to join him. "This motorcycle only seats one," he says stoically, adding, "just because you bailed me out doesn't mean you own me." As he cycles out of sight, the girl hollers behind his departure, "Call me!"

Charlie exhibits the same demeanor in his dialog with the college boys:

> Student: "I've seen more action in a zoo than in this club."
>
> Charlie: "From what side of the cage, boy?"

It is only fitting that he'd end up employed at a working-class drifter's stereotypical destination: a traveling carnival.

Charlie, on the road, notices pretty Cathy Lean (Joan Freeman) in a car with her father and an older woman (Leif Erickson and Barbara Stanwyck). He shouts flirtatiously, and the father angrily runs him off the road, destroying his bike and guitar. Charlie insists the man pay. The older woman, introduced as Maggie, insists he will, and offers Charlie a ride to the next town. She ends up hiring him to work in her carnival.

This transitional scene establishes the narrative in the same manner that the opening scene explains the Charlie character. Charlie now has a love interest in the girl, a conflict with her father, and a supporter via Maggie. He also has a job where he can exhibit his toughness, pursue the girl, and, eventually utilize his singing ability. From this point the film explores at least the superficial possibilities of each.

The script, and John Rich's direction, uses isolated sequences to present Charlie's pursuit of Cathy. While walking on the carnival grounds for the first time, he abruptly kisses her. She reacts in anger, but Charlie maintains his confidence. She agrees to go up on the Ferris wheel with him for a private ride, but they are caught by her father. He is the one character in the film who does not like Charlie. The others, including various workers and a fire-breathing performer he befriends, are all welcoming and supportive. Charlie comes off as friendly and likeable, even choosing to respond to the father's anger with lighthearted comments. He seems unfazed, likely realizing he can leave as soon as his motorcycle and guitar are repaired.

Barbara Stanwyck's veteran status pays off in that she effortlessly steals every scene she is in. Even Elvis Presley's formidable presence is overshadowed by her own forceful charisma. Elvis likely stepped back and allowed the actress to carry the scenes in which they appear together. He was very respectful of his fellow actors, especially those who had a history. He would talk to Stanwyck between scenes and tried to learn from her. Unlike, say, Angela Lansbury, who disliked working in a Presley movie, Stanwyck was quite fond of Elvis and patiently answered any questions he had about acting.

The studio's first choice of Mae West for the role eventually played by Stanwyck is an interesting thing to ponder. West reportedly turned the role down because she wanted top billing alongside Elvis, which is something the Colonel would never allow. Other accounts report that she wanted to play his love inter-

Nice shot of the filming of *Roustabout* with Elvis and Barbara Stanwyck performing a scene

est. In any case, while West might have turned in a good performance in such a role, Ms. Stanwyck does brilliantly in what would be her final theatrical film.

In *Elvis Aaron Presley*, Presley was said to not get along well with director John Rich, and his bodyguards recall that Rich made Elvis do several takes on a certain scene while the singer was suffering from a bad case of the flu, complete with a fever. Elvis patiently did as he was told, take after take, without a problem, but afterward he privately indicated his disgust.

This does not take away from Rich's work on the film. He frames scenes with several rides going on in the background, offering movement that offsets the actors playing a scene in the foreground. Rich alternates between medium shots, long shots, and close-ups, while his establishing shots try to encompass the vastness of the active carnival setting. There is a cleverness to his choices for night scenes, depicting the area with fewer customers and a slower pace. Even in close-up there are people milling about in the background, maintaining the carnival atmosphere. The framework is solid and effective.

Once Charlie's motorcycle and guitar are repaired, he has settled pretty comfortably in carnival life and continues to pursue Cathy, with whom he has become increasingly more smitten (rebuffing the advances of an aggressive carnival performer played by Sue Ane Langdon). In order to attract people to the carnival game he is asked to manage, Charlie pulls out his guitar and starts singing. Soon he is promoted as a major attraction and gets the attention of a rival carnival owner.

Veteran western character actor Pat Buttram plays the owner of the rival carnival, testing his Mr. Haney character whom he would play on TV's *Green Acres* the following year. Buttram would later state that Haney was inspired by Presley manager Colonel Tom Parker, whom he observed while doing *Roustabout* and the earlier *Wild in the Country*. In *Roustabout*, Haney is Harry Carver, who has garnered the nickname of the Undertaker for putting small-time carnivals out of business. He has his sights set on Maggie's carnival, which is already in trouble with creditors. Charlie's singing is promising enough to possibly get her out of debt. The loyal Charlie ignores Harry's overtures.

Elvis plays Charlie as a man in search of meaning. He does not seem completely comfortable with his drifter status or his inability to stay out of trouble. The virginal Cathy is nicer than the women he is accustomed to (as represented by the girl who bailed him out of jail earlier in the movie—a loose waitress with a thing for Charlie). Charlie sees an anchor here, a work ethic, and the fact that the carnival is a traveling one causes him to relate to it on a personal level. At one point Maggie says to him, "What do you know about family?" Charlie abruptly, and angrily, responds, "Nothing!" Despite the continued conflict with Cathy's father, he senses a familial grounding at the carnival. Harry's promise of more money and greater prestige can not shake his loyalty. It might have earlier, indicating that Charlie's own personality is changing. Elvis has enough understanding of acting nuance to convey this effectively.

The narrative continues to present its story through isolated scenes with a sequence in which Cathy must position herself in the dunk tank and be submerged in the cold water whenever a decent throw smacks the lever that releases her. A loudmouthed former minor league pitcher (Steve Brodie, who had picked a fight with Elvis in *Blue Hawaii*) tries to attract his equally boisterous date (Jane Dulo) by repeatedly knocking Cathy in the water. Charlie is chagrined that Cathy's father would assign her to such a post, and even more upset that Cathy must be repeatedly dunked in the cold water. Charlie interrupts the man's game, and a fight is averted, but the man discovers his wallet is missing. Cathy's father is blamed and taken to jail. Later that night, Charlie finds the wallet. He is sidetracked before turning it in, and the father ends up spending the night in jail. When Cathy and Maggie discover this, Charlie is blamed for purposely withholding the evidence. Frustrated, Charlie quits and goes to Harry Carver's carnival as the star singing attraction.

It is likely just coincidence that the best musical number in the movie, Jerry Leiber and Mike Stoller's "Little Egypt," is the one performed once Charlie joins Harry's rival company. Charlie's eventual return to Maggie's carnival, saving it from bankruptcy, even gaining the begrudging support of Cathy's father, is shown to be because he is in love with Cathy. Charlie has seen the light. He is now a carny, accepting its semireligious existence that the fortune-teller earlier describes as "all we have." The ending seems to wrap up too quickly. But the central character's redemption is complete.

Critics were unimpressed with both the film and the soundtrack, but *Roustabout* was a hit at the box office and its soundtrack flew to the top of the chart, knocking off a Beach Boys live album. It would remain there for a week before being replaced by *Beatles '65*. It would be Presley's last number one album until 1973. While the *New York Times* did not bother reviewing the movie, *Variety* stated:

> Elvis Presley-starrer, *Roustabout,* is a gaudily-staged, tritely-scripted film looming as a box office smash, based on lure of Presley name and co-billing of Barbara Stanwyck and expensive quality of the Technicolor, Techniscope frame provided for 11 Presley songs. Good cast tries its best to cope with nonsense but it's losing battle. Miss Stanwyck's talents—she's had four Academy Award nominations in distinguished career—are totally wasted. Miss Freeman hasn't much to do except wring her hands when father and boyfriend get in fights, but does it prettily. Standouts in smaller roles are Pat Buttram as owner of rival carny and Steve Brodie, obnoxious customer in baseball-tossing game.

The original story for *Roustabout* had Elvis Presley's character drummed out of the army for running under fire, a far different perspective on the character than what ended up in the film. Allan Weiss, who penned the original story, believed Elvis had remarkable acting talent and wanted to provide a more challenging character. Rewrites were ordered, and according to *Careless Love*, Weiss later stated, "They wanted me to keep things shallow. They just wanted a framework in which they could put some songs." Despite this, Weiss and cowriter Anthony Lawrence's screenplay were nominated for a Writer's Guild Award as Best Screenplay for a Musical, losing to *Mary Poppins*.

One of the things that upset Elvis Presley was an article in the *Las Vegas Desert News and Telegram* during the shooting of *Roustabout,* which stated:

> Would you believe that Richard Burton and Peter O'Toole owe part of their current success to Elvis Presley? These two brilliant Shakespearian-trained actors, winning worldwide acclaim for their performances in *Becket*, might not have had the opportunity to star in the picture, were it not for Sir Swivel Hips. Don't laugh, it's not that Elvis refused the role of Henry II or Becket. No, Elvis helped finance *Becket* indirectly. Producer Hal Wallis, who has made Presley's biggest hits, also produced *Becket*. Says Wallis, "In order to do the artistic pictures, it is necessary to make the commercially successful Presley pictures. But that doesn't mean a Presley picture can't have quality too." At the moment, Wallis is shooting *Roustabout* starring Elvis. The story may not be the greatest, but O'Toole and Burton can't sing like Elvis either.

As described in *Careless Love*, Presley confronted Wallis and asked, "When do I get to do my *Becket*?" Presley associate Jerry Schilling stated: "Elvis didn't have a problem doing musical comedies, he just didn't want to do ten of them, one after the other."

Along with the aforementioned "Little Egypt" and "Poison Ivy League," the rocker "Hard Knocks" and the ballad "Big Love, Big Heartache" are good Presley soundtrack tunes. None were radio hits, however, so the album's climb to number one on the charts remains a bit curious, although impressive. Oddly, the title song originally written for the movie, "I'm a Roustabout," was replaced by the song "Roustabout" prior to production. The former, written by the dependable Otis Blackwell ("Don't Be Cruel," All Shook Up," "Return to Sender") and Winfield Scott, was much more of a rocker in the Presley style, and there is no explanation for why it was replaced with the simpler song used in the movie.

This would be the last time Elvis rose to the occasion and tried to find something of substance in one of his movie roles. As his films, and his soundtracks, settled even more firmly into formula comedies, Elvis put forth little effort. His talent was so strong, it was difficult to discern that he is doing only the very least to put over a scene or a song. But beginning with his next film, *Girl Happy*, Elvis had given up on the possibility of being taken seriously as a movie actor. In a 1972 interview for *Elvis on Tour*, Presley would recall:

> I thought they would get a new property for me, or give me a chance to show some acting ability, to do an interesting story. But it did not change. I became very discouraged. No amount of money could give me self-satisfaction. I would like to have had something more challenging than Hollywood's image of what they thought I was.

Roustabout resulted in a lawsuit due to Elvis Presley's performance of the Leiber-Stoller song "Little Egypt," which had been a minor hit for the Coasters in 1961. An actual dancer who performed as Little Egypt sued in court, stating she gave no permission to use her name for a character in the movie. She lost the case.

Actor-dancer Christopher Riordan was making his second appearance in an Elvis Presley movie and had fonder memories in an interview:

> I hated doing *Viva Las Vegas*. I was a bit of a snob, and thought after working with Fred Astaire it was a comedown to do an Elvis movie. Plus, the choreographers treated me very rudely. So when I was called to do *Roustabout*, I wasn't interested. However the opportunity to have a role and not just be a dancer, and to work with Barbara Stanwyck convinced me to take the part. I didn't realize that a mutual friend had mentioned to Elvis that I was a single parent who had won custody of my son, which was not common back then. He admired that, and came up to me on the set of *Roustabout* and said, "nice to see you again." I couldn't believe he even noticed me on the other picture. I later was put on a list of people he wanted in his movies, and was the only male on that list. He made sure I was nearby during a scene. He liked to look over at me and smile or sneer. I have never forgotten his kindness and support. He was a wonderful person.

It is worth noting that around the time of *Roustabout*, Elvis hired a man named Larry Geller as his hairstylist. Geller would get very close to Elvis and turn him on to spiritual books like *The Prophet*. This expansion of Presley's spirituality is said to have had a psychological effect during a period where he felt creatively limited and frustrated. Unfortunately, his prescription drug taking also increased as his career became less and less significant on the charts and the films he did not enjoy making achieved box office success beyond what Elvis thought they were worth.

Roustabout was the first movie Elvis Presley filmed in 1964. It began production in March, about a month after the Beatles made a triumphant appearance on *The Ed Sullivan Show*. During this appearance, Ed Sullivan famously read a good luck telegram on the air from Elvis and the Colonel. Presley's cousin Billy Smith told Alanna Nash in *Elvis Aaron Presley*:

> It made it seem like Elvis was a fan, but also like he wasn't worried about their success and what it might do to his. Elvis was very threatened by The Beatles, but he tried to hide it. The Beatles were like early Elvis in that they were rebellious, they had that hard-driving rock and roll going, and they were brand spanking new.

Following on the Beatles' success, other British acts including the Rolling Stones, the Dave Clark Five, Herman's Hermits, and the Kinks all came over to the United States and achieved success with music that was innovative and challenging, just as Presley's 1950s work had been.

The music industry changed very rapidly and consistently, progressing past what Elvis had established, ironically due to his enormous, towering influence on the work of these British groups. Elvis would play Beatles records and tell his music company, Hill and Range, "This is the sound I want again." But he continued to be given mediocre songs to fill up a soundtrack album for his latest formula movie. He was said to do dozens of takes on songs, trying to find some kind of hook to make them more interesting, and would become increasingly more frustrated at his inability to elevate this material above the dismissably mediocre. His associates also recall that he would stack new songs in piles like good, medium, and not good. Soon the good stack would be so small, some songs from the medium stack would have to be added. It was a frustrating time for Elvis Presley's creativity, and it continued to get worse. Colonel Parker's idea to "make 'em fast, make 'em cheap" was resulting in monetary profits, but there is little foresight to doing the same thing the same way until it peters out completely. The Beatles, Stones, Kinks, and other groups were vibrant and exciting with their new twist on the style Elvis had established a decade earlier. And soon the Beatles would be making movies as well.

CHAPTER 19

Girl Happy
(MGM, 1965)

Director: Boris Sagal
Screenplay: R. S. Allen
Producer: Joe Pasternak
Cinematographer: Phillip H. Lathrop
Editor: Ruth Roland
Assistant directors: Jack Aldworth and Wallace Jones
Makeup: William Tuttle
Hairstylists: Sydney Guilaroff and Larry Geller
Vocals: The Jordanaires
Technical advisor: Colonel Tom Parker
Cast: Elvis Presley, Shelley Fabares, Harold J. Stone, Gary Crosby, Joby Baker, Jimmy Hawkins, Nita Talbot, Mary Ann Mobley, Fabrizio Mioni, Jackie Coogan, Peter Brooks, John Fielder, Chris Noel, Lyn Edgington, Gail Gilmore, Pamela Curran, Rusty Allen, Ralph Lee, Dan Haggerty, Tommy Farrell, Richard Reeves, Mike De Anda, Norman Grabowski, Milton Frome, Alan Hanley, Hank Jones, Kent McCord, Beverly Adams, George Cisar, Theresa Cooper, Nancy Czar, Stasa Damascus, Jim Dawson, Darren Dublin, Ted Fish, Julie Payne, Red West, Les Tremayne, Olan Soule.
Songs (in the order performed):
  "I Got News for You" (performed by Nita Talbot)
  "Do the Clam" (written by Ben Weisman, Sid Wayne, and Dolores Fuller; performed by Elvis Presley)
  "Girl Happy" (written by Doc Pomus and Norman Meade; performed by Elvis Presley)
  "Cross My Heart and Hope to Die" (written by Ben Weisman and Sid Wayne; performed by Elvis Presley)
  "Do Not Disturb" (written by Bill Giant, Bernie Baum, and Florence Kaye; performed by Elvis Presley)
  "Spring Fever" (written by Bill Giant, Bernie Baum, and Florence Kaye; performed by Elvis Presley)

"Wolf Call" (written by Bill Giant, Bernie Baum, and Florence Kaye; performed by Elvis Presley)
"Fort Lauderdale Chamber of Commerce" (written by Sid Tepper and Roy C. Bennett; performed by Elvis Presley)
"Puppet on a String" (written by Sid Tepper and Roy C. Bennett; performed by Elvis Presley)
"I've Got to Find My Baby" (written by Joy Byers; performed by Elvis Presley)
"The Meanest Girl in Town" (written by Joy Byers; performed by Elvis Presley)
"Startin' Tonight" (written by Lenore Rosenblatt and Victor Millrose; performed by Elvis Presley)

The *Girl Happy* soundtrack album went to number eight on the charts
"Do the Clam" went to number 21, while "Puppet on a String" reached number 14 on the charts

Released April 14, 1965
Filmed June 5–August 28, 1964
96 minutes
Technicolor
Aspect Ratio: 2.35:1
Gross: $3,250,000
Released to DVD by Warner Home Video

Girl Happy is the start of what many consider to be a real low point in Elvis Presley's movie career, where the films settle completely into the formula established by *Blue Hawaii* without highlights like *Viva Las Vegas* or *Roustabout*. In a 1972 interview for *Elvis on Tour*, Elvis would sum up his movie career dismissively: "I was doing a lot of pictures close together, and they got very similar. I'd read the first four or five pages and I knew it was just a different name with 12 new songs, and the songs were mediocre."

This was especially evident in *Girl Happy*, a musical comedy that is pure formulaic fluff. And while it is reasonably entertaining on its own terms, it lacked the energy of *Viva Las Vegas* and the dramatic edge of *Roustabout*. It was the first in a steady succession of similarly formulaic Elvis movies as Presley describes in the above quote. In the same 1972 interview he went on to state, "At a certain stage I had no say so, I didn't have final approval of the script. I couldn't say this is not good for me. I don't think anybody was consciously trying to harm me, it's just that Hollywood's image of me was wrong." And it was the image that is being presented in *Girl Happy*. Although the soundtrack resulted in one minor hit, the silly "Do the Clam," and the title tune was a good, upbeat, Doc Pomus composition, much of the music is pretty weak, especially compared to the British Invasion tunes that were permeating the radio airwaves at the time *Girl Happy* was in release.

Roy Carr and Mick Farren stated in *Elvis: The Illustrated Record*:

> 1965 promised to be a revolutionary year for rock and roll with the Beatles, the Rolling Stones, and Bob Dylan breaking into previously uncharted territory, while bands like the Who, the Yardbirds, and the Byrds were determinedly struggling up the success ladder. Elvis now made his first contribution of the year (with "Do the Clam") and it proved to be anything but innovative. The rule seemed to have become: three films a year, no studio records, and if the soundtrack music doesn't fill the quota, the balance can be made with re-issues.

Elvis's next hit record was a re-release of his 1960 recording "Crying in the Chapel," a gospel-inspired R&B ballad that had been a hit for Sonny Til and the Orioles in 1950. The Presley version was released appropriately at Easter in 1965, right around the time *Girl Happy* hit theaters. It would be his last hit until the very end of the decade.

Carr and Farren are correct in stating that at this point in Presley's movie career, the formula was to shoot fairly low-budget movies filled with enough songs for a soundtrack album. Each would have a thin plot with no real challenge for Elvis. They would be lightweight entertainment for his many fans.

In this one, Elvis (curiously playing a character named Rusty, which had been Ann-Margret's character's name in *Viva Las Vegas*) and his band look forward to spending time in California during their usual winter break from performing at a gangster-owned clubs in windy Chicago. However, their success is drawing good crowds, so the head of the club where they are currently finishing their contract decides to hold them over indefinitely. They want to refuse, but realize it would be unhealthy to do so. When they find out that the gangster's daughter, Valerie (Shelley Fabares), is vacationing in Florida with two friends (Chris Noel and Lyn Edgington), and he is worried about temptations and safety, they talk him into allowing them to travel down there and act as her chaperones. He agrees, and they get to go to Florida as planned.

There are several telling things in these opening scenes that establish the plot. First, Harold J. Stone as Big Frank the club owner was best at playing comic villains and that is how he portrays the character here. He is only menacing within the context of comedy. There is no dramatic edge at all, even from a character who is supposed to be the heavy. It is purely comical, as Stone's rant about his daughter's safety and the temptations she'll face is pure sitcom fodder. Elvis and his three bandmates (Andy, Wilbur, and Doc) are afraid to bring up their request to go to Florida. Elvis carefully cons the befuddled father into sending them to keep an eye on his daughter. So Elvis is the leader on- and offstage. Second is the very fact that Elvis is part of a band, not a solo performer as in his other movies. The success of the Beatles made rock groups all the rage, so Elvis was cast as part of a four-man ensemble. Finally, whenever the three bandmates are on-screen, the background music plays "Three Blind Mice," perhaps in relation to the symbolic blindness or cluelessness of the characters, or maybe to compare them to the Three Stooges, whose theme song of "Three Blind Mice" is very strongly identified with their characters. In 1964 when this movie was being filmed, the Three Stooges were very popular fare on television, so much so that they re-formed and were actively making feature-length movies for the younger set. Of the actors playing band members in *Girl Happy*, veteran actors Joby Baker and Jimmy Hawkins (whose career dated back to childhood) were cast with Gary Crosby (son of Bing and the only actual musician among the three).

Once the four of them get to Florida, they combine their task of looking after the gangster's very attractive daughter Valerie and scoping out the other women. It is left pretty much up to Elvis to pay attention to Valerie while the band members from this point are ogling the other girls and comically striking out. The film concentrates mostly on vignettes until its focus centers on Rusty and Valerie gradually falling for each other, the latter being unaware that her father hired Rusty.

The plot is very standard but somehow there is a sense of fun permeating the proceedings, so that the formulaic fluff is engaging enough to make it one of the better examples of this type of Elvis movie. Elvis himself was dissatisfied, but according to an interview with Chris Noel, who appeared in the movie as one of Shelley Fabares's friends:

> Elvis never showed that he was unhappy. He was always on time, always knew his lines and his marks, and always worked hard to do his best. He wanted to make the movie as good as he could, and he joked around with everyone, making us all feel comfortable. I never heard him make a single negative remark about the songs in the movie, or his corny dialog, or anything else. Whatever he may have thought of things privately, in public he knew that as the star of the movie he had a responsibility to all of us. He got along with everyone. In professional terms, he was a dream to work with.

Shelley Fabares agreed with Noel. Appearing in the first of three movies she would make with Elvis Presley, in an interview with Frankie Verocca, Fabares recalled:

> Elvis and I hit it off immediately. I had just gotten married, so I wasn't interested in him romantically, and the fact that I liked him

Elvis liked working with Shelley Fabares in *Girl Happy*

on a completely different level made him more comfortable with me. We had a lot of fun and I think this was the best of the three pictures I made with him. We laughed from beginning to end.

Whenever Elvis was asked in later years who his favorite female costar was, he would always say Shelley Fabares, not Ann-Margret.

The on-screen chemistry between Presley and Fabares was discernible, and the characters presented an even more interesting dynamic. Rusty is there to essentially "babysit" Valerie, and since she wears glasses, he dismisses her as the brainy type and has little interest (she attracts a comical brainy male stereotype played by Peter Brooks). There is an interesting underlying theme lurking beneath the *Girl Happy* scenario that confronts the burgeoning women's liberation movement. Valerie wants to be left alone and on her own. Her father states, "If I had a son, ok, let someone else's father worry," indicating that women are not allowed such freedoms. Valerie's quest gives some attention to the evolution of women in society as reaching for the same freedoms as their male peers had long enjoyed. The film never develops this subliminal idea, however. After Valerie is pegged as "brainy," Rusty instead pursues the elusive Deena (Mary Ann Mobley) as a challenge. He changes his mind when Valerie strips to a swimsuit and reveals herself as beautiful. The screenplay does little to develop the characters, even at a more superficial level. Big Frank and the intellectual Brentwood (Peter Brooks) are stereotypes. There is even an Italian character (a throwback to *Viva Las Vegas*) who manages to distract Valerie's attentions for a while.

Douglas Brode in his 2006 book *Elvis Cinema and Popular Culture* stated:

> The Elvis of *Loving You* and *King Creole* is gone; he here resembles the despised Wendell Corey and Walter Matthau characters. The boy who swore to make the world a better place has co-opted by the system he set out to change, now serving as a cynical centerpiece of all he opposed in his idealistic youth.

Throughout the film, Elvis does, as Chris Noel indicated, try to have fun in his role. A comical sequence in which Rusty must break into a prison to rescue Valerie, then dress as a girl to sneak back out, is presented in an offbeat comic manner and an edginess he likely enjoyed.

Director Boris Sagal was able to sense Presley's dissatisfaction with the sort of film he was making, and took the singer aside to advise him. He stated that Elvis should just take some time off and study acting, refine his rough edges, and insist on roles that tapped into his proven ability as an actor. Elvis was pleased with Sagal's understanding, but realized such a thing would be impossible.

While Elvis was filming *Girl Happy*, the first Beatles film, *A Hard Day's Night*, was released. Unlike the Presley movies, *A Hard Day's Night* was embraced by the critical intelligentsia for director Richard Lester's innovative cinematic approach to the group's attempt to respond to, and live with, their massive success. It explored this in a humorous manner, the group coming off like hip Marx Brothers amidst a whirlwind of funny vignettes and top-level original songs. It remains one of the finest English-language films ever produced. Along with the changes in the music world, there were events in the real world to which younger people were responding. According to Presley associate Marty Lacker in *Elvis Aaron Presley*:

> He supported civil rights. This was the time of all the uprisings by the blacks, especially in the South. Television news was full of the civil rights marches and demonstrations, with film of black people all over Alabama and elsewhere getting beaten to a pulp. He didn't like to see anybody beat on. Colonel always drummed it into his head not to take sides on politics because he said it was bound to offend somebody, no matter which side Elvis took. He could have been a force in that regard because Southern people, particularly, liked him. But he didn't speak out because of what Colonel had

told him. So that's why Elvis never talked politics. And he never voted.

When *Girl Happy* showed up in the spring of 1965, Howard Thompson of the *New York Times* seemed to take in stride that this now represented the type of picture Elvis would be doing.

> Elvis Presley has been hopping all over the map in recent years for movie locales. "Girl Happy," his latest color musical, opening yesterday at the Forum and other houses, lands him at Fort Lauderdale, Florida "where the boys are," remember? Thousands of them, avidly eyeing thousands of beach cuties come spring. That's the text of El's new Metro release. This time, though, the entertainment runs thin. El and three pals in a music combo arrive on the scene to keep an eye on their boss's daughter, Shelley Fabares, and a cute chick she is. And guess what happens. That's it—that's the picture. Even with a large throng of clean-cut youngsters and some fetching Fort Lauderdale backgrounds woven in for travel-poster picturesqueness, the picture meanders familiarly. The saving grace is the steady stream of tunes, as rhythmical as they are unoriginal, belted out by the star and the other youngsters. That's one thing—for those who care—you can always count on in a Presley frolic.

Theater owners, however, were pleased with this latest Elvis Presley vehicle, calling it in *Box Office* "a ticket-happy, customer-pleasing playdate for a welcome change." It had been discovered back with the box office receipts of *Blue Hawaii* that a colorful piece of fluff with comedy and songs were the ingredients for a successful Elvis Presley picture. *Girl Happy* is not as good a movie as *Blue Hawaii*, but it managed to emerge among the top 15 percent of box office hits in 1965.

One odd thing about the film's title tune, which is arguably the best song in the movie, is that the recording was sped up in the studio. Some state it was to make it more lively and upbeat; others claim it was an attempt to make thirty-year-old Elvis sound younger. Both are ridiculous reasons (regarding the former, Elvis did several takes on his songs before he was satisfied, and this one could have been performed at a quicker tempo on any number of these takes).

For his next film, *Tickle Me*, Elvis Presley works with a budget so small, there were no original songs. Another lightweight musical comedy, *Tickle Me* was a good example of how said formula could result in some measure of success. The producer was Ben Schwalb, who had a history of making good low-budget products. The studio was Allied Artists, a poverty row studio that desperately needed a hit to keep from folding. The screenwriters were Edward Bernds and Ellwood Ullman, who were decidedly out of their element in that

Magazine ad promoting *Girl Happy*

their past collaborative work had been comedies featuring the Three Stooges and the Bowery Boys. Norman Taurog was back as director. And, as a money-saving measure, not one original song was used. The music in *Tickle Me* was culled from old recordings Elvis had already done. Despite all of this, it somehow turned out to be one of the more agreeable examples of formulaic product during this period of Elvis Presley's musical career.

CHAPTER 20
Tickle Me
(ALLIED ARTISTS, 1965)

Director: Norman Taurog
Screenplay: Edward Bernds and Ellwood Ullman
Producer: Ben Schwalb
Cinematographer: Loyal Griggs
Editor: Archie Marshek
Assistant directors: Jack Aldworth, Wallace Jones
Makeup: Wally Westmore
Hairstylists: Nellie Manley and Larry Geller
Original music: Walter Scharf
Vocals: The Jordanaires
Technical advisor: Colonel Tom Parker
Cast: Elvis Presley, Julie Adams, Jocelyn Lane, Jack Mullaney, Merry Anders, Bill Williams, Edward Faulkner, Connie Gilchrist, Francine York, Barbara Werle, John Dennis, Grady Sutton, Romo Vincent, Allison Hayes, Ines Pedroza, Lilyan Chauvin, Angela Greene, Dorian Brown, Dorothy Konrad, Eve Bruce, Jackie Russell, Linda Rogers, Laurie Burton, Jean Ingram, Ann Morrell, Richard Reeves, Christopher Riordan, Taggart Casey, Louie Elias, Robert Hoy, Kenner Kemp, Charles Sherlock, Bert Stevens, Jack Tomek, Peggy Ward, Red West.
Songs (in the order performed):
  "(It's a) Long Lonely Highway" (written by Doc Pomus and Mort Shuman; performed by Elvis Presley)
  "It Feels So Right" (written by Fred Wise and Ben Weisman; performed by Elvis Presley)
  "(Such an) Easy Question" (written by Otis Blackwell and Scotty Moore; performed by Elvis Presley)
  "Dirty Dirty Feeling" (written by Jerry Leiber and Mike Stoller; performed by Elvis Presley)
  "Put the Blame on Me" (written by Kay Twomey, Fred Wise, and Norman Blagman; performed by Elvis Presley)

> "I'm Yours" (written by Don Robertson and Hal Blair; performed by Elvis Presley)
> "Night Rider" (written by Doc Pomus and Mort Shuman; performed by Elvis Presley)
> "I Feel That I've Known You Forever" (written by Doc Pomus and Alan Jeffries; performed by Elvis Presley)
> "Slowly but Surely" (written by Sid Wayne and Ben Weisman; performed by Elvis Presley)
>
> "(Such an) Easy Question" reached number 11 on the charts
>
> Released June 30, 1965
> Filmed October 12–November 24, 1964
> 90 minutes
> Technicolor
> Aspect ratio: 2.35:1
> U.S./Canada gross: $3.4 million; worldwide gross: $4 million
> Released to DVD by Warner Home Video

Elvis Presley continued his series of formula musical comedies with this lightweight effort that even Elvis admitted was a fun movie. *Tickle Me* featured Elvis as Lonnie Beale, a rodeo star who decided to take a job at a ranch during the off-season. When he arrives, he discovers this ranch is a weight loss spa for young women, all of whom happen to be trim and pretty.

Tickle Me was written by Edward Bernds and Ellwood Ullman, whose other credits included several films for the Three Stooges and the Bowery Boys. Elvis enjoyed doing comedy, and despite some subsequent criticism for the occasional slapstick, *Tickle Me* was an amusing trifle that remained entertaining throughout.

The story behind *Tickle Me* was that Allied Artists hadn't had a hit movie since *Billy Budd* in 1962 after enjoying strong success in the 1950s with the low-budget Bowery Boys comedies that had remained extremely popular after the studio inherited the series from Monogram Studios. Producer Ben Schwalb had produced the Bowery Boys movies, and believed a carefully budgeted Elvis film could save the studio from financial collapse. He approached the Colonel, who agreed to do the film. However, unlike what has been reported in previous studies, Elvis did not take a cut in salary for doing this film. A good chunk of the budget was his salary, and he also received his usual 50 percent of the profits.

It was Schwalb's idea to bring in Ullman and Bernds, with whom he had worked on the Bowery Boys series. Colonel Parker approved of them as screenwriters, but Schwalb's request to have Bernds direct the film was refused. Parker preferred to have someone Elvis was familiar with, so Norman Taurog was

TICKLE ME 173

Elvis at an all-girl dude ranch in *Tickle Me*

brought in to direct *Tickle Me*. In another cost-saving measure, no new songs were recorded for the film. A handful of album cuts that had previously been recorded and released were used instead, coming out on extended play and single play records to promote the movie.

Cowriter Edward Bernds recalled in an interview:

> Elvis was very shy and polite when Elwood and I met him, but he was genuinely impressed with our credentials. He liked the idea that we had worked with the Three Stooges and the Bowery Boys, and looked forward to doing that type of comedy. If you'll notice during the early part of the picture, when Elvis is just arriving at the spa, he is distracted by the pretty girls and trips over a table and chairs. I was on the set the day that was filmed. He stumbled over it in a comic manner, but without going overboard with his reactions, and it turned out to be charming and funny. Afterward he came to me and to Norman Taurog, the director, and wanted to be assured that it was funny. He worked hard and really wanted to do a good job. I thought the picture came out just fine.

Despite being comical in a more slapstick vein than previous Elvis movies, the dynamics are structured in adherence to the Presley formula. Elvis had a manly type job, a silly sidekick, an angry rival, a pretty girl he had to chase and convince, and a boss to whom he had to report. However within this established framework there were thematic alterations. His boss was a woman, his rival was a comic heavy, his sidekick was independently creative, and the pretty girl was central to the existing plot.

It is natural that the boss, Vera Radford, is a woman, in that she is running a girls' health ranch. Julie Adams plays the role that seems to be at least somewhat inspired by the Barbara Stanwyck part in *Roustabout*. She is tough, uncompromising, and yet also kind, defending Lonnie when other workers complain that his singing is distracting the girls from their tasks. Jack Mullaney plays the obligatory sidekick Stanley Potter, his resourcefulness making him more than the wayward follower with whom Elvis is usually saddled. Western movie veteran Edward Faulkner is Brad Bentley, the angry rival. Brad is not the same sort of begrudgingly respected rival found in other Elvis movies. He instead plays a comic foil, Faulkner rising to the occasion by playing up the comedy.

Jocelyn Lane, as Pam Merritt, is the pretty female costar. Jocelyn Lane's role was originally offered to Bridget Bardot, who was intrigued by the role but ultimately chose not to come to America from France to play it. Lane was chosen due to her resemblance to Bardot. It is she who carries the dramatic subplot of a gold mine left to her by her grandfather, and the evil rustlers who plot to take it from her. Naturally, Lonnie comes to her rescue, with silly Stanley at his side. The crooks' attempt to secure the gold by "haunting" the cabin is in the same manner as a Three Stooges comedy such as *Hot Scots* (1947) written by Ullman, *Merry Mavericks* (1951) written and directed by Bernds, or *The Bowery Boys Meet the Monsters* (1954), which they cowrote and Bernds directed. Elvis rises to the occasion, offering eye-bulging double takes with as much dedication as Huntz Hall or Shemp Howard had ever exhibited. The monster masks in *Tickle Me* were created by Ellis Burman Sr., who is generally known as having created the first commercially available line of studio-quality monster masks.

There is a continual sense of fun to *Tickle Me* that extends beyond the usual Elvis musical comedy, and the singer responds by calling attention to the proceedings, occasionally breaking the fourth wall and looking directly into the camera (at the audience)—a comic effect used in earlier cinema, most notably by Oliver Hardy in his films with Stan Laurel. According to an interview with actress Francine York, who appeared in the film, the sense of fun permeated the set between takes as well.

> Elvis was wonderful—kidding around all the time—joking—really wonderful. Norman Taurog was an old school director who knew how to handle actors. He was kind of old by this time, but I liked him so much—he was very nice and complimentary to me.

York's big scene in *Tickle Me* was when Lonnie is teaching her how to effectively shoot a bow and arrow, getting very close to her, and causing Pam to get jealous. Francine York recalls:

> I knew how to shoot a bow and arrow, so it was perfect for the scene—Norman Taurog asked us to do the scene over again and Elvis said "shucks I could stay like this all day." He was such a sweet, inspiring presence on the set.

The bulk of *Tickle Me* centers around the basic goings-on at the ranch, as starlets are whipped into tip-top shape. Merry Anders is quite amusing as Estelle, a perpetually hungry lady who tries to entice Stanley into giving her more food. Connie Gilchrist offers fun as a harried housekeeper. Veteran comedy actor Grady Sutton is a welcome presence as a wealthy investor who along with his wife is served a full steak dinner, which Estelle attempts to pilfer. It is all very simple and pleasant, with a great deal of slapstick punctuating the situational humor.

The context of the Elvis music is such that he breaks into song while working, distracting the girls from their exercises, as well as from watching Brad show off, much to his chagrin. For instance, when Brad is about to show the girls his diving expertise, an Elvis song takes them away from the pool. His angry reaction causes him to lose his balance and plummet into the pool in a typical slapstick manner. Faulkner mentioned in an interview that he enjoyed camping it up for his comical role in this movie:

> I had worked with Elvis on *G.I. Blues*, but it was such a small part, I think I was only on the picture for two days, so I was surprised that he remembered me when I came on the set. I had mostly been doing westerns because that was what had been in vogue when I entered the movie business in 1958. But with *Tickle Me* I got to do more comedy, and that was always a lot of fun. Elvis was a good actor, and very easy to work with. We had a great time.

Christopher Riordan related in an interview that he continued to be impressed with Elvis as well: "No matter what the scene was, he did it as if it were *Hamlet*. Even as he became more disillusioned, he was always professional."

The songs in *Tickle Me* were cherry-picked from past Elvis albums, with the idea that none had previously been released as a single. While this does mean that the film features no original songs, it also means that it features some of the best music in any Presley movie of the sixties. This includes "Dirty Dirty Feeling" and "It Feels So Right" from the landmark *Elvis Is Back* album (1960), "Put the Blame on Me" from the *Something for Everybody* album (1961), "Night

Rider," "I'm Yours," "(Such an) Easy Question," and "I Feel That I've Known You Forever" from *Pot Luck* (1962), and two songs from former soundtrack albums that had not been featured in the movies: "Slowly but Surely" from *Fun in Acapulco* and "Long Lonely Highway" from *Kissin' Cousins*. The musical numbers are the best since *Viva Las Vegas* despite not being originally recorded for this movie. "(Such an) Easy Question," written by Otis Blackwell and Winfield Scott, stayed on the Hot 100 Chart for eight weeks and peaked at number 11. It hit number one on the Easy Listening Chart and stayed there for two weeks. "I'm Yours," written by Don Robertson, spent 11 weeks on the Hot 100 Chart, peaking at number 11, and made it to the top spot during its three-week stay on the Easy Listening Chart. Of course the idea that Elvis songs were now doing better on the Easy Listening Chart was even greater evidence of how much he'd been eclipsed by groups like the Beatles and the Rolling Stones.

Presley's cousin Billy Smith recalled for Alanna Nash in *Elvis Aaron Presley*:

> The Beatles hit it big and the whole British Invasion started. The music was exciting and it was different. It made Elvis look out of touch. And pretty soon The Beatles started making movies too. *A Hard Day's Night* and *Help!* had a lot of wit to them. And here's Elvis doing *Girl Happy* and *Tickle Me*.

Despite it still being a lightweight musical comedy, *Tickle Me* allowed Elvis to step back and observe the silliness, not only by playing straight to the campy goings-on around him, but by engaging in slapstick and breaking the fourth wall by addressing the audience. The sense of fun spread throughout the cast, and all who commented on it remembered it as one of the more enjoyable experiences. Julie Adams, a veteran actress who had scored legendary status in *Creature of the Black Lagoon* a decade earlier, remembered in an interview Elvis "doing everything beautifully" in the film.

Elvis had a flair for comedy and the idea of doing a straight comedy script seemed to appeal to him, based on the supporting actors' recollections that he appeared to be happy and enthusiastic during filming. And he continued to recall this movie favorably, as well as the people in it. Edward Faulkner recalled in an interview:

> A few years later I was shooting a picture at MGM and Elvis was making a movie nearby. I got on the set, and stood behind the cameraman. Elvis was rehearsing a scene with his back to the camera. When he turned, he saw me and stopped the scene, grabbed two chairs, and sat and chatted with me, asking about my wife and family, and how things were going with work. We were both from the south, so when we got together it was just a couple of old farm boys.

> He closed the set for twenty minutes just to visit with me. He was such a nice guy. It's a shame what later happened to him.

Howard Thompson of the *New York Times*, often sympathetic to Elvis movies, was unhappy with this one, stating:

> Elvis Presley had better watch his step after *Tickle Me*, his latest color musical film, which arrived yesterday at the Palace and other houses. This is the silliest, feeblest and dullest vehicle for the Memphis Wonder in a long time. And both Elvis and his sponsors, this time Allied Artists, should know better. In such trim packages as *Viva Las Vegas* and *Fun in Acapulco*, the Presley formula—colorful settings, tunes and pretty girls aplenty—took on real, tasty sparkle. But yesterday's flapdoodle should strain the indulgence of the most ardent Presley fans. See for yourself, girls. It looks made up as it goes along.

Variety, however, appeared to better understand the comedy's perspective in their review:

> Presley takes his character in stride, giving a performance calculated to appeal particularly to his following. His comedy timing is right for most of the slapstick. . . . [Elvis] gets good comedy backing from a competent cast and a flock of young beauties cavorting in near-Bikini attire. Romance and sub-plot are offered in the shapely person of Jocelyn Lane . . . Miss Lane delivers a sharp enactment of the gal Presley falls for, and Julie Adams makes the most of her role as ranch owner. Jack Mullaney shines as a naïve character. Merry Anders is an always-hungry ranch patron, and Edward Faulkner is in for a comedy part as swimming instructor.

Theater owners responded happily as *Tickle Me* was offered for good rental terms and patron response was favorable. According to *Box Office*, a theater owner in Rochester, New York, stated, "Definitely Presley's best picture to date and we have played all of them. Has a little bit of everything in it to keep everyone happy. Songs, girls, suspense, comedy, all add up to customer happiness." Meanwhile, a Texas theater owner raved: "Here is a movie that is the best yet. Nothing but good can be said about this fine Elvis film. The color was tops. The acting was well above the ordinary. Elvis' songs were well liked by my teenagers. Don't pass it up. It will do good business any day of the week."

The Colonel put together a promotional campaign that included RCA purchasing Elvis Presley's custom gold-appointed white Cadillac limousine, sending it on a tour of the country to promote this film. Packages of colored "tickle feathers" and feather pens were also given out as promotional items. As a result,

Magazine ad celebrates the box office success of *Tickle Me*

the film already made enough at the box office to save Allied Artists from bankruptcy after being in release for a month. It eventually became the fifth-highest-grossing movie in the studio's history, and ended the year as number 30 among *Variety*'s list of Big Rental Pictures of 1965. Satisfied with having done what he'd set out to do, producer Ben Schwalb retired with this as his final production after 20 years of producing movies.

Elvis Presley won a 1966 Golden Laurel Award for Best Male Performance in a Musical Film for his work in *Tickle Me*. It was to be the only acting award Elvis would receive in his entire film career.

CHAPTER 21
Harum Scarum
(MGM, 1965)

Director: Gene Nelson
Screenplay: Gerald Drayson Adams
Producer: Sam Katzman
Cinematographer: Fred Jackman, Jr.
Editor: Bart Lewis
Assistant director: Eddie Saeta
Makeup: William Tuttle
Hairstylists: Sydney Guilaroff, Larry Geller
Vocals: The Jordanaires
Technical advisor: Colonel Tom Parker
Cast: Elvis Presley, Mary Ann Mobley, Fran Jeffries, Michael Ansara, Jay Novello, Phillip Reed, Theodore Marcuse, Billy Barty, Dick Harvey, Jack Constanzo, Larry Chance, Barbara Werle, Brenda Benet, Gail Gilmore, Wilda Taylor, Vicki Malkin, Ryck Rydon, Richard Reeves, Joey Russo, Suzanne Covington, Maja Stewart, Les Tremayne, Art Gilmore, Carolyn Carter, Eileen Diamond, Robert Lamont, Judy Durell, Red West, Ralph Lee, Hugh Sanders
Songs (in the order performed):
"Harum Scarum" (written by Peter Andreoli, Vince Poncia Jr., and Jimmie Crane; performed by Elvis Presley)
"Golden Coins" (written by Bill Giant, Bernie Baum, and Florence Kaye; performed by Elvis Presley)
"Go East Young Man" (written by Bill Giant, Bernie Baum, and Florence Kaye; performed by Elvis Presley)
"Shake That Tambourine" (written by Bill Giant, Bernie Baum, and Florence Kaye; performed by Elvis Presley)
"Animal Instinct" (written by Bill Giant, Bernie Baum, and Florence Kaye; performed by Elvis Presley)
"Wisdom of the Ages" (written by Bill Giant, Bernie Baum, and Florence Kaye; performed by Elvis Presley)
"Hey Little Girl" (written by Joy Byers; performed by Elvis Presley)

> "So Close Yet So Far (from Paradise)" (written by Joy Byers; performed by Elvis Presley)
> "My Dearest Serenade" (written by Stanley Jay Gelber; performed by Elvis Presley)
> The soundtrack album reached number eight on the charts
> Released December 15, 1965
> Filmed March 15–April 19, 1965
> Produced by Four Leaf Productions for release by Metro Goldwyn Mayer
> Alternate title: **Harem Holiday**
> 95 minutes
> Metrocolor
> Aspect ratio: 1.66:1
> U.S. gross: $1.5 million
> Released to DVD by Warner Home Video

Harum Scarum is not only Elvis Presley's weakest film, it also contains perhaps the least interesting collection of songs in all of his movies. How the soundtrack album lasted on the charts for 11 weeks, rising to a respectable number eight, is anyone's guess.

The movie has at least a modicum of potential. Elvis was interested in the idea of playing in a costume picture, as he was a great admirer of silent movie superstar Rudolph Valentino, intrigued at how he was able to project so successfully with his eyes. He liked director Gene Nelson, having worked with him on *Kissin' Cousins* the year before. He was so pleased with his sheik costume, he wore it home to show Priscilla. She recalled in *Elvis and Me*:

> Elvis was excited about the film when he first started shooting, He thought this would be a part he could really sink his teeth into. His morale plummeted. *Harum Scarum*'s plot was a joke, the character he played a fool, and the songs he sang disasters. The film turned out to be yet another disappointment, an embarrassing one at that.

Elvis became so frustrated doing take after take of the songs for this movie, never managing to make them above the mediocre, he eventually gave up, told the musicians to lay down their tracks, and then added his vocal later on.

The plot hints at the possibility that *Harum Scarum* is attempting to be a send-up of an Elvis Presley movie. He plays a singer who does action movies, his latest being a desert adventure entitled *Sands of the Desert*. While on a promotional tour in the Middle East, he is captured by assassins who take his on-screen exploits as fact, and want him to carry out an assassination. This basic idea offers some potential for parody, which is not explored, nor does the comedy attempt

Elvis was initially pleased to be doing a costume picture, but *Harum Scarum* turned out to be one of his weakest films

to investigate the conflict between a person and a screen image (Elvis had said in interviews that "it's hard to live up to an image"). Instead, *Harum Scarum* settles comfortably into the formulaic niche, only without any good music or scenes to sustain it effectively.

The general dynamic of *Harum Scarum* is not unlike a Bob Hope movie. Elvis, the central figure, continues to make wisecracks no matter how much danger he is in. Elvis's character does not exhibit Hope's base cowardice, and also unlike Hope, the jokes are not particularly funny. Bob Hope had a coterie of top-level comedy writers punching up his dialog. Elvis relied on the feeble script he was provided. Jay Novello, in the comic sidekick role, is not unlike the character Walter Brennan played in Bob Hope's *The Princess and the Pirate* (1944). The sets for *Harum Scarum* were left over from the 1927 silent *King of Kings*, the

Press kit ad for *Harum Scarum*

costumes from the 1944 *Kismet*. It was just a cheap, lifeless, dull vehicle, the low point perhaps being a clumsy dance number performed by a little girl, with Elvis pretending to be impressed with the youngster's performance.

As noted in an interview with Alanna Nash, actress Mary Ann Mobley, the leading lady in this movie, stated: "Elvis would joke about the movies. When we were making *Harum Scarum*, he said, 'This isn't going to change history, is it?' The sad thing is that Elvis was a better actor than the movies allowed him to be."

Upon viewing the finished film for the first time, even Colonel Parker realized they had a turkey on their hands. He stated in a letter to MGM that it would take "a 55th cousin to P. T. Barnum to sell this picture." His suggestion was to add a talking camel as narrator, in order to make it seem as if the silliness of the script was intended. The studio rejected his idea.

Critics were also unimpressed with this latest Presley offering. *Variety*'s October 7, 1965, review seemed to think Presley's charisma would sustain the weak production:

> If Presley were any more relaxed, Perry Como and Bing Crosby would have to retire, but he gets into the general spirit of things and he's Elvis. With anybody but Elvis Presley to gun possibilities this would be a pretty dreary affair at the box-office. Elvis, however, apparently can do no wrong—even if producers do manage—and *Harum Scarum,* which suffers from a lack of imagination in providing star with a substantial showcase but enabling him to belt out eight song numbers, will probably meet with response similar to Presley's past entries.

However Vincent Canby of the *New York Times* was dismissive:

> "Something terrible is about to happen" mutters an inscrutable Japanese actor early in *Ghidrah, The Three-Headed Monster*, and during the next three hours his prophecy comes only too true. It is hard to imagine a more perfect blending of witlessness than this double bill of *Harum Scarum*, the latest Elvis Presley vehicle, and *Ghidrah*, an all-star Japanese monster film . . . Elvis is prettier than Ghidrah, and has two fewer heads, but both characters are definitely the product of the special effects department. Mr. Presley wanders through the improbable whimsies of *Harum Scarum* with all the animation of a man under deep sedation, but then he had read the script, which has to do with a Hollywood star, a mythical Arab kingdom and some oil rights. Every line of dialogue sounds like a song cue, and about every other one actually is.

Even the moviegoers, who often disagreed with the critics, were not impressed when *Harum Scarum* showed up at their local theater. Exhibitors commenting in *Box Office* magazine stated:

> Not up to his others. The plot of the story was not interesting enough to hold attention. Presley's worst movie yet. Didn't bring a crowd. We can forgive one like this, but no more. The least of the Elvis Presleys. The worst Presley picture to date. I heard folks telling others not to go see it.

However, at least one theater reporting to *Box Office*, in the small town of Foreman, Arkansas, was pleased with the movie, stating: "Nice color and a good plot. Did fair for us considering we had a ball game and dance against us. It's a fine picture. Don't miss it. Play it."

Harum Scarum reached number 11 on the *Variety* list of national weekly box office hits, earning $2 million. At the end of the year it was listed at number 40 among the top grossing movies of 1965. The soundtrack album, containing a souvenir picture of Elvis in costume, enjoyed an 11-week stay on the Billboard LP chart, peaking at number eight.

But despite this level of success, Elvis knew he had produced a turkey. At the end of filming, Elvis presented director Gene Nelson with an autographed picture, on which he inscribed: "Some day we'll do it right." Even Colonel Parker, who did not seem to care about film aesthetics as long as they made money, was disappointed in the movie, advising the studio to get it out quick and enjoy some first-run box office success before word of mouth destroyed the film financially. However, to the Colonel's delight, *Harum Scarum* became a moneymaker.

Lamar Fike told Alanna Nash in *Elvis Aaron Presley*:

> As far as the movie years were concerned—and by that I mean the sixties—they might have been years of incredible frustration on the whole, but they were also years of incredible money. And when you've already been paid for the pictures, and you've already spent half the money, you've got to do them. All of those pictures were pre-signed. So Elvis had no choice.

CHAPTER 22
Frankie and Johnny
(UNITED ARTISTS, 1966)

Director: Fred de Cordova
Screenplay: Alex Gottlieb and Nat Perrin
Producers: Alex Gottlieb and Edward Small
Cinematographer: Jacques R. Marquette
Editor: Grant Whytock
Assistant director: Herbert S. Green
Makeup: Dan Greenway
Hairstylists: Joan St. Oegger and Larry Geller
Vocals: The Jordanaires
Technical advisor: Col. Tom Parker
Cast: Elvis Presley, Donna Douglas, Harry Morgan, Sue Ane Langdon, Nancy Kovack, Audrey Christie, Robert Strauss, Anthony Eisley, Joyce Jamison, Jerome Cowan, Henry Corden, Dave Willock, Naomi Stevens, Cliff Norton, Jack Littlefield, James Millhollin, Billy Benedict, Dick Winslow, Robert Williams, Richard Reeves, Eddie Quillan, George Klein, Earl Barton, Judy Chapman, Dee Jay Mathis, Wilda Taylor, Larri Thomas
Songs (in the order performed):
　"Come Along" (written by David Hess; performed by Elvis Presley)
　"Petunia the Gardener's Daughter" (written by Sid Tepper and Roy C. Bennett; performed by Elvis Presley and Eileen Wilson)
　"Chesay" (written by Fred Karger, Ben Weisman, and Sid Wayne; performed by Elvis Presley)
　"What Every Woman Lives For" (written by Doc Pomus and Mort Shuman; performed by Elvis Presley)
　"Frankie and Johnny" (written by Alex Gottlieb, Fred Karger and Ben Weisman; performed and Elvis Presley and Eileen Wilson)
　"Look Out Broadway" (written by Fred Wise and Randy Starr; performed by Elvis Presley, Eileen Wilson, and Ray Walker)
　"Beginner's Luck" (written by Sid Tepper and Roy C. Bennett; performed by Elvis Presley)

> "Down by the Riverside / When the Saints Go Marching In" (performed by Elvis Presley)
> "Shout It Out" (written by Bill Giant, Bernie Baum, and Florence Kaye; performed by Elvis Presley)
> "Hard Luck" (written by Ben Weisman and Sid Wayne; performed by Elvis Presley)
> "Please Don't Stop Loving Me" (written by Joy Byers; performed by Elvis Presley)
> "Everybody Come Aboard" (written by Bill Giant, Bernie Baum, and Florence Kaye; performed by Elvis Presley)
>
> The soundtrack album reached number 20 on the charts
> "Frankie and Johnny" made it to number 25 on the charts
>
> Released March 31, 1966
> Filmed May 25–June 30, 1965
> Produced by Edward Small Production for United Artists
> 87 minutes
> Technicolor
> Aspect Ratio: 1.66:1
> U.S. gross: $2,050,000
> Released to DVD by MGM Home Video

Frankie and Johnny was at least somewhat of a departure from the Elvis Presley movie formula in that it was a period piece, set during the 1920s. As with many Presley movies, the supporting cast was filled with such welcome veterans as Harry Morgan, Robert Strauss, Cliff Norton, Jerome Cowan, Billy Benedict, James Millhollin, and Eddie Quillan. The female lead is Donna Douglas, at the time enjoying strong popularity from her stint on television's *Beverly Hillbillies*. Sue Ane Langdon, from *Roustabout*, appears playing a similar role. The screenplay was written by coproducer Alex Gottlieb, who had produced Abbott and Costello films, from a story by Nat Perrin who had written for the Marx Brothers. Director Fred de Cordova did a nice job of keeping the frame bustling with movement during the medium shots that required background. And yet, with all of these ingredients, *Frankie and Johnny* is nearly as weak as the previous *Harum Scarum*, which is the low point of Elvis Presley's film career.

The film is based on the traditional song which is sometimes credited to songwriter Hughie Cannon. The song was inspired by an actual murder where a woman named Frankie Baker (1876–1952) shot her lover Allen (aka Albert) Britt in the abdomen after he won a slow-dancing contest with a woman named Alice Pryor. Songwriter Bill Dooley composed "Frankie Killed Allen" shortly after this case. It was the writer of "Won't You Come Home Bill Bailey," Hughie Cannon, who came out with the first published music of "Frankie and Johnny" in 1904 under the title "He Done Me Wrong." It uses the names Frankie and Johnny, and calls the other woman as Nellie Blye. It is this version, using these names, on which the Elvis Presley film is most closely based.

Elvis is Johnny, a successful entertainer whose addiction to gambling results in the chagrin of Frankie, played by Donna Douglas. Harry Morgan is a fellow gambler, and the two scheme to discover surefire bets. Perpetually broke, Johnny often asks Frankie for money. After a visit to a fortune-teller, Johnny is told a redhead is good luck, so he hooks up with auburn-haired Nellie Blye (Nancy Kovack), while also being pursued by Mitzi (Sue Ane Langdon). The film plods along with more lackluster musical sequences and, considering the level of talent penning the script, surprisingly little humor. Presley's smart quips are beneath his ability, while the soundtrack boasts only one truly great song, the bluesy "Hard Luck," which was not released as a single. The music has a period feel, which is appropriate, but a song like "Petunia the Gardener's Daughter" results in a stiff, embarrassed performance by Elvis, who was said to have recorded dozens of takes on this number, never being pleased with the outcome.

Variety was pleased with the film, stating:

> *Frankie and Johnny* is a sure-fire box office entry. It's Elvis all the way in a story built loosely around the classic folk song, coupled with a dozen or so tunes, pretty girls and Technicolor. Frederick de Cordova directed the Edward Small production, which hits the mark as pleasant entertainment, and is certain to be another Presley money-winner. Elvis is Elvis. He sings and acts, apparently doing both with only slight effort. *Frankie and Johnny* proves to be nothing more than an hour and a half romp, providing a showcase for Presley's songs. He does 12 of them, including the title tune.

While this is a rather positive review it is also a very telling one. Reviewers, like the anonymous one for *Variety*, had resigned themselves to the fact that Elvis Presley movies were of a certain type, that they held some merit for being successful within their limited niche, and no more should be expected. In a sense this is true, and perhaps the same can be said for John Wayne's movies of the same period, as he'd long since become a cinematic icon. The difference is that the John Wayne formula was netting some minor classics like Henry Hathaway's *The Sons of Katie Elder* (1965)[1] and Howard Hawks's *El Dorado* (1966). Elvis Presley's formula settled lazily on lightweight musical comedy with reduced budgets.

There are some visual aspects of *Frankie and Johnny* that make it, at the very least, effective in its presentation. Along with the aforementioned period music, the authenticity of the 1920s era, including the costumes and the sets, are realistic and colorful. It presents the period as living up to its Roaring Twenties tag

Elvis and Donna Douglas in *Frankie and Johnny*

with a sense of carefree fun and Presley's wry humor as the luckless, wayward Johnny. But within this framework, the movie simply plods along with no real impact, the performances being earnest, but easy, and nobody truly rises above the flaccid material.

This might not have happened had Ann-Margret taken the role of Frankie. She owed a movie to producer Edward Small, and there was serious talk about casting her opposite Elvis in an attempt to recapture the magic of *Viva Las Vegas*. The spark between the two would have been palpable, certainly more impactful than what exists between Elvis and Donna Douglas. Douglas, at the time very popular on television, used the occasional film role to break away from being typecast. It didn't work. Further offers were not forthcoming. *Frankie and Johnny* was to be her final theatrical movie.

Douglas had another, more serious problem during production. She actually did fall in love with Elvis Presley. According to all accounts, there was no romance between the two. Elvis had been getting spiritual teaching from his current hairstylist, Larry Geller. It interested Douglas who, like Elvis, had come from a Christian background, and she enjoyed talking to him about it. They talked a lot during filming, and a closeness was formed. As with most productions, once the movie was made Elvis moved on to his next venture, leaving Douglas so heartbroken that she had trouble returning to her television show; its producers had to console the actress and help her work through her broken heart.

The title song, one of over 250 versions of the tune that had been recorded over the years, did poorly on the charts, lingering on Billboard's Top 100 for eight weeks, and never rising above number 25. The soundtrack album fared little better, making it to number 20. Curiously, the soundtrack was re-released in 1976, with three tracks missing, by the low-budget Pickwick label. It is the only movie soundtrack to be re-released by this label, which collected Presley songs (many from movie soundtracks) and released various albums throughout the 1970s. Sometimes this was effective. The 1971 Pickwick release *C'mon Everybody* gathers some of the better soundtrack songs, including the title track from *Viva Las Vegas*, "King of the Whole Wide World" from *Kid Galahad,* and others. When Elvis died in 1977, RCA re-released all of his soundtrack albums, including some that had been out of print for years. However they were unable to re-release the complete soundtrack to *Frankie and Johnny* because of the truncated Pickwick album released months earlier. It would not be until 2010 when the complete soundtrack to *Frankie and Johnny* would once again be made available.

This was the third movie version of *Frankie and Johnny* to be released, after one in 1930 (under the title *Her Man*) and another in 1936. A 1991 movie by this title, starring Michelle Pfeiffer and Al Pacino, was more closely based on Terrence McNally's 1987 play *Frankie and Johnny in the Clair de Lune.*

Many young people had, by 1966, left Elvis for the Beatles. Several remaining Elvis fans were waiting for him to answer their success with something interesting and exciting. Releasing a dull 1920s musical during the year the Beatles were coming out with *Rubber Soul* and *Revolver* was not likely to distract Beatles fans. Audiences seemed unenthused as well. The film finished at number

47 among box office draws for 1966, a very poor showing for an Elvis Presley movie. While some theaters reported good attendance and crowd reaction, one theater did so poorly with *Frankie and Johnny* that the owner proclaimed in *Box Office* magazine, "Elvis is out!" *Frankie and Johnny* barely grossed $2 million. In some cities, it was paired in a double feature with a revival of the Beatles film *Help!* to bolster box office.

For his next movie, producer Hal Wallis decided to have Elvis revisit the setting that resulted in his biggest hit. But when one compares the upcoming *Paradise, Hawaiian Style* to the box office triumph *Blue Hawaii*, it is a painfully strong indicator how far Elvis Presley had fallen.

CHAPTER 23
Paradise, Hawaiian Style
(PARAMOUNT, 1966)

Director: Michael D. Moore
Screenplay: Allan Weiss and Anthony Lawrence
Producer: Hal Wallis
Cinematography: W. Wallace Kelley
Editor: Grant Whytock
Assistant director: James A. Rosenberger
Makeup: Wally Westmore
Hairstylists: Nellie Manley and Larry Geller
Vocals: The Jordanaires
Technical advisor: Colonel Tom Parker
Cast: Elvis Presley, Suzanna Leigh, James Shigeta, Donna Butterworth, Marianna Hill, Irene Tsu, Linda Wong, Julie Parrish, Jan Shepard, John Coucette, Grady Sutton, Doris Packer, Don Collier, Phillip Ahn, Mary Treen, Gi Gi Verone, Jackie Brown, Sandy Kawelo, Fred Carson, Steve Brodie, Edy Williams, Channing Hale, Red West
Songs (in the order performed):
"Paradise, Hawaiian Style" (written by Bill Giant, Bernie Baum, and Florence Kaye; performed by Elvis Presley)
"Scratch My Back (Then I'll Scratch Yours)" (written by Bill Giant, Bernie Baum, and Florence Kaye; performed by Elvis Presley and Marianna Hill)
"Stop Where You Are" (written by Bill Giant, Bernie Baum, and Florence Kaye; performed by Elvis Presley)
'This Is My Heaven" (written by Bill Giant, Bernie Baum, and Florence Kaye; performed by Elvis Presley)
"House of Sand" (written by Bill Giant, Bernie Baum, Florence Kaye; performed by Elvis Presley)
"Queen Wahine's Papaya" (written by Bill Giant, Bernie Baum, and Florence Kaye; performed by Elvis Presley and Donna Butterworth)
"Datin'" (written by Fred Wise and Randy Starr; performed by Elvis Presley and Donna Butterworth)

> "Drums of the Islands" (written by Sid Tepper and Roy C. Bennett; performed by Elvis Presley)
> "A Dog's Life" (written by Sid Wayne and Ben Weisman; performed by Elvis Presley)
> "Sand Castles" (written by Herb Goldberg and David Hess; performed by Elvis Presley)
> "Bill Bailey, Won't You Please Come Home" (written by Hughie Cannon; performed by Donna Butterworth)
>
> The soundtrack album reached number 15 on the charts
>
> Released July 15, 1966
> Filmed August 7–29, 1965
> 91 minutes
> Technicolor
> Aspect ratio: 1.66:1
> U.S. gross: $2.5 million
> Released to DVD by Paramount Home Video

Paradise, Hawaiian Style is today considered another weak Elvis Presley formula musical, but while it did not do the box office numbers of *Blue Hawaii*, it was Presley's most financially successful film of 1966. Once again Hal Wallis offered top-level production values, and the location filming in Hawaii framed each scene nicely. However, the movie suffers from the same creative limitations as the past several Presley films. The plot is too simple, the songs are lackluster, the humor is forced and stilted, while Elvis has so little enthusiasm. He appears to have gained a discernible amount of weight for this movie. Director Michael Moore, who had been an assistant on several earlier Elvis productions, carefully shoots his star in an effort to hide his excess weight, but it remains evident throughout the film.

As in *Blue Hawaii*, Elvis is a pilot who attempts to find success in the tourist business in *Paradise, Hawaiian Style*, but the threadbare plot is just an excuse to stop for some songs. Oddly, a few of the musical numbers feature Elvis singing duets with child actress Donna Butterworth. In fact, only Ann-Margret in *Viva Las Vegas* sings more duets with Elvis than Miss Butterworth does in this movie. Butterworth recalled in an interview with Joe Krein:

> I was born in Pennsylvania. I lived there until I was three years old, then we moved to Hawaii. My biggest dream was to meet Elvis, and at that time *Paradise, Hawaiian Style* was in the works and I had already done a few things professionally. I was in *The Family Jewels* with Jerry Lewis, which was released by Paramount. So I was happy to find out that they wanted me in the Elvis film. They were doing a lot of the filming practically in my back yard so that was great.

Elvis attacked by kids in *Paradise, Hawaiian Style*

Besides the several duets with Elvis, Donna Butterworth is also spotlighted in her own number, a version of "Won't You Come Home Bill Bailey."

If we follow the pattern of the Elvis movies, it seems like something of a natural step to offer a film that not only utilizes past successful ideas like colorful scenery and pretty girls, but now extends to present a family-oriented perspective as well. This idea had been investigated a bit in earlier films like *Girls! Girls! Girls!* and *It Happened at the World's Fair*, but even Vicki Tiu in the latter film did not have the level of screen time or prominence that Miss Butterworth enjoys in *Paradise, Hawaiian Style*.

While Elvis maintains an effectively cool demeanor throughout the film, which remains effective despite his softer, heavier appearance, his wry one-liners give way to slapstick in at least one scene. Elvis had investigated slapstick's possibilities in *Tickle Me*, as it had been cowritten by scenarists who'd worked with the Three Stooges and the Bowery Boys. In *Paradise, Hawaiian Style* the slapstick scene involves Elvis and a woman (Julie Parrish) transporting several show dogs by plane. The dogs are uncooperative, and Elvis and Julie must deal with their antics, but Elvis finds time to sing a song. What was natural and funny in *Tickle Me* seems forced and unimpressive in *Paradise, Hawaiian Style*.

The slender plot thread, dismissible songs, upstaging by a child actress, and silly comedy appeared to be quite acceptable to audiences at that time, based on

Elvis attacked by dogs in *Paradise, Hawaiian Style*

comments from period theater owners in *Box Office*: "Thank goodness for Elvis. You can always hear the cash register jingle with his pictures. A very good film. You can't beat a Hal Wallis Presley."

It is interesting that the producer responsible for settling Elvis into a pat formula was being praised for the very reason Presley himself felt boxed in and creatively limited. Elvis appears to have given up, as his lack of enthusiasm is evident for perhaps the first time. Presley has always been noted for professionalism and turning in an earnest performance despite the material. However, by the time he made *Paradise, Hawaiian Style*, it appeared his responsibility was such that he would do only as contracted and no more. While those who worked on the movie with Elvis recall he spent far more time in his trailer than usual, actress Donna Butterworth recalls him as friendly and in a good mood.

Most newspapers did not bother reviewing *Paradise, Hawaiian Style*, believing that an Elvis movie had a ready-made noncritical audience and that the films had become indistinguishable from each other. *Variety*, however, liked the film, their review exhibiting an surprising level of enthusiasm:

> Hal Wallis . . . returns singer to the island state in this gaily-begarbed and flowing musical. Seldom has the panorama and terrain of Hawaii been utilized to such lush advantage, beautifully caught in the finest tints of Technicolor and providing star with an atmospheric backdrop for the type of yarn he's best suited for . . . girls and songs. It's a natural for Presley fans, who seem to be legion, and carries strong exploitation potential. One particular sequence is a comedy gem: Presley loses control of his chopper while transporting six dogs of various breeds to a canine show on another island. Simultaneously, the helicopter stunting takes on a load of thrills, some of the best ever filmed for this form of locomotion. Presley delivers one of his customary ingratiating portrayals, in usual voice and adept at comedy.

When we look at *Paradise, Hawaiian Style* in the twenty-first century, it appears to be a much lesser version of superior Elvis musicals. At least movies like *Girls! Girls! Girls!* and *G.I. Blues* retain a campy sense of fun decades after their release, and Elvis is always an engaging personality. But a movie like *Paradise, Hawaiian Style* cannot be saved by its colorful cinematography and beautiful locations. It is not a good movie, and Elvis was completely justified in approaching it with somewhat less than his usual charisma.

Toward the end of August 1965, Elvis completed location filming in Hawaii and returned to California to shoot interior scenes. It was at this time that he agreed to meet with the Beatles, who had been requesting a meeting with their idol since arriving in the United States a couple of years earlier. At this point, the Beatles had surpassed Elvis in popularity, taking all but his most diehard fans. Their films were witty and funny, their music was exciting and vibrant. They were what Elvis started out as, and what he should have continued to be.

Elvis was certainly aware of this. According to Presley cousin and associate Billy Smith in *Elvis Aaron Presley*, when the singer would do a recording,

> he'd ask for the bass to be brought forward a little more in places. And he wanted his voice mixed down, and the music brought up louder, even if it overrode his voice sometimes. He thought RCA was bringing out his voice too much. He'd say "those New York sons of bitches! They're screwing with my music!" Because a lot of times they took the tapes from the recording sessions up there to mix 'em. And he'd explain how he wanted it done. He'd play a Beatles record and say "This is what I am looking for here. I want that drive back. And I

don't want my voice to be brought out front. If it's there, I want the background singers brought out with me."

In the same book, Presley associate Marty Lacker concurred: "They used to cut these acetates for Elvis after the sessions, and we'd listen to 'em. The acetates sounded better than the actual records did after the Colonel finished screwing with them. Colonel would tell RCA, 'no, I want my boy's voice up a little more.'"

Once the time came when a meeting between Elvis Presley and the Beatles could take place, the logistics were finally worked out. Paul McCartney recalled in *The Beatles Anthology*:

> We tried many times to meet Elvis. Colonel Tom Parker, his manager would just show up with a few souvenirs, and that would have to do us for a while. We didn't feel brushed off we felt we deserved to be brushed off. After all, he was Elvis, and who were we to dare to want to meet him? But we finally received an invitation.

The Beatles arrived on the evening of August 27, 1965, and recalled that Elvis Presley was seated on a large couch. Music was playing (Paul McCartney remembers it being the song "Mohair Sam" by Charlie Rich), the television was on, but the sound was off (something the Beatles often did as well, according to McCartney). Paul McCartney recalled, "We were in awe. He was our idol, and there he was. We were speechless and he sat there waiting for us to say something. It was quite awkward at the start."

Elvis finally broke the ice by stating, "Look, if you guys are going to just sit there and stare at me, I'm going up to bed!" They all laughed, and Elvis had three guitars brought out for John, George, and Paul, apologizing to Ringo for not having any drums. Elvis himself played bass, as he was currently learning the instrument.

McCartney further recalled:

> That was the greatest. Elvis was into the bass, so there I was, "Well, let me show you a thing or two, El . . ." Suddenly he was a mate. It was a great conversation piece for me. I could actually talk about the bass, and we sat around and just enjoyed ourselves. He was great. Talkative. Friendly and a little bit shy. We expected that, we hoped for that.

It is often wondered why there were no pictures taken and nothing was recorded during this momentous occasion. McCartney explained that this was not considered a photo op, but a private meeting.

The Beatles were there for four hours, Ringo drumming on a chair during the jam session, then joining some of Presley's associates in a pool game. At one point John Lennon asked why Elvis didn't start touring and doing some good rock and roll music again. Elvis, understanding that the Beatles were already trapped by their massive stardom, confided that he'd love to do that, but he had commitments regarding movies that he'd signed contracts for ahead of time. McCartney recalls Elvis not being terribly impressed with his movie career.

> It was one of the great meetings of my life. I think he liked us. I think at that time, he may have felt a little bit threatened, but he didn't say anything. We certainly didn't feel any antagonism. I only met him that once, and then I think the success of our career started to push him out a little, which we were very sad about, because we wanted to coexist with him. We invited him and his people to come see us the next day. He said he had to be at the studio.

Marty Lacker recalled in *Elvis Aaron Presley*, "The next afternoon several of us went to where The Beatles were staying and they were overjoyed to see us. John pulled me over and said, 'Last night was the greatest night of my life.'"

Meeting the Beatles was not the only encounter with British singers that Elvis had while filming *Paradise, Hawaiian Style*. Lacker remembered:

> Herman's Hermits were big at the time, and Peter Noone came over to where we were shooting one day. Elvis talked to him for a little while and Noone figured he'd trap Elvis into giving him a compliment. He asked Elvis his favorite group. Elvis said, "well I sort of like them all." Noone persisted, though, and said, "but who is your *favorite* group?" And I said under my breath "the LAPD." And without blinking an eye, Elvis said, "the Los Angeles Police Department." Everybody broke up laughing, and Noone just froze. He didn't know what to say.

Elvis also met Welsh singer Tom Jones during filming. Jones, a huge fan, was floored when he discovered Elvis was also a fan of his, and proceeded to sing excerpts of songs from Jones's latest album.

Paradise, Hawaiian Style enjoyed reasonable success, but during production Elvis was reminded of the changing trends in popular music. While the newcomers were inspired by his work, his reliance on formula movies with lackluster soundtracks were causing his legacy to be overshadowed. Many wondered if there was any aspect of the "real" Elvis Presley left in the ersatz Hollywood Elvis.

CHAPTER 24

Spinout
(MGM, 1966)

> *Director:* Norman Taurog
> *Screenplay:* Theodore Flicker and George Kirgo
> *Producer:* Joe Pasternak
> *Cinematographer:* Daniel L. Fapp
> *Editor:* Rita Roland
> *Makeup:* William Tuttle
> *Hairstylists:* Sydney Guilaroff and Larry Geller
> *Vocals:* The Jordanaires
> *Technical advisor:* Colonel Tom Parker
> *Cast:* Elvis Presley, Shelley Fabares, Diane McBain, Dodie Marshall, Deborah Walley, Jack Mullaney, Will Hutchins, Warren Berlinger, Jimmy Hawkins, Carl Betz, Cecil Kellaway, Una Merkel, Frederick Worlock, Deanna Lund, Dave Barry, James McHale, Joe Esposito, Red West, Jean Marie Ingels, Inge Jaklyn, Joanne Medley, Virginia Wood, Nancy Czar, Thordis Brandt, Arlene Charles, Phyllis Davis, Judy Durell, Gay Gordon, Josh Harding, Jay Jasin, Jeanmarie, Fredda Lee, Sheryl Ullman.
> *Songs* (in the order performed):
> "Spinout" (written by Sid Wayne and Dolores Fuller; performed by Elvis Presley)
> "Stop Look and Listen" (written by Joy Byers [as Joe Byers]; performed by Elvis Presley)
> "Adam and Evil" (written by Fred Wise and Randy Starr; performed by Elvis Presley)
> "All That I Am" (written by Sid Tepper and Roy C. Bennett; performed by Elvis Presley)
> "Never Say Yes" (written by Doc Pomus and Mort Shuman; performed by Elvis Presley)
> "Am I Ready" (written by Sid Tepper and Roy C. Bennett; performed by Elvis Presley)
> "Beach Shack" (written by Bill Giant, Bernie Baum, and Florence Kaye; performed by Elvis Presley)

> "Smorgasbord" (written by Sid Tepper and Roy C. Bennett; performed by Elvis Presley)
> "I'll Be Back" (written by Sid Wayne and Ben Weisman; performed by Elvis Presley)
>
> The soundtrack album reached number 18 on the charts
> The title song reached number 40
>
> Released October 17, 1966
> Filmed February 23–April 16, 1966
> Released in England as *California Holiday*
> 90 minutes
> Technicolor
> Aspect ratio: 2.35:1
> U.S. gross: $3 million
> Released to DVD by MGM Home Video

Perhaps it is due to previous weak Elvis Presley movies, but *Spinout* emerges as a very pleasant lightweight musical comedy in the manner of *Girl Happy* or *Tickle Me*. While it certainly adheres to the standard formula for a typical Elvis movie and is a far cry from *Viva Las Vegas*, let alone the more challenging *Jailhouse Rock, King Creole,* or *Flaming Star*, there is some fun to be had with *Spinout*, and the soundtrack features a few tracks that rise somewhat above the usual movie fodder.

Viva Las Vegas was at least part of the inspiration for *Spinout*. The film did not originally intend to feature Elvis as a race car driver, but the Colonel, remembering the success of *Viva Las Vegas*, instructed the screenwriters to "fit in a racing car." Screenwriter George Kirgo had written the Howard Hawks–directed *Red Line 7000* (1965), so coming up with a racing theme for this Elvis movie was no particular challenge.

Elvis plays Mike McCoy, who sings lead in a traveling rock and roll band and drives race cars. Millionaire Howard Foxhugh wants Mike to drive his Fox Five car in an upcoming race. Mike wants to race his own Cobra 427. Meanwhile Howard's daughter, Cynthia, is smitten with Mike and wants to trap the carefree bachelor into a relationship. At the same time, Les, the female drummer of Mike's band, is equally smitten with him and chagrined that he simply considers her one of the boys. Finally, a female author has been spying on Mike to observe his behaviors for her book, *The Perfect American Male*, having chosen Mike as one of her subjects.

Several dynamics are at work here and each is worth some discussion. First is the casting of Carl Betz as father Howard to Shelley Fabares as daughter Cynthia. Betz and Fabares famously played father and daughter on television's *Donna Reed Show*, which had just ended its long run. Howard represents the

Poster for *Spinout*

wealthy establishment. Cynthia is the spoiled rich girl. Both try to crowd Mike's freedom to make his own choices.

Since bands were now popular, Presley's character is part of a band. As in *Girl Happy* in which the "Three Blind Mice" theme played whenever the bandmates appeared on camera, there is another Three Stooges homage in *Spinout*. Jimmy Hawkins plays a character named Larry. Jack Mullaney's character is Curly. Elvis, the leader, is Mike (not Moe), but with the same first letter and single syllable. Deborah Walley, as Les, is forever reminding the others "I'm a girl!" and is especially bothered that Mike overlooks her in so cavalier a manner.

Diane McBain, as the author using Mike as a subject for her latest book, is similar to the older women in earlier movies like *Follow That Dream*. Her interest in Mike is based solely on his outward magnetism, despite pretending to some level of depth by studying him for a book project. Mike, constantly proclaiming the freedom of bachelorhood as the only way he'll live, avoids any level of commitment to the three women.

The relationship between Mike and Cynthia is central to the plot. Cynthia is set in her belief that her father will provide any request, including booking Mike's band to play at her birthday party. Mike responds to her in the same way that Elvis's character had in previous films to similarly snobby rich girls, such as the spoiled nymphette in *Blue Hawaii*. However, when Elvis's character in the 1961 film puts the girl over his knee and spanks her, it presented him as ersatz parent, disciplining an unruly child. In 1966, on the cusp of a new generation's perspective regarding gender roles, Mike's threat in *Spinout* to put Cynthia over his knee makes Elvis appear to represent the old-school attitude in a new cultural world. He never does spank her. The threat is an idle one.

As with many of his formula musicals, music is only the catalyst to get what he really wants. His characters just so happen to have great singing talent, and it is used as a means to an end rather than as the end itself. Mike sings with his band to raise money for his racing car. Once a rugged individualist in *Loving You* or *King Creole*, Elvis now travels with a group. He is part of a community.

There are a few light, amusing moments in *Spinout*; one highlight is when Mike convinces a wealthy older couple that they should get away on a second honeymoon, allowing him to watch their expensive home. It is next door to the Foxhughs' house. The older couple is played nicely by veterans Cecil Kellaway and Una Merkel (in her last movie).

Unlike other formula musicals, *Spinout* allows Elvis to fulfill his character's desires to the very end. All of the women interested in Mike are married off to tangential characters. The film concludes with Mike remaining happily single. No woman has trapped him, yet they all end up in relationships that promise the bliss they'd hoped for with Mike.

Norman Taurog, the most prolific director of Elvis Presley movies, once again puts his stamp on the proceedings by keeping the situations fast paced and lightly funny. Nothing heavy handed, no fancy filmmaking, Taurog allows the situations to sustain on their own merit, wisely relying on the talent and charisma of the performers. But that's really all a film like *Spinout* has to boast.

The Elvis Presley movies, at this point, were so completely mired in formula that a film like *Spinout*, which is at least as good as *G.I. Blues*, emerges as a veritable oasis in the desert. Elvis continued to desire a role in a movie with a good script, a strong director, and few or no songs. He told friends that he'd be perfectly willing to take a supporting role in a major film, recalling Frank Sinatra's success in *From Here to Eternity* after several light musicals, which established Sinatra as a good dramatic actor. Presley was, at the very least, as good an actor as Sinatra was, and he realized it. But, as Presley associates continue to admit today, Elvis never stood up to the Colonel. Meanwhile, Colonel Parker continued to believe that success was measured by monetary value rather than creative fulfillment.

When compared to the recent *Paradise, Hawaiian Style*, in which Elvis was discernibly aloof in his role, *Spinout* presents him as having some level of enthusiasm. Much of it was due to Shelley Fabares once again appearing as his leading lady. His comfort with director Taurog was another factor. Ideas from previous Elvis movies abounded (the leading lady and band dynamic from *Girl Happy*, the race car idea from *Viva Las Vegas*) but these elements were proven and remained effective enough. The race footage was exciting and competently filmed.

The songs in *Spinout* are generally unremarkable when compared to earlier material like *Jailhouse Rock* or even *Viva Las Vegas*, but the soundtrack was much better than those found in *Harum Scarum, Paradise, Hawaiian Style,* and *Frankie and Johnny*. "I'll Be Back" is a little-known gem.

The soundtrack album for *Spinout* contained a song that was not featured in the movie, Bob Dylan's "Tomorrow Is Such a Long Time." From a historical perspective, it is quite unnerving that the powers that be chose to bury this song as an extra on a soundtrack album rather than release it as a single and promote it. Dylan was quite important to popular music's culture in 1966, releasing the album *Blonde on Blonde*, which is a masterpiece by any standards. The fact that Elvis recorded a Dylan song would show him as coexisting comfortably among the new wave of rock and rollers, reworking one of their compositions in his own inimitable style. Unfortunately, the choice to bury the song as an extra on the *Spinout* soundtrack makes it among the lesser-known Presley tracks from this period.

Variety was pleased with *Spinout,* stating:

> *Spinout* is an entertaining Elvis Presley comedy-tuner, in which four gals compete for his attention between nine new songs. Well-produced

by Joe Pasternak, and directed with verve by Norman Taurog, pic has Elvis as the leader of a touring rock-roll group. Racing car plot line adds another lure for the young market, while many comedy situations maintain interest. Presley fans will rally to the box office, and other drop-ins will likewise be diverted by this Metro release.

The *New York Times*, however, was far less impressed:

> Mr. Presley, to be precise, has made more than 20 films, but the minor variation this time is that he prefers racing cars and bachelorhood to the cuties his crooning captivates. There are, to be exact, Diane McBain, Deborah Walley and Shelley Fabares as the charmers vying for his hand. But our handsome hero, who loves his Duesenberg more than any dame, manages to sing eight songs [the reviewer must have slept through the ninth], win the big road race and remain footloose and fancy free. "I'll Be Back," he chants in one number, which should be a welcome hint only to those juveniles whose motors he starts racing.

But it is the moviegoers' reaction that mattered most to Presley's management, and theaters indicated a favorable reaction. A Vermont theater owner reported to *Box Office* magazine that "Elvis Presley's *Spinout* from Metro Goldwyn Mayer, is one of Elvis's best action pictures for some time and had plenty of singing too. We played this to one of the largest crowds we have played to for some time, and all enjoyed the picture." Meanwhile up in Quebec, Canada, the report in the same magazine raved: "Elvis is back and one of his best in a long time. We have lost some Elvis fans and this one should bring them back."

The indication that even some Elvis fans were becoming disillusioned after *Harum Scarum*, *Frankie and Johnny*, and *Paradise, Hawaiian Style*, and that *Spinout* could bring them back, is further indication that this film had a general consensus as being a better example of the Elvis movie formula at its most effective.

And while Elvis never felt particularly comfortable as part of the whole Hollywood scene, his stardom was not lost on fellow film actors and remained quite strong, despite having settled into predictable movies and relying on the soundtracks for his record output. Shelley Fabares recalled in an interview with Frankie Verocca being in the MGM studio commissary during the production of *Spinout*:

> Elvis was supposed to meet me there for lunch. The place was packed with movie stars all having their lunch. Elvis came in and looked around for me and before I could even wave him over, everything in the commissary just stopped. They all turned and looked at Elvis and then got up and moved toward him. Now these were not a bunch of

fans, these were top movie stars at MGM. Elvis turned around and left. I have never seen anything like it.

Spinout grossed $3 million at the box office based on U.S. and Canada rentals, which was reasonably good for 1966. Apparently moviegoers expected the very formula that Elvis Presley movies now offered, and when in the mood for lightweight musical comedy, the latest Elvis picture was welcomed. However, fans who had a deeper interest in rock and roll and were following its progression dismissed Elvis as someone whose relevance was clearly from another time. And while in retrospect we recognize that Presley would reclaim his throne as king a couple of years later, during the time these movies were released audiences accepted them as they were presented. And while they remained profitable, those profits were no longer at the level they had been.

CHAPTER 25
Easy Come, Easy Go
(PARAMOUNT, 1967)

Director: John Rich
Screenplay: Allen Weiss and Anthony Lawrence
Producer: Hal Wallis
Original Music: Joseph J. Lilley
Cinematographer: William Marguiles
Editor: Archie Marshek
Makeup: Wally Westmore
Hairstylists: Nellie Manley and Larry Geller
Vocals: The Jordanaires
Technical advisor: Colonel Tom Parker
Cast: Elvis Presley, Dodie Marshall, Pat Priest, Pat Harrington, Jr., Skip Ward, Sandy Kenyon, Frank McHugh, Ed Griffith, Read Morgan, Mickey Elley, Elaine Beckett, Shari Nims, Diki Lerner, Robert Isenberg, Elsa Lanchester, Tom Hatten
Songs (in the order performed):
   "Easy Come, Easy Go" (written by Sid Wayne and Ben Weisman; performed by Elvis Presley)
   "The Love Machine" (written by Gerald Nelson, Fred Burch, and Chuck Taylor; performed by Elvis Presley)
   "Yoga Is as Yoga Does" (written by Gerald Nelson and Fred Burch; performed by Elvis Presley and Elsa Lanchester)
   "You Gotta Stop" (written by Bill Giant, Bernie Baum, and Florence Kaye; performed by Elvis Presley)
   "Sing You Children" (written by Gerald Nelson and Fred Burch; performed by Elvis Presley)
   "I'll Take Love" (written by Dolores Fuller and Mark Barker; performed by Elvis Presley)

No chart success

Released March 22, 1967
Filmed September 12–October 31, 1966

Alternate title: *A Girl in Every Port*
95 minutes
Technicolor
Aspect ratio: 1.85:1
U.S. gross: $1,950,000
Released to DVD by Paramount Home Video

By the time he made *Easy Come, Easy Go*, the Elvis formula was no longer achieving the same box office success, having continued to dwindle for some time. And although this was a Hal Wallis production, it was missing the lush, colorful scenery and scene-for-scene songs. In fact, *Easy Come, Easy Go* is a fairly drab-looking movie, and has the smallest song count since *Kid Galahad* in 1962. It has the distinction of being the final Elvis Presley movie produced by Hal Wallis, and for including the worst of all Elvis movie songs.

This was not originally to be an Elvis Presley movie at all. It was planned as a vehicle for the surf rock duo Jan and Dean. But when Jan Berry was injured in a serious car crash in April 1966, putting him in a coma for two months, the film was revamped as the next Elvis Presley vehicle.

Easy Come, Easy Go features Elvis in his third branch of the service, having been in the army for *G.I. Blues* and the air force in *Kissin' Cousins*. As a navy frogman seeking a buried treasure, Elvis plays a character more interested in money than girls. The basic plot narrative moves quite slowly and the songs are generally pretty mellow except for the title track and the up-tempo "You Gotta Stop," a song Elvis changed from its original title "Stop, You're Wrong." Backing vocals were recorded for the Ray Charles composition "Leave My Woman Alone," but Elvis never recorded his vocal for it. Another song, "She's a Machine," was dropped from the film, because Elvis hated it so much.

The real low point of the film is the ridiculous novelty number "Yoga Is as Yoga Does," which Elvis sings in a duet with veteran actress Elsa Lanchester. Perhaps the prevailing heads determined that Elvis was no longer part of the youthful counterculture and thus included a scene to parody one of the excesses of that culture. It is intended as a comic scene, with Elvis tying himself up in knots, attempting to fit in with the others. He draws upon his ability to express comic reaction, which he'd used in earlier movies and more effective scenes. But rather than enhance the comic element, it just seems more forced. The song, although a novelty number, is at a level of silliness that simply emphasizes how badly Presley's significant legacy had plummeted.

Director John Rich, who helmed the Elvis movie *Roustabout*, was again behind the director's chair with this movie. Although satisfied with how *Roustabout* turned out, Rich was not interested in directing another Elvis movie. According to John Rich, he was completely taken aback when Wallis expressed his own indifference, stating, "Just put them through their paces." Colonel Parker had trouble securing advance money for promotional purposes, something that had never been a problem earlier. And once the movie was released, it grossed under $2 million, while the extended play soundtrack sold only around 30,000 copies, the worst-selling Elvis record ever.

Elvis himself was more disillusioned than ever. According to Peter Guralnick in *Careless Love*:

> [Elvis] felt more estranged from Hollywood than ever, as he stoically endured a movie that no one seemed to want to make and faced the inescapable conclusion that, after all these years, to these people he was nothing more than a joke. Most of the time he just followed directions; he had learned long ago that it was all about finding your mark, and then just having whatever fun there was to be had along the way.

Elvis was arriving late for wardrobe fittings, and for recording sessions.

Longtime character actor Frank McHugh, in his final movie, is typically enjoyable, while actresses Dodie Marshall and Pat Priest are pleasant support (the latter just having completed a stint as Marilyn on TV's *The Munsters*). And while Elsa Lanchester duets with Elvis in the film's worst song, her flamboyant performance as a yoga instructor is otherwise amusing. The cast is rounded out by familiar faces like Pat Harrington and Skip Ward.

Easy Come, Easy Go was released in 1967. In music, the Beatles continued to progress with their masterpiece, *Sergeant Pepper's Lonely Hearts Club Band*. Rock music was further redefined by Jimi Hendrix's debut album, *Are You Experienced*. Cinema was advancing with films like Arthur Penn's *Bonnie and Clyde*, which gave thirties-era gangsters the wild child sensibilities of sixties youth, and Mike Nichols's *The Graduate,* which addressed the youth culture on their own terms. A film, and soundtrack, like *Easy Come, Easy Go* made Elvis Presley seem like an anachronism. After creating the very subculture that continued to advance, Elvis was now responding to its progression with parody, and not particularly well.

Variety liked the film, calling it

> another well-made Hal B. Wallis production starring Elvis Presley, this time as an underwater demolitions expert who finds lost treasure. Good balance of script and songs, plus generally amusing performances by a competent, well-directed cast, add up to diverting entertainment. Commercial prospects are bright for Paramount release in general situations, particularly drive-ins.

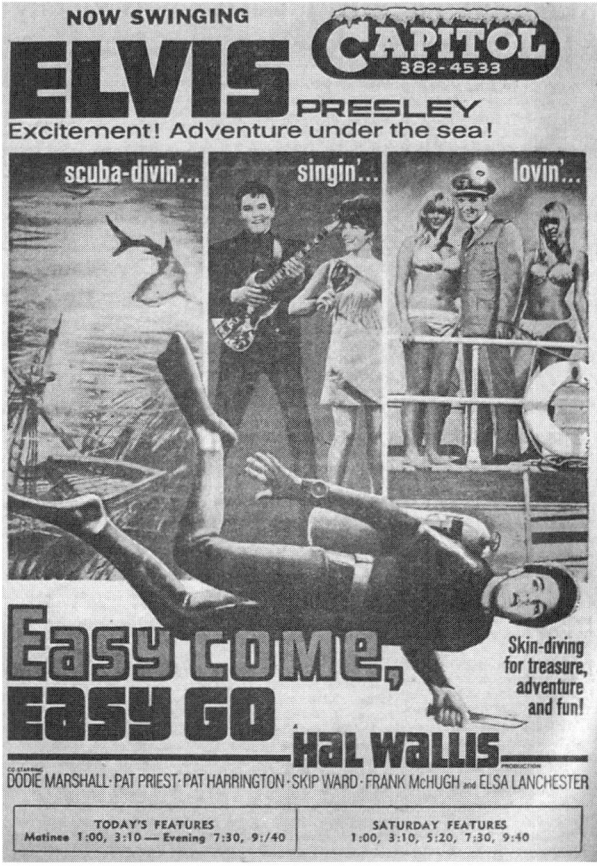

Newspaper ad for *Easy Come, Easy Go*

It appears that *Variety*'s critic simply realized what to expect from a new Elvis Presley movie and responded accordingly. Rather than assess *Easy Come, Easy Go* as a film, he approached it as an Elvis movie, and decided it was perfectly good of its kind. Maybe in the wake of the Monterey Pop crowd, Elvis now seemed tame and acceptable when only ten years earlier he was approached as dangerous and frightening. Obviously the image had been tamed. But rather than adapt with his audience and explore different ideas, Elvis succumbed to anticreative management. Recording songs by the top songwriters of the era, including Bob Dylan, Lennon-McCartney, Jagger-Richards, Goffin-King, Gamble-Huff, and others, would have netted him challenging material that allowed him to rise to the occasion. Allowing for roles in films that gave him stronger stories, better direction, and parts he could creatively explore would also have been beneficial. But Elvis Presley was packaged and sold in a manner that was at odds with his own perspective. And, as he candidly told the Beatles and others who would listen, he was pre-signed for the films and had to accept the scripts he was given.

Hal Wallis was the producer who signed Elvis, and had made money with him as he once had with the comedy team of Dean Martin and Jerry Lewis. But Wallis realized that Elvis was no longer the commodity he once had been, which is why little production value was offered this latest effort, and why Wallis chose to make it his last Elvis Presley picture. Elvis would continue to fulfill his contract away from Paramount. *Easy Come, Easy Go* only reached number 50 among the top grossing films of 1967, a poor showing for an Elvis Presley picture. It was an unhappy conclusion to Elvis Presley's tenure with Hal Wallis, but some will note that Elvis Presley's next movie release was actually filmed just prior to *Easy Come, Easy Go*. In fact, *Double Trouble* had just wrapped six days before Elvis started work on *Easy Come, Easy Go*. At least with *Double Trouble* there was some attempt to merge the Elvis movie formula with what worked for the Beatles. But popular culture was progressing so rapidly by this time in the 1960s, it was just too difficult for Elvis to keep up. *Double Trouble* was, at least, an improvement and with a somewhat better soundtrack. Still, Elvis remained in the career doldrums. The fact that his future held such triumphs as the 1968 TV special and the Memphis sessions the following year was, at this point, unrealized.

CHAPTER 26
Double Trouble
(MGM, 1967)

Director: Norman Taurog
Screenplay: Jo Heims, from a story by Marc Brandel
Producers: Irwin Winkler and Judd Bernard
Cinematographer: Daniel Fapp
Editor: John McSweeney, Jr.
Makeup: William Tuttle
Hairstylists: Mary Keats and Larry Geller
Technical advisor: Colonel Tom Parker
Cast: Elvis Presley, Annette Day, John Williams, Yvonne Romain, the Wiere Brothers (Harry, Herbert, and Sylvester), Chips Rafferty, Norman Rossington, Monte Landis, Michael Murphy, Leon Askin, John Alderson, Stanley Adams, Maurice Marsac, Walter Burke, Helene Winston, Bob Homel, Peter Balakoff, George Dee, Luke Gerard, John Harding, Bob Bergy, Hal Bokar, Barry Cole, Chester Hayes, Mary Hughes, Robert Isenberg, Bob Johnson, Murray Kamelhar, George Klein, Ralph Smiley, Billy Smith, Christopher Riordan, Rick Teagarden, Jack Teagarden, Bill Snyder, Ray Saunders, Audrey Saunders, Ted DeWayne

Songs:
  "Double Trouble" (written by Doc Pomus and Mort Shuman; performed by Elvis Presley)
  "Baby, If You Give Me All Your Love" (written by Joy Byers [as Joe Byers]; performed by Elvis Presley)
  "Could I Fall in Love" (written by Randy Starr; performed by Elvis Presley)
  "Long Legged Girl (With the Short Dress On)" (written by J. Leslie McFarland [as Leslie Macfarland] and Scotty Moore; performed by Elvis Presley)
  "City by Night" (written by Bill Giant, Bernie Baum, and Florence Kaye; performed by Elvis Presley)
  "Old MacDonald" (written by Randy Starr; performed by Elvis Presley)
  "I Love Only One Girl" (written by Sid Tepper and Roy C. Bennett; performed by Elvis Presley)

> "There's So Much World to See" (written by Sid Tepper and Ben Weisman; performed by Elvis Presley)
> "It Won't Be Long" (written by Sid Wayne and Ben Weisman; performed by Elvis Presley)
>
> No chart success
>
> Released April 5, 1967
> Filmed July 11–August 30, 1966
> Alternate title: *You're Killing Me*
> 90 minutes
> Technicolor
> Aspect ratio: 2.35:1
> U.S. gross: $1.6 million
> Released to DVD by Warner Home Video

Double Trouble was filmed just prior to *Easy Come, Easy Go*, which went into production less than two weeks after shooting completed on this film. It was released less than two weeks after the release of *Easy Come, Easy Go*. So the films played practically on top of each other in theaters, sometimes on the lower half of double bills. *Double Trouble* is superior, despite its rather obvious and desperate attempt to emulate what producers thought successful in the Beatles movies. It is ironic that this idea was an attempt to update Presley's movie image, as the Beatles had moved on creatively from the *Help!* period by this time, having released a few subsequent albums in which their style evolved further. The Beach Boys had released *Pet Sounds* the previous year, and Bob Dylan offered *Blonde on Blonde*. The Beatles' *Sergeant Pepper's Lonely Hearts Club Band* was again redefining rock and roll's concept, and Jimi Hendrix brought it to a heavy-metal edge with *Are You Experienced.*

The world of *Double Trouble* was a swinging mod world of pat situations with no hippie communes, no civil rights movement, no Vietnam, and no student unrest. During the year that gave us *Bonnie and Clyde, The Graduate, Cool Hand Luke,* and *In Cold Blood*, a film like *Double Trouble* (or *Easy Come, Easy Go*) seemed as out of touch with the youth market as Bob Hope's *Eight on the Lam*.

The songs are at least better than what Elvis had offered in his previous movie, and he continues to project a wry comic sensibility with his performance, which works. Elvis seems to enjoy working with the bombastic Wiere Brothers, who are no funnier in this picture than in any other they invaded, and the cast is rounded out by veterans like John Williams, Chips Rafferty, and Norman Rossington. Thus, it is a merry little comedy mystery with music, pure fluff within the limitations of the Elvis movie formula, and sufficient under those specific terms.

There are some elements that made it topical for an older audience. Spy thrillers were popular, especially those set in foreign locales. Elvis plays Guy Lam-

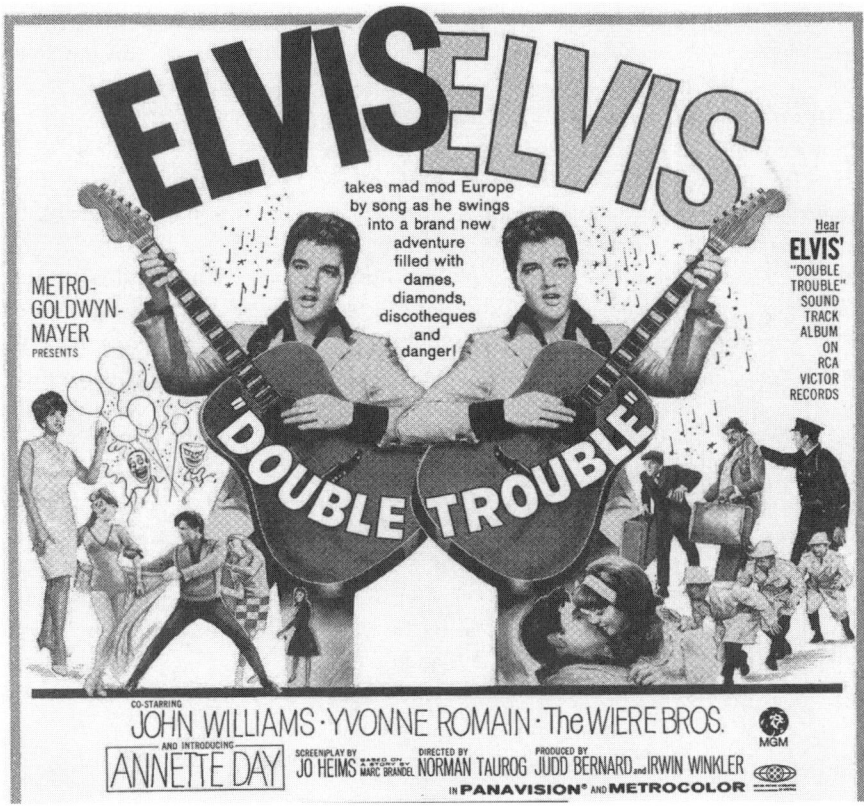

Press kit ad for *Double Trouble*

bert, an American singer in London and Antwerp. Guy meets heiress Jill Conway (Annette Day appearing in her only movie) who becomes infatuated with him. The plot deals essentially with Jill leading Guy through a series of adventures involving spies and jewel thieves. There is a basic structure to the narrative, but it is just a backdrop for songs and lightweight situations. The Wiere Brothers, a comedy act, attempt to provide some manner of comic relief.

Elvis was once again unimpressed with the songs he was given to sing in *Double Trouble*, and continued to arrive late to recording sessions. As a manner of convenience, MGM moved the recording sessions to the soundstage, which had poor acoustics, further annoying Presley. He also continued to be dismayed by the way production revamped his own ideas regarding the way the songs should be presented. When he finally spent hours trying to make something out of the song "Old MacDonald," Elvis became fed up and the studio had to use an incomplete, seventh take as the master. The session ended with Elvis recording "Long Legged Girl (With the Short Dress On)," which is probably the best song in the movie. Elvis's leading lady, eighteen-year-old Annette Day, had been working in her parents' antique shop in London when she was discovered and cast in this movie, despite no prior acting experience (producers felt she had the right look for the part).

During the filming of *Double Trouble* Elvis had the opportunity to meet singer Jackie Wilson, whom he had admired since seeing him perform with Billy Ward's Dominoes more than ten years earlier. He went to see Wilson perform and Jackie later visited the set. Another encounter was with singer James Brown, with whom Elvis shared a mutual admiration. Brown had called Graceland often in an attempt to meet Elvis, but always when the nocturnal singer was sleeping. When told James Brown was in attendance at the Wilson show, Elvis went to Brown's table (something he rarely did—he usually waited for others to approach him). Upon being introduced Brown said to Presley, "Man you sure do sleep a lot!" According to Presley associate George Klein in *Careless Love*, "Elvis almost fell on the floor laughing. He said, 'Aw James you know how it is being a night person.' And James said, 'I know brother' and slapped Elvis' hand."

Elvis remained friends with these men until the end of his life. Some reports indicate that Elvis contributed to *American Bandstand* host Dick Clark's fundraising efforts toward Jackie's medical bills when he suffered a massive stroke in 1975 (he outlived Elvis, dying in 1984, but remained in a coma). An openly distraught James Brown was the first to arrive at Elvis Presley's funeral in 1977.

Variety, which had been oddly impressed with *Easy Come, Easy Go*, was unhappy with *Double Trouble*, calling the movie "extremely lightweight" and stated:

> Presley plays an American singer touring foreign discotheques, and scene shifts from London, where two femmes enter his life, to Bruges and finally Antwerp. Intertwined in his travels, and femmes chasing him, are a couple of eccentric jewel thieves who have planted a fortune of diamonds in his luggage, mysterious attempts on his life and his arrest for allegedly kidnapping one of the kittens who happens to be a rich heiress 17-going-on-18. Plottage seldom plays too important a part in Presley films but here is utter confusion. Presley as usual gives a pretty fair account of himself despite what's handed him. He delivers in customary style, entirely at home in his character.

Double Trouble was once again overlooked by the *New York Times* film reviewers, as they appeared to have given up on Elvis movies.

Theater owners, reporting to *Box Office* magazine, were also less impressed with this effort, one theater in South Carolina reporting: "We are always happy to have Elvis in anything, but I sure hope he will be given better roles. Am still waiting for more like *Blue Hawaii* or *Viva Las Vegas*."

Double Trouble did even worse at the box office than *Easy Come, Easy Go* had done. While the previous movie was number 50 in *Variety*'s end of the year reports, this one sunk even lower, to number 58. It didn't help that Paramount decided to saturate the market by re-releasing older Elvis movies like *Girls! Girls! Girls!* and *Fun in Acapulco*, sometimes in a double feature. In one issue of *Box Office*, revivals of *Viva Las Vegas* and *Girls! Girls! Girls!* were doing weekend dates at some theaters while *Double Trouble* was beginning its initial run at another, and *Easy Come, Easy Go* was ending its run at still another. Add to this the fact that many Elvis movies were playing on television as well, scoring impressively high ratings.

The year 1967 might be the lowest in Elvis Presley's career since he first achieved fame. Despite being awarded a Grammy for his gospel album, *How Great Thou Art*, and his marriage to Priscilla Presley that year, Elvis was enjoying little chart success or box office success.

CHAPTER 27
Clambake
(MGM, 1967)

Director: Arthur H. Nadel
Screenplay: Arthur Browne, Jr.
Producers: Jules Levy, Arnold Laven, Arthur Gardner
Cinematographer: William Marguiles
Editor: Ernest R. Rolf (Tom Rolf)
Makeup: Dan Greenway
Hairstylists: Judith Cory, Larry Geller
Technical advisor: Colonel Tom Parker
Cast: Elvis Presley, Shelley Fabares, Will Hutchins, Bill Bixby, Gary Merrill, James Gregory, Suzie Kaye, Harold Peary, Marj Dusay, Jack Good, Olga Kaya, Angelique Pettyjohn, Sam Riddle, Wallace Earl, Sue England, Lee Krieger, Arlene Charles, Steve Cory, Lisa Slagle, Christopher Riordan, Charlie Hodge, Red West, Melvin Allen, Herb Barnett, Teri Garr, Dal McKennon, Robert P. Lieb, Jonathan Kramer, Joe Esposito, Richard Davis, Francis Humphrey Howard, Corbin Bernsen
Songs (in the order performed):
"Clambake" (written by Ben Weisman and Sid Wayne; performed by Elvis Presley)
"Who Needs Money?" (written by Randy Starr; performed by Elvis Presley and Ray Walker)
"A House That Has Everything" (written by M. Arnold, J. Morrow, and C. Martin; performed by Elvis Presley)
"Confidence" (written by Sid Tepper and Roy C. Bennett; performed by Elvis Presley)
"You Don't Know Me" (written by Eddy Arnold and Cindy Walker; performed by Elvis Presley)
"Hey, Hey, Hey" (written by Joy Byers [as Joe Byers]; performed by Elvis Presley)
"The Girl I Never Loved" (written by Randy Starr; performed by Elvis Presley)
"How Can You Lose What You Never Had" (written by Ben Weisman and Sid Wayne; performed by Elvis Presley)

> The soundtrack album reached number 18 on the charts
> Two songs not in the movie, "Big Boss Man" and "Guitar Man," were featured as extras on the soundtrack album. "Big Boss Man" reached number 38 on the Billboard charts.
>
> Released December 4, 1967
> Filmed March 10–11, March 28–April 27, 1967
> 99 minutes
> Technicolor
> Aspect ratio: 2.35:1
> Released to DVD by Warner Home Video

In *Clambake*, Elvis Presley is dressed in a rhinestone-laden cowboy outfit, the very type of gear his character in *Loving You* had rejected. Elvis in the late 1960s had become what 1950s Elvis hated, and the result is another of his weakest films and most unimpressive soundtracks. Priscilla Presley recalled in *Elvis and Me* that Elvis himself felt this movie was rock bottom and continued to refer to it as his worst: "He would call me from the set and complain how bad the movie was." Costar Shelley Fabares remembered in an interview how Elvis would mutter, "What are we doing here?" while setting up for a scene.

Here we have a *Prince and the Pauper* dynamic as Elvis plays Scott Hayward, a rich boy who feels trapped by his wealth. Scott leaves his family and drives to Florida in a 1959 Chevrolet Corvette Stingray Racer in an attempt to sort out what he wants to do with his life. When Scott stops for gas, he meets Tom Wilson (Will Hutchins), who is on his way to take a job as a waterskiing instructor at a hotel in Miami. Tom remarks that Scott must have it made, so Scott gets the idea to switch identities with Tom so he can find out how people will react to him as an ordinary person. Tom, meanwhile, gets to pretend to wealth.

This setup could almost be assessed as an attempt to present the singer as 1950s Elvis—the one who went against the established ways and carved his own path. The key difference is that Elvis Presley was from a modest background, not a pampered rich boy who simply wants to investigate what "ordinary life" might be like. Elvis and Will Hutchins sing a duet that calls out their switched identity dynamic, with Hutchins dubbed by singer Ray Walker of the Jordanaires. The song "Who Needs Money" is filmed as Scott drives Tom's vehicle, while Tom is in Scott's Corvette, the two men trading vocals from their own perspective. It was a rock-bottom example of the standard to which musical Elvis movies had sunk—ordinary musical numbers without a shred of substance.

Scott must then maintain the facade of a waterskiing instructor once they reach the hotel, while Tom enjoys his role as a pampered wealthy guest. Another guest, Dianne Carter (Shelley Fabares), insists on waterskiing lessons once she

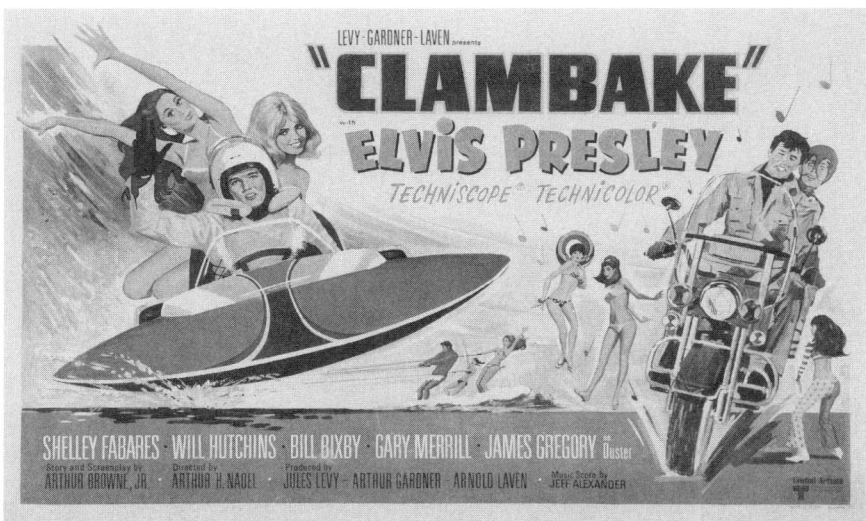

Lobby card for *Clambake*

sees Scott, but proves herself to be quite adept on the water. She just wants to attract the attention of another wealthy guest, James Jamison (Bill Bixby). Dianne admits to being a gold digger and assumes Scott is also. He ends up falling for Dianne, despite his misgivings about her approach.

Bill Bixby, having completed his run as the nervous Tim O'Hara on television's *My Favorite Martian*, and prior to his sobering performance on TV's *The Courtship of Eddie's Father*, is especially effective as the smarmy rich boy who expects to have whatever he wants. Jamison is the antithesis of Scott, who disdains wealth privilege. Bixby plays up his character with flamboyant zeal, offering perhaps the best comic performance in the movie. His pretentious manner, conflict with Scott, expectations regarding Dianne, and reaction to his own comeuppance are all played effectively for laughs.

In a tangential plot, Scott resourcefully uses some material that his father's company once manufactured without success to rebuild a damaged boat so he can drive it in a race. The boat builder, Sam Burton (Gary Merrill), allows him to stay in the shop overnight working on perfecting the solution he got from his father—a coating that was flawed because it loses strength when wet. Once he accomplishes this, he repairs the high-performance boat and enters it in the annual Orange Bowl Race, which Jamison has won the last three years in a row. Scott wins the race and reveals his identity to Dianne, who promptly faints.

The plot tangent is interesting because it presents another aspect to the character Elvis is playing. For all his privilege, Scott is also educated and capable,

able to create the necessary chemistry to make the solution effective. Jamison's lofty beliefs are borne from the expectation that he always comes out on top. Scott realizes he must work to achieve such a status, despite both men coming from equally wealthy backgrounds.

Elvis was unhappy with *Clambake*'s script as soon as he read it, so he did little to prepare for the film. When he arrived on the set, the studio was displeased to find that he had gained 30 pounds, looking heavier than he had in any of his previous movies. Also, only a day or so into the shoot, Elvis fell at home and hit his head, getting a mild concussion. His doctors stated that he should rest, so filming did not resume until nearly three weeks later.

Despite his misgivings, Elvis still tried to have some fun on the set. Costar Will Hutchins recalled on the Western Clippings website:

> I'm sure if the Colonel had allowed him to accept meatier roles, he'd have won an Oscar. He was the most talented fellow I ever worked with. Sometimes I'd feel a tad lost. One-take Elvis and twenty-take Hutchins. He'd give me a grin, a pat on the back, a comforting word—he'd make me feel like his salary! Behind his mischievous eyes I sensed an abiding melancholy. I figured he'd grown weary of making the same flick over and over and over. Sort of like the myth of Sisyphus—a guy pushes a huge boulder up a steep hill throughout eternity only to have the boulder elude him and roll down to the bottom. I figured Elvis was saddened by the emergence of the Beatles and their rise to the top.
>
> One day Elvis invited me into his trailer. He put an LP on the turntable. I reckoned I was about to be the first kid on my block to hear his latest album. Instead, what issued forth was the mellow voice of the great French actor Charles Boyer reciting love poems. We're all onions. No one ever came close to peeling away Elvis' multi-layers to get to his rich core.

Elvis would always cite *Clambake* as his worst movie (and *King Creole* as his best), and it remains one of the least interesting examples of his standard formula. Thus, it is surprising to read *Variety*'s rave review:

> Elvis Presley has the benefit of superior mounting throughout in his latest, *Clambake*, carrying such a title because of a fast and colorful musical production number. The Jules Levy-Arthur Gardner-Arnold Leven [*sic*] production is one of the singer's top offerings to date, backed by a legitimately-premised story line, melodic songs, acceptable acting and winding with a spectacular water race. Film has all the makings of being one of Presley's heaviest grossers.

However, Howard Thompson of the *New York Times*, who had been far more understanding regarding Elvis Presley's movies than Bosley Crowther had been, stated:

> Elvis Presley hit a real Christmas clinker yesterday with "Clambake," a silly, tired little frolic that could have used a few clams. Even stanch Presley admirers—and we're one of them when he delivers the likes of "Fun in Acapulco" and "Viva Las Vegas!"—will have to strain to justify this one . . . it's mighty slim, Presley pickings. The bikini-clad rock 'n' roll cuties aren't bad, but Elvis has surrounded himself with better. Likewise the tunes, and composer Jeff Alexander has done considerably better. Even the scenery, in contrast to the sun-drenched authenticity of those other two pictures, is fairly pallid.

The only good song in the film is Eddy Arnold's ballad "You Don't Know Me," which Elvis gives a soulful reading. The soundtrack album's two bonus tracks, "Big Boss Man" and "Guitar Man," were among the better rockers Elvis had recorded in some years. It showed him that relying on movie soundtrack recordings was less effective than what he could do in the studio.

A lot was going through Presley's mind by this point. According to Elvis associate Billy Smith in *Elvis Aaron Presley*:

> Elvis' contract with MGM was nearly up and Colonel started re-evaluating things. In the early years, when Elvis was hot, Colonel told him, "You're Elvis Presley. You'll get a million dollars a picture and sometimes a percentage. All you got to do is show up on time and take the money and run." Even the studio heads said, "Good ol' Elvis. He'll ride a hog through a blizzard if that's what the script calls for." The Colonel saw two things—One: that the pictures had worn out their welcome and Elvis was getting hard to sell. And two, that Elvis was flat refusing to do anymore. Elvis told Colonel that he'd quit the business before he'd sign another movie contract. And Colonel saw he was dead serious.

At one time wanting to be another James Dean or Marlon Brando, Elvis was now so completely disillusioned with the movies he had been making, he truly took a stand. *Clambake* was the experience that put him over the edge.

Elvis still had a few films left on his contract for the remainder of 1968 and one in 1969. Once he completed those, he planned to be finished with Hollywood forever. He was considering returning to live performances (he had not done a live show since 1961) and was negotiating for a Christmas special to be broadcast at the end of the year. Despite his initial enthusiasm, and discernible potential, for acting in movies, Elvis was no longer getting good scripts with top directors and fewer songs. He no longer was allowed a more challenging movie if he agreed to do the occasional musical. His films had now lapsed into the deadening formula that drew on none of his creativity. Elvis had to do something important and return to relevance in show business. He wanted to remove himself from what his career had become and re-invent it once again. But before that was possible, he had a few more movies to do. And it can be argued that his next film, *Stay Away, Joe*, while not following the formulaic pattern as closely as something like *Clambake*, was an even worse movie.

It was obvious that Elvis remained in a rut as far as his movies were concerned, and he simply filled out his contract as effectively as he could.

CHAPTER 28
Stay Away, Joe
(MGM, 1968)

Director: Peter Tewksbury
Screenplay: Michael Hoey and Burt Kennedy, from Dan Cushman's novel *Stay Away, Joe*
Producer: Douglas Laurence
Cinematography: Fred J. Koenkamp
Editor: George W. Brooks
Assistant director: Dale Hutchinson
Makeup: William Tuttle
Hairstylist: Sydney Guilaroff
Vocals: The Jordanaires
Cast: Elvis Presley, Burgess Meredith, Joan Blondell, Katy Jurado, Thomas Gomez, Henry Jones, L. Q. Jones, Quentin Dean, Anne Seymour, Douglas Henderson, Angus Duncan, Mike Lane, Susan Trustman, Warren Vanders, Buck Kartalian
Songs (in the order performed):
  "Stay Away, Joe" (written by Sid Wayne and Ben Weisman; performed by Elvis Presley)
  "Lovely Mamie" (sung briefly, no writing credit; performed by Elvis Presley)
  "Dominic" (written by Sid Tepper and Roy C. Bennett; performed by Elvis Presley)
  "All I Needed Was the Rain" (written by Fred Wise and Ben Weisman; performed by Elvis Presley)
  "Stay Away" (written by Sid Tepper and Roy C. Bennett; performed by Elvis Presley)

No chart success

Released March 8, 1968
Filmed October 4–November 18, 1967
Running Time: 102 minutes
Metrocolor
Aspect ratio: 2.35:1
Released to DVD by Warner Home Video

For the entire first half hour of *Stay Away, Joe*, Elvis throws himself at his buddies, they throw themselves back, and everyone is rolling around in a good-natured brawl. This roughhousing then gives way to a party with music, dancing, and more brawling. All this takes place after Elvis comes riding into the area on the back of a bull.

Made after production ended on *Speedway* but released earlier, *Stay Away, Joe* has Elvis playing a Native American again for the first time since *Flaming Star* and, like the earlier film, there are few songs on the soundtrack. The difference is, this loosely structured mishmash of a movie is not only poorly executed, it perpetuates the sort of stereotyping of Native Americans that the earlier film avoided. *Stay Away, Joe* ranks alongside the likes of *Harum Scarum* as among the very worst of Elvis Presley's movies.

The opening of the film benefits from Peter Tewksbury's direction. Primarily a TV director, Tewksbury takes advantage of the Arizona location scenery by filming the opening credits with expansive overhead shots and long shots. The opening moments, with Elvis driving madly, attempting to herd cattle and ending up with the car submerged in a swamp, is fast and amusing. Unfortunately, the film never builds from this sequence. The next several scenes are a succession of brawls, dances, and other physical activities for half an hour with no semblance of a plot or narrative structure. It is completely disjointed and devoid of entertainment value.

In what exists of a plot that is eventually introduced, Elvis plays Joe Lightcloud, a Navajo who persuades his congressman (Douglas Henderson) to give him 20 heifers and a prize bull so he and his father (Burgess Meredith) can prove that the Navajos can successfully raise cattle on the reservation. If they succeed, the government will agree to help all the Navajo people in a similar fashion. During Joe's welcome home party, his friend Bronc (L.Q. Jones) barbecues the prize bull. Joe hastily borrows a lazy bull named Dominick, which shows no interest in the heifers. A subplot features Mamie Callahan (Quentin Dean), who can't keep away from the girl-chasing Joe, much to the dismay of her shotgun-wielding mother (Joan Blondell). The screenplay was adapted from the failed Broadway musical *Whoop-Up,* which had been based on the Dan Cushman novel. The movie retained many of the same plot devices and characters from the play, including Joe's grandfather who refuses to live in a house, preferring his teepee.

While there is some semblance of an idea in which Native Americans prove a valid point to the U.S. government about the effectiveness of their traditions, it is buried amidst a series of unmotivated brawls, physical gags, and chase scenes. With the paucity of songs, we don't even get the chance to see Elvis stop the action and break into a good, rocking musical number. It's just a seemingly endless series of unrelated physical sequences. One song, which Elvis purported to hate passionately, is "Dominic," which he serenades to a bull.

Press kit ad for *Stay Away, Joe*

The headier problem with *Stay Away, Joe* is the film's depiction of Native Americans as shiftless and conniving. While at one point the film attempts to have satiric fun with this premise (the elderly patriarch, played by Thomas Gomez, chastises his son for being unable to read smoke signals, stating, "Lot of good sending you to school, can't read own language"), but most of the film is spent in carefree brawling and roughhousing, and the characters are incompetent stereotypes. Perhaps it can be argued that stereotyping is inherent in comedy, but even the eventual review in *Variety* noticed a problem:

> Basic story—contemporary American Indians who are portrayed as laughable incompetents—is out of touch with latter day appreciation of some basic dignity in all human beings. This is not meant as a demand that minority groups be depicted in uptight emotional dramatic situations, but rather that, in a desired comedy setting, there be some shading in characterizations. At best, film is a dim artistic accomplishment; at worst, it caters to out-dated prejudice. Custer himself might be embarrassed—for the Indians.

Variety had usually been pretty receptive to Elvis Presley movies, even as they wallowed in the consistent formula that they hadn't strayed from since *Girl Happy* three years earlier. But the magazine were generally unimpressed with *Stay Away, Joe,* further stating:

> Apparent goal was to soft-pedal the songs, and strengthen dramatic impact via casting of versatile pro thesps. Achievement is partial; the true breaks are minimal, and logical, but, in contrast to older Presley pix—where there generally was a developed plot—this one ranks among the weakest.

Director Tewksbury tries to dress up the visuals with some nice camera angles, including an overhead shot of Katy Jurado putting away groceries while carrying on a dialog with Meredith. They are surrounded by cluttered furnishings, offering an example of how they live and function. The three-camera process the director uses benefits from good editing, cutting to each person as they speak. The overhead shots Tewksbury uses throughout the film continues to take advantage of the location scenery.

But for a film this disjointed, the director's visual sense offers little enhancement to a dreary movie experience. However, this was not the consensus when the film was first released. *Film Daily* liked *Stay Away, Joe* much better than *Variety* had, stating: "It doesn't matter that credibility is stretched. What matters is that the picture evokes a mood of mirth and happy frenzy that is catching." Meanwhile, theater owners praised the film to *Box Office* and talked about good attendance, with such statements as:

> Stay Away Joe brings good comedy back. It is short on songs, but long on comedy and good at that. I'd almost decided that no one knew how to make a comedy anymore. This is excellent. One of the best grossing Elvis Presley movies in a long time Elvis is getting better and the roles he plays are better suited to him.

Still, the movie was a lowly number 65 among the annual box office lists in *Variety*.

The supporting cast can't be faulted. Burgess Meredith, Joan Blondell, Katy Jurado, and Thomas Gomez were all seasoned veterans, while newcomer Quentin Dean had already scored in Norman Jewison's *In the Heat of the Night* the year before. The direction is good, and the scenery, when utilized, frames the action nicely. But *Stay Away, Joe* remains an artistic failure.

CHAPTER 29

Speedway
(MGM, 1968)

Director: Norman Taurog
Screenplay: Phillip Shuken
Producer: Douglas Laurence
Cinematography: Joseph Ruttenberg
Editor: Richard Farrell
Assistant director: Dale Hutchinson
Makeup: William Tuttle
Vocal Accompaniment: The Jordanaires
Cast: Elvis Presley, Nancy Sinatra, Bill Bixby, Gale Gordon, William Schallert, Victoria Paige Meyerink, Ross Hagen, Carl Ballantine, Poncie Ponce, Burt Mustin, Harry Hickox, Christopher West, Beverly Powers, Richard Petty, Buddy Baker, Cale Yarborough, Dick Hutcherson, Tiny Lund, G. C. Spencer, Roy Mayne, Harper Carter, Bob Harris, Michele Newman, Courtney Brown, Dana Brown, Patti Jean Keith, Carl Reindel, Gari Hardy, Charlotte Stewart, Sandy Reed, S. John Launer, Dee Carroll, Arlene Charles, Karen Hamilton, Sharon Garrett, William Keene, Barbro Hedstrom, Morgan Hill, Marilyn Jones, Charlie Hodge, Robert Stevenson, Hal Riddle, Rita Rogers, Sheryl Ullman, Claude Stroud, Dianne Stanley, Kathy Nelson, John McDonnell, Jamie Michaels, Sally Mills, Ward Ramsey, Tom McCauley, Ralph Ano, Robert James, Gary Littlejohn, George Cisar
Songs (in the order performed):
"Speedway" (written by Mel Glazer and Stephen Schlaks; performed by Elvis Presley)
"Let Yourself Go" (written by Mel Glazer and Stephen Schlaks; performed by Elvis Presley)
"Your Time Hasn't Come Yet, Baby" (written by Mel Glazer and Stephen Schlaks; performed by Elvis Presley)
"He's Your Uncle, Not Your Dad" (written by Mel Glazer and Stephen Schlaks; performed by Elvis Presley)
"Who Are You, Who Am I" (written by Mel Glazer and Stephen Schlaks; performed by Elvis Presley)

"Your Groovy Self" (written by Lee Hazlewood; performed by Nancy Sinatra)
"There Ain't Nothing Like a Song" (written by Mel Glazer and Stephen Schlaks; performed by Elvis Presley)
"Five Sleepy Heads" (written by Mel Glazer and Stephen Schlaks; performed by Elvis Presley)
"Western Union" (written by Mel Glazer and Stephen Schlaks; performed by Elvis Presley)
"Mine" (written by Mel Glazer and Stephen Schlaks; performed by Elvis Presley)
"Goin' Home" (written by Mel Glazer and Stephen Schlaks; performed by Elvis Presley)
"Suppose" (written by Mel Glazer and Stephen Schlaks; performed by Elvis Presley)

Released June 12, 1968
Filmed June 26–July 23, 1967
94 minutes
Metrocolor
Aspect ratio: 2.35:1
Budget: $1.5 million (estimated); gross: $3 million
Released to DVD by Warner Home Video

Filmed before *Stay Away, Joe* but released afterward, *Speedway* was the final Elvis film that adhered to the formula originally set by the success of *Blue Hawaii*. Elvis is in a macho-type job, surrounded by pretty girls, and overcoming conflicts in an easy, affable manner. It is colorful, and there is music. This formula was financially successful for years, but once it became the only type of movie Elvis was offered, box office receipts started falling. Elvis would begrudgingly agree to do these lightweight musicals that netted further dividends via the soundtrack album, with the understanding that he would also be allowed the occasional dramatic role that was separate from his singing. Once that method was abandoned and Elvis was exclusively doing musicals (beginning with *Girl Happy* in 1965), his fans began outgrowing them.

The world of 1968 was far different than in 1965, and even more removed from 1961. Racial inequality, protests, Vietnam, student movements, and other issues affecting young people seemed nonexistent in the Elvis Presley movie world. This is where things were simple, innocent, tuneful, colorful, and shallow. It was not perceived as escapist entertainment by the masses, who were embracing the more maverick cinema of *Bonnie and Clyde*, *The Graduate*, and *The Good, the Bad and the Ugly*, making the Elvis movies seem a bit too simple and old fashioned. Music was making tremendous strides very quickly, with artists like Jimi Hendrix reinventing rock guitar and the Beatles ceaselessly changing their approach to something deeper and more challenging.

Speedway was more of the same, Elvis once again playing a race car driver (the idea men desperately attempting to have *Viva Las Vegas*–level box office) and again casting a noted female as the lead actress (Nancy Sinatra, a friend of Presley's since he returned from the army and appeared on her father's TV show). The music was weak, with the notoriously bad "He's Your Uncle, Not Your Dad" among the songs on the soundtrack.

Behind the scenes, Priscilla was becoming more suspicious of Elvis's relationships with his leading ladies, and thus was in California and visiting the set while *Speedway* was being filmed.[1] It was while Elvis was filming *Speedway* that Priscilla called him from Palm Springs to deliver the news that she was pregnant with their first child.

Maybe it was this news that perked up Elvis and made him appear more upbeat during the filming, or perhaps it was also due to being surrounded by old friends like Nancy, Bill Bixby, and director Norman Taurog, but *Speedway* is one of the better formula pictures, and performed more successfully at the box office than any of his films since *Tickle Me* three years earlier. In fact, its box office receipts were nearly double the gross of *Stay Away, Joe* and *Double Trouble* combined. But this was hardly reason enough to continue making movies, especially since Elvis didn't want to continue making them. As a result, Elvis was allowed to finish the remainder of his movie contract working outside of the established formula.

In this one, Elvis plays race car driver Steve Grayson, whose manager and friend, Kenny Donford (Bill Bixby), has mismanaged his winnings. As a result, Steve finds himself in trouble with the Internal Revenue Service for back taxes. Susan Jacks of the IRS (Nancy Sinatra) is assigned to keep an eye on Steve with the intention of taking any prize money he wins racing and putting it toward his $150,000 debt. Of course she ends up falling for Steve. There is some typical comedy, and Gale Gordon (then popular on television for his work with Lucille Ball) is an amusing presence as (of course) a banker. The film features guest appearances by several of the top stock-car drivers of the time, including Richard Petty, Buddy Baker, Cale Yarborough, and Tiny Lund. The soundtrack album netted no hit songs, and only reached number 72 on the charts.

Nancy Sinatra gets a solo number, written by then-boyfriend Lee Hazlewood, and it appears on the *Speedway* soundtrack, making her the first artist to have her own solo number on an Elvis album. Nancy was not the first choice to play Susan. Petula Clark, at the time riding high on the charts with several hits, was originally sought for the role, but she chose instead to do Francis Ford Coppola's *Finian's Rainbow* opposite Fred Astaire (making her Astaire's final dance partner). Clark would make history in 1968 by dueting with Harry Belafonte on her own television special, touching his arm as the two of them sang. Chrysler, the show's sponsor, feared Southern viewers' reaction to her touching a black man, and demanded another take be used. Clark refused, and destroyed all other

Elvis and Nancy Sinatra in *Speedway*

takes, delivering the finished program to the network with the touch intact. The show received high ratings and critical acclaim. Her career at its height, she was unable to appear in *Speedway*.

The *New York Times*, which had skipped reviewing many of the Elvis movies during this period, decided to take a look at this one. The paper was not impressed:

> Just another Presley movie—which makes no great use at all of one of the most talented, important and durable performers of our time. Music, youth and customs were much changed by Elvis Presley 12 years ago; from the 26 movies he has made since he sang "Heartbreak Hotel" you would never guess it.

Even *Variety*, usually pretty sympathetic to Elvis movies, was unimpressed, but still worked hard to be positive:

> Under Norman Taurog's know-how comedy direction even some of the silliness in the Phillip Shuken script gets by as entertainment, but the story lacks the legitimacy of better Presley starrers. However, with Presley in there swinging in his usual style and his own particular brand of lightness, the feature stacks up as an okay entry.

One of the more interesting reviews came from Roger Ebert, who had just started reviewing movies in Chicago the year before. Ebert considered *Speedway* a breath of fresh air, stating:

> You may not believe this, but I was inspired to see Elvis Presley's "Speedway" because of this week's Essay in Time magazine. There were other reasons, too. I hadn't seen an Elvis movie since last summer's *Easy Come, Easy Go*, and after a week of war movies (Mexican, Second and Vietnam) the idea of a nice, relaxed, simple musical held allure. . . . He is as respectable on the screen as Dick Powell ever was, and his recent movies hold no hint of the swivel hips my generation remembers from the Ed Sullivan shows of 1956. Elvis is excessively proper in behavior with his various dates. . . . And so it goes, with Elvis buying a station wagon for a poor family, and Elvis arguing with the tax man, and Elvis climbing into his Plymouth, and Nancy Sinatra still desperately trying, at this late stage of her career, to sing. *Speedway* is pleasant, kind, polite, sweet and noble.

So formula Elvis had finally taken hold, the rocking rebel of the 1950s being completely obliterated by this safe counterpart whose movies achieved success for their old-fashioned way of ignoring any issues. They were clean, wholesome, lightweight, and forgettable. Elvis was ready to abandon his movie career, began preparing a Christmas TV special, and arranged for his final few movies to be more interesting and challenging. The powers that be, realizing the Elvis formula was no longer relevant, allowed Presley to work outside the formula. This resulted in a series of films that, while not among his best, are certainly a lot different than what we might expect.

Speedway's success may have indicated that while the Elvis movies were light and clueless, they might have continued to serve something of a purpose as being a pleasant escape from the seriousness of life, as Roger Ebert indicated. Elvis was more interested in different roles and settings.

Theater owners were pleased, offering these comments to *Box Office*: "This is one of the best Elvis Presley pictures. Song, speed, comedy. This one has it all. The music score is the best one of the year. And Nancy Sinatra is double WOW. Good business. Kids loved it." *Speedway* grossed more than Presley's last nine movies and came in a respectable number 40 among the top box office grossers of 1968. But that was not enough to keep the formula active.

While the race car idea that had been used in the wildly successful *Viva Las Vegas* was not quite as potent when revisited for *Spinout* or *Speedway*, the latter two movies are not to be confused. Douglas Brode in his book *Elvis Cinema and Popular Culture* stated:

> Those who dismiss the Presley musicals invariably see *Spinout* and *Speedway*, owning to similar titles, as the films that are easiest to confuse—the ultimate proof that, by this point, all were produced cookie-cutter fashion, the same script endlessly recycled. When closely considered, though, *Speedway* is the antithesis of *Spinout*. They are the two most different films in the oeuvre. Until *Spinout*, the Presley persona had arced with each successive 1960s picture away from the "good life" that defined male behavior during the early 1960s. In *Spinout*, he experienced a panic attack at the thought that he was transforming into something more mature. Elvis in *Speedway* embodies the opposite of what he'd become in the film. Here, the playboy image is embodied by Kenny (Bixby). Steve (Elvis) finds it offensive. The great irony is that Steve never considers dumping Kenny despite many slights.

It was around this time that Colonel Parker started looking for other deals outside of the movies, realizing that the films were not pulling in the same level of box office as they once had. Elvis was understandably nervous about his stature in entertainment and wanted to return to concentrating on music rather than relying on lackluster soundtrack songs foisted upon him by songwriters with limited skill from the Hill and Range music company.

Elvis was considering a return to live touring, and some time back in the studio for something other than a movie soundtrack, perhaps to appear on television. What he knew for sure is that he wanted to get away from feeling so trapped in Hollywood movies that were projecting an image that embarrassed him. A good indicator of how far his music career had sunk was the release of the compilation album, *Elvis Gold Records Volume 4*, which, despite coming out in February 1968, contained mostly songs from before 1965 and some dating back to 1960, rather than (like previous volumes) being a compilation of his most recent hits. Presley's most recent hits were soundtrack songs that were not hits at all.

The potential of Elvis Presley's unfulfilled movie career continued to hamper his importance to the development of popular music. Something had to change. Elvis had everything to gain, and everything to lose.

CHAPTER 30
Live a Little, Love a Little
(MGM, 1968)

Director: Norman Taurog
Screenplay: Michael A. Hoey and Dan Greenburg, from Greenburg's novel *Kiss My Firm but Pliant Lips*
Producer: Douglas Laurence
Cinematography: Fred J. Koenekamp
Editor: John McSweeny, Jr.
Assistant director: Al Shenberg
Cast: Elvis Presley, Michele Carey, Don Porter, Rudy Vallee, Dick Sargent, Sterling Holloway, Celeste Yarnall, Eddie Hodges, Joan Shawlee, Ann Doran, Mary Grover, Emily Banks, Michael Keller, Merri Ashley, Phyllis Davis, Ursula Menzel, Susan Shute, Edie Baskin, Gabrielle, Ginny Kaneen, Susan Henning, Morgan Windbeil, Benjie Bancroft, Robert Isenberg, Joe Esposito, Lonnie Burr, Thordis Brandt, Mari Aldon, Bruce Hoy, John Hegner, Veronica Ericson, Russ Bender, Heidi Winston, Marcia Mae Jones, Myrna Ross, Gayle Rogers, Hiroko Wanatabe, John Wheeler, Brooke Mills, Morgan Jones, Britt Lomond, Hal Riddle, Gayle Rogers, Bartlett Robinson, Paul Sorenson, James Oliver, Vernon Presley
Songs (in the order performed):
"Wonderful World" (written by Guy Fletcher and Doug Flett; performed by Elvis Presley)
"Edge of Reality" (written by Bill Giant, Bernie Baum, and Florence Kaye; performed by Elvis Presley)
"A Little Less Conversation" (written by Mac Davis and Billy Strange; performed by Elvis Presley; choreographed by Jack Baker)
"Almost in Love" (written by Luiz Bonfá and Randy Starr; performed by Elvis Presley)

No chart success. On its re-release in 2002, "A Little Less Conversation" topped the charts in the United Kingdom, but had little success in the United States.

Released October 23, 1968
Filmed March 11–May 24, 1968
90 minutes
Metrocolor
Aspect ratio: 2.35:1
Released to DVD by Warner Home Video

Live a Little, Love a Little gets kudos for venturing away from formula, but as with *Stay Away, Joe*, it appears that the formula is what structured even the weakest Elvis Presley movies. There is no hook to this film's narrative, and despite limiting the songs and allowing for a more adult theme (Elvis is a photographer for a girlie magazine), the general plot is confusing and ultimately unresolved.

Live a Little, Love a Little starts off like a comedy, with Elvis being pursued by a flighty woman's exuberant Great Dane. The woman (Michele Carey) is representative of the free spirit types from this era, never revealing her identity to Elvis or to us. She changes her name for different people and different moods, kidnaps Elvis, redirects his life, affects his career, and makes him angry. In fact, he seems angry and confused throughout the film and never really gets any conclusions or offers comeuppance. He is baffled by the woman, her relationships with other people (from her ex-husband to delivery boys), and this plot idea fluctuates with the plot of Elvis attempting to work as a photographer for two rival magazines.

The cast is interesting. Dick Sargent of TV's *Bewitched* is Carey's timid ex-husband who has never really left her world, Sterling Holloway and Eddie Hodges are delivery people, Rudy Vallee and Don Porter are rival magazine editors. The girl's Great Dane is reported in several sources as Elvis Presley's own dog, Brutus, but Priscilla Presley insists it was a trained dog for the movie. And the pace is fast, with Elvis racing in a dune buggy from the girl's place to his two jobs that are precariously housed in the same office building. But nothing is ever concrete or gets resolved; it all remains very messy and confusing.

There are highlights. Elvis sings very little, but "A Little Less Conversation," sung to actress Celeste Yarnall, is the best song and became an unlikely hit in a remix version over 20 years later. The song did only average business in the United States, but in other countries it reached number one. On the Elvis Australia website, Yarnall remembered Elvis in an interview:

> I adored Elvis. When I met him for the first time he immediately put me at ease. We had to film our kissing first and neither of us heard the director say, "Cut!" For me, it was love at first kiss! We became

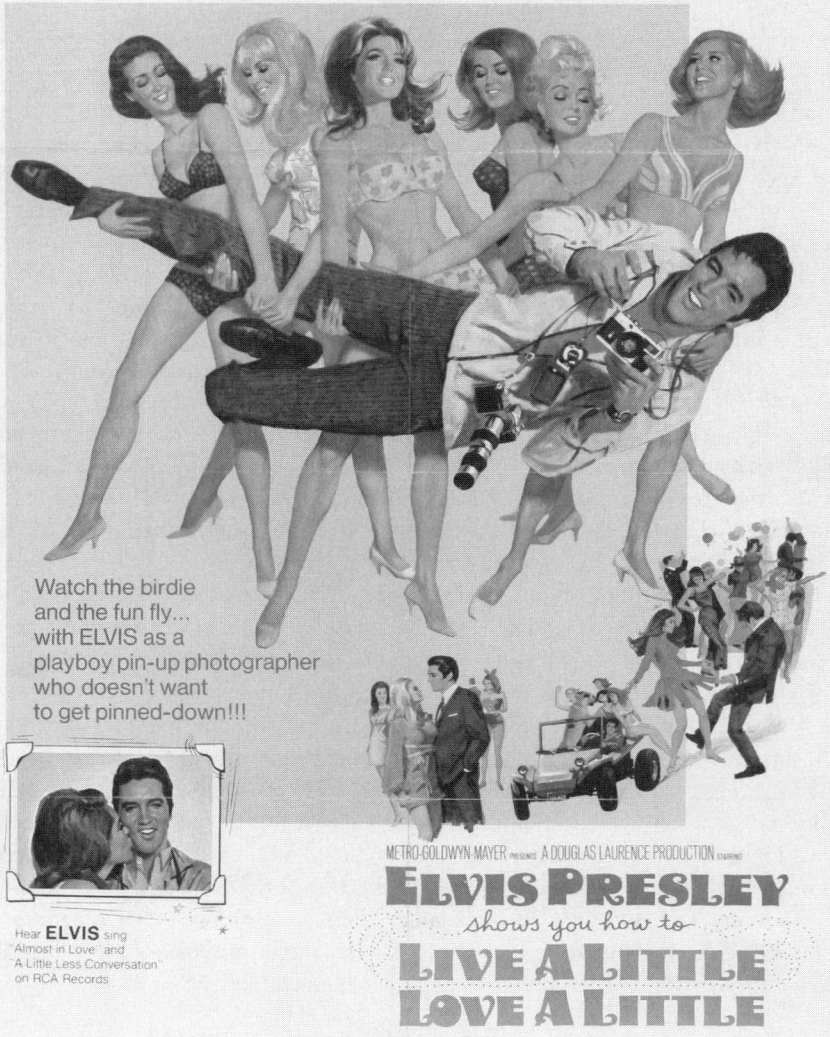

Poster for *Live a Little, Love a Little*

> very good friends. He was warm and kind and full of love. He had this tremendous desire to please people. We watched the funeral of Martin Luther King, Jr. together over lunch in his trailer. He cried. He really cared deeply.

This was not only Elvis Presley's final film with favorite director Norman Taurog, but Taurog's final film in his long career. He retired from directing and began teaching filmmaking at the University of California School of Cinema. Taurog lived 25 more years, but went blind toward the end of his life. He briefly served as director of the Braille Institute.

Variety usually enjoyed the Elvis movies, but they were not impressed with *Live a Little, Love a Little*, stating:

> Story peg—why has Michele Carey effectively kidnapped him?—is sidetracked in banal plotting and trite dialog until the answer not only doesn't matter, it is barely noted at all . . . Songs are dull, physical values are standard, and mediocrity prevails . . . Below average b.o. prospects loom for Metro on general duals.

The film's box office performance was so poor, it did not even see release in some countries, including the United Kingdom. Theater owners were generally unimpressed with this offering as well, reporting in *Box Office*: "One of the poorer grossing Elvis pictures but still playable" and "A little rough for Elvis but they handled it very well." At least one theater seemed pleased with the very differences that turned off other viewers, stating, "Elvis is getting to be a better actor all the time and many people feel the same way."

Live a Little, Love a Little, for all its many flaws, can at least be praised for attempting to investigate another area of the Elvis screen persona—how he would react to having his control taken from him. His screen character never seems to have much control in this movie. There is even a scene where he goes home and finds that all of his belongings are gone and other people are living there. The woman, posing as his sister, moved him out and into her place. This lack of control is unlike the usual Presley persona, but its carefree and irresponsible nature is akin to late sixties idioms. Elvis, being the victim, represents the older perspective.

Elvis was always a good actor, but the material was not always on his side. This is especially true with the confusing narrative, forced risque attitude, and wasted talent that permeates *Live a Little, Love a Little*. Shortly after completing this film, Elvis Presley began work on his triumphant 1968 TV special. It would be perhaps the finest performance of his career.

CHAPTER 31

Elvis: The Elvis Comeback Special

A string of formula lightweight musical comedies and a singing career that relied on unimpressive soundtracks from those movies were what Elvis Presley had to offer during the second half of the 1960s. Meanwhile, the Beatles, the Rolling Stones, Jimi Hendrix, and a number of other artists who had been originally influenced by Elvis were taking the music in new directions. Elvis had been following the trajectory of his career without giving any notice to the progress in musical depth and lyrical content that had permeated the mainstream and made his work seem out of touch. After the release of the gospel song "Crying in the Chapel" in 1965 (which was already five years old at the time), Elvis had generated no chart action with his music, and his films were no longer attracting strong box office numbers.

In June 1968 Elvis Presley was to perform a music special for NBC. And he was nervous. He realized where his status was in entertainment, and knew that if this special was not a success, it could end his career. It seems impossible that a star of Elvis Presley's magnitude had fallen to this level in his career, but the progression of the music he created had left him far behind. His films were sometimes simple and enjoyable, but there was no impact, no progress, no achievement. They were the sort of movies one might watch and find superficially entertaining, but forget just as quickly. Working far beneath his potential, Elvis now had something to prove, perhaps even more than when he came out of the army in 1960.

Elvis had not performed live since 1961. He had not appeared on television since Frank Sinatra's *Welcome Home Elvis* special in 1960 when he returned from the army. But that time he was returning in triumph, his past work having exploded onto popular culture in a manner that rarely occurs. This time, Elvis needed to remind people of a past that they had forgotten. His importance had been eclipsed by the string of movies and soundtracks that seemed archaic in the wake of films like *A Hard Day's Night* and albums like *Are You Experienced* and *Aftermath*.

Colonel Tom Parker, Presley's manager, continued to exhibit the same anticreative decision making that resulted in Elvis's steadily dwindling film career; he wanted Elvis to do a standard Christmas special, similar to what Bing Crosby might have done, where he would sing a few standards, offer a benediction, and bid farewell. Elvis did not want that, and confided to producer Steve Binder that he needed something stronger that would force people to take notice. Elvis realized that he had a choice—to return to his roots as the most important rock and roll artist of the century, or to continue the career trajectory that offered films like *Harum Scarum* and songs like "Yoga Is as Yoga Does."

Elvis had enough of the Colonel's decisions. Presley associate Lamar Fike told Alanna Nash for *Elvis Aaron Presley*:

> The way Colonel structured the original deal with NBC was for a TV special and a movie. He did it over the phone. Afterwards he got a telegram from Tom Sarnoff at NBC, Burbank, which read "Confirming our phone conversation, we have a deal for production of one Elvis feature and one TV special according to terms discussed between us during last couple of days. Congratulations to both of us." Colonel sent a copy off to Elvis in Memphis, and Elvis fired a telegram back: "Is that the best you could do? Respectfully yours, Elvis."

Presley's cousin Billy Smith stated to Nash: "He could have done this so much earlier. But he had to be shoved into a corner and almost kicked before he would bite."

Elvis reportedly still had some trouble standing up to the manager he credited with bringing him from his dirt-poor Tupelo existence to wealth and fame. According to *Careless Love*, he would privately tell producer Binder, "Don't budge, your plan is what I want to do!" Binder put Elvis in total creative control of the program, assisting in production areas that were outside of Presley's area. "I just want to get back to my music," he said.

And get back he did. *Elvis* opened with a close-up of Elvis snarling, "If you're looking for trouble, you came to the right place," the camera then panning back to reveal him trimmed down to his best shape in years, clad in a full-length black leather suit designed by Bill Bellew. This was not the Elvis of *Girl Happy* and *Paradise, Hawaiian Style*. This was the rebel rocker who came out of the South and exploded onto the conservative music scene. This was the man who inspired all that had been going on musically while he'd been in Hollywood making movies. This was the king reclaiming his throne.

The strongest portion of the special featured Elvis sitting comfortably with longtime musician partners Scotty Moore and D. J. Fontana (as well as associates

Elvis scored with his comeback special in December 1968

Charlie Hodge and Alan Fortas) as he played through some of his classic songs while surrounded by ecstatic audience members, and told amusing stories. He lifted the side of his upper lip in a sneer and said, "Remember this? I made 29 pictures looking like this!" He recalled a concert he did in the fifties where the vice squad threatened to arrest him for his lascivious hip-swiveling, stating, "All I could move was my little finger," proceeding to demonstrate while singing "Hound Dog." Elvis indicated that his favorite current bands were the Beatles and the Byrds.

Elvis presented every part of his music that had made him so significant. He barreled through hard rock numbers with hip-swiveling gusto. He gave a soulful reading of "Love Me Tender," and a bluesy presentation of "One Night." He sang gospel, pop, and closed the show with the emotionally stirring "If I Can Dream," showing that he was not above songs with insightful lyrics that confronted the world of today that had seemed to pass him by. Elvis returned to his rightful place at the head of the line. It was a triumph the likes of which had not been seen before, and not since. On completion of taping the special, an exhausted Elvis took a vacation to Palm Springs to recuperate.

The special aired in December. When it concluded, according to *Elvis Aaron Presley*, Presley associate Marty Lacker phoned Elvis and told him, "If you did one thing tonight, you showed people the real Elvis Presley instead of the guy in those movies." Elvis thanked him for saying that.

Critics raved about the performance, which is fascinating in and of itself because entertainment journalists ten years before had attacked Elvis for the same reasons they were now praising him. *Rolling Stone*, which was quickly becoming an important fixture in music journalism since its debut in November 1967, praised Elvis heavily and called the special the finest performance of his career.

Roy Carr and Mick Farren in *Elvis: The Illustrated Record* stated:

> It was like watching a man rediscover his strength, charisma and self respect. It reminded a world that had been all too near forgetting, just how great Presley could be when given the chance. The rock and roll was the wildest he had produced since he'd come out of the army. The gospel music was treated with respect; both it and the ballads were presented without the layers of saccharine that had, all too sadly, become the Presley hallmark over the years.

Critic Jon Landau stated in *Careless Love*: "There is something magical about watching a man who has lost himself find his way back home."

The special was seen by 42 percent of the viewing audience, making it the most watched program of the year, and a huge ratings success for NBC. Elvis realized how much he had missed the excitement of performing live, presenting his music to eager audiences. He decided that he would return to the studio in Memphis and cut an album of diverse songs that exhibited his versatility as a singer. He also told his management to start making arrangements for a full-time touring schedule.

But first he had to finish the last few movies on his contract.

CHAPTER 32

Charro!
(NATIONAL GENERAL PICTURES, 1969)

> **Director:** Charles Marquis Warren
> **Screenplay:** Charles Marquis Warren, from a story by Frederick Louis Fox
> **Producer:** Charles Marquis Warren
> **Cinematography:** Ellsworth Fredericks
> **Editing:** Al Clark
> **Assistant director:** Leslie Gorall
> **Makeup:** Gene Bartlett, William Reynolds
> **Music:** Hugh Montenegro
> **Cast:** Elvis Presley, Ina Balin, Victor French, Barbara Werle, Solomon Sturges, Lynn Kellogg, Paul Brinegar, Harry Landers, Tony Young, James Almanzar, Charles H. Gray, John Pickard, Garry Walberg, Duane Grey, Rodd Redwing, J. Edward McKinley, Robert Luster, James Sikking, Robert Karnes, Christa Lang, John Patino, Arnie Frank, Charlie Hodge, Jacqui Brandt, Megan Timothy, Kathleen Darc
>
> Released March 13, 1969
> Filmed July 22–August 30, 1968
> Alternate title: *Come Sundown, Come Hell*
> 98 minutes
> Gross: $1.5 million

Charro! has been said to be the film that Colonel Parker arranged in the deal with NBC that also included the TV special. In fact, it was a later film, *Change of Habit*, that was part of the NBC deal. *Charro!* was released by National General Pictures, whose only connection to TV networks was working with CBS on a few projects. After filming the special in June in 1968, Elvis took a vacation and then spent July and August working on this western. *Charro!* features no songs other than the title tune sung over the credits. It is produced, written, and directed by Charles Marquis Warren, who had a long track record with movie

Poster for *Charro!*

and TV westerns. It was exactly the type of movie Elvis had been wanting to make for over a decade.

Originally, Elvis was not scheduled to make a western at all. As early as March 1968, Elvis was set to do a Matt Helm type of detective spoof called *That Jack Valentine*. The script for this movie, written by Paul Gaer, had been floating around for about a year. Gaer was originally set to direct and filming was to take place in London. By the time Elvis was considered, Arthur Nadel had replaced Gaer as producer-director and Nancy Sinatra was being considered as the female lead. However, once Elvis was busily working on the TV special in June, Nadel was replaced by Charles Marquis Warren, and the idea for *That Jack Valentine* was dropped in place of a western, *Come Sundown, Come Hell*. Marquis would produce and direct from his own screenplay, which was based on a story by Fredrick Louis Fox.

While *Charro!* is often called a spaghetti western because Elvis sports a grizzled beard and Hugo Montenegro provides the score, *Charro!* is actually structured like a vintage B western, and may very well be the last of its kind. Victor French is sufficiently villainous as head of the outlaw gang with whom Elvis (as Jesse Wade) once rode. The outlaws have committed crimes that they want to pin on their erstwhile member, so they burn his neck with a branding iron and distribute "Wanted" posters that name Jesse as the culprit, and the scar on his neck as an identifying feature. Jesse seeks vengeance on the outlaw gang in order to clear his name.

Elvis is very commanding in the title role, maintaining the unsmiling persona that he'd always tried to cultivate, especially earlier in his film career. The supporting cast is strong, and the story is solid. The screenplay rests on the sort of hackneyed dialog that often permeated B westerns ("My name's Wade. Jess Wade. Mean anything to you?" or "Just make a move. That's all I ask, just make a move"). Perhaps this sort of dialog might not be feasible as late as 1969, but it works reasonably well in context. Warren's direction makes great use of the Arizona location scenery with wide-angle overhead shots as the men are riding, and medium shots framing the action with colorful negative space.

Fans at the time might have concluded that because Elvis had triumphed in the TV special, he was now returning to more serious films rather than the conventional lightweight musicals he'd been grinding out for most of the 1960s. But what Elvis was actually doing was finishing out the remaining movies on his contract so that he could return to live touring. Because the formula musicals were no longer guaranteeing big box office numbers, Elvis was allowed to stretch a bit. *Charro!* finally affords Elvis the opportunity to do a straight movie with no songs. The irony is that the title is his character's nickname, and it loosely translates to "singer."

Variety's review of March 12, 1969, was not terribly impressed, stating:

> Presley strolls through a tedious role that would have driven many another actor up the wall. . . . Even more at fault than Presley, who has occasionally responded in the past to the demands of a good director, is Charles Marquis Warren, who takes credit (or blame?) for the script, the direction and even part of the production.

Perhaps a film like *Charro!* looks better now as an older movie from an unidentifiable period than it did in 1968–1969 among more progressive westerns like *Butch Cassidy and the Sundance Kid* (1969) and *Once Upon a Time in the West* (1968). The *New York Times* was similarly unimpressed:

> His mouth hidden behind the mask of a stubble-like beard, his hair powerfully slicked into place, his walk modest and his manner retiring, Presley appears thoroughly tamed. He treats his part rather as a minor embarrassment, and he seems determined not to push himself in a role that could have used a stronger personality to fill the lapses in the story and the wide open spaces in the dialogue. Of course Presley saves the town. The issue was never in doubt, and not even the rudiments of conflict or of suppressed loyalties exist within the central character.

The rudiments of standard western filmmaking are all here. Elvis is shown taming a wild horse, drinking with a cupped hand out of a swamp, moving slowly and methodically through town as he seeks out the outlaw gang, the former flame who wanted him to go straight, and a sheriff friend, in his quest to clear his name. Montenegro's musical score aptly enhances each scene, helping to drive the action and heighten the suspense. *Charro!* has a great look, a great sound, good acting, and a typical western script. It is by no means great cinema, but it is perfectly competent, and probably the most satisfying Elvis Presley movie since *Viva Las Vegas*.

Apparently *Charro!* was originally much more violent, but a lot of the more violent scenes were edited prior to the film's release. While the executives at NBC were open to Elvis doing a serious western film that could not only capitalize on his name, but also on the popularity of what Clint Eastwood was doing, they realized that violence at the same level as the Eastwood movies might alienate a portion of Presley's loyal fan base. Compromises, therefore, were made between the creative vision and the more business-oriented aspects of the production.

Charro! was not a box office hit, pretty much breaking even. Elvis's fee was nearly half of the film's budget. However at least one theater owner in Texas was quite pleased with the results, stating in *Box Office*: "*Charro!* is what I have been needing to make up for the losses on other pictures. It's different from the usual Elvis line, but people accepted it and we enjoyed good attendance. If I could get one movie a month of this caliber, I'd be very pleased."

Elvis had one more movie on his MGM contract and the movie Colonel Parker had arranged for him to do through NBC along with the TV special. As he concluded his film career, he was finally being allowed to work outside the formula by which he felt creatively limited, but only because this formula no longer made the same money as it once had. A film like *Charro!* is a reasonably good example of what might have been. It is not as strong a western as *Flaming Star* had been, but it is certainly more interesting than musicals like *Harum Scarum* and *Easy Come, Easy Go*.

Presley's acting in *Charro!* was sufficient for a decidedly undemanding role. Had his films been completely separate from his music career, as he so desired, perhaps the standard Elvis movie would have been something more like *Charro!* rather than something like *Clambake* (it is unrealistic to believe that every Elvis Presley movie would have been the caliber of *Jailhouse Rock* or *King Creole*). And Elvis would probably have felt a lot happier and more creatively fulfilled. In any case, the *New York Times* was wrong. Elvis was satisfied with his role in *Charro!* and was pleased with the finished film. But it was not enough for him to continue a movie career that had consistently let him down.

CHAPTER 33
The Trouble with Girls
(MGM, 1969)

Director: Peter Tewksbury
Screenplay: Arnold Peyser and Lois Peyser
Story: Mauri Grashin, from the novel ***Chautauqua*** by Day Keene and Dwight V. Babcock
Producer: Lester Welch
Cinematography: Jacques R. Marquette
Editor: George W. Brooks
Assistant director: John Clark Bowman
Makeup: William Tuttle
Hairstylist: Mary Keats
Cast: Elvis Presley, Marlyn Mason, Nicole Jaffe, Sheree North, Edward Andrews, John Carradine, Anissa Jones, Vincent Price, Joyce Van Patten, Pepe Brown, Dabney Coleman, Bill Zuckert, Pitt Herbert, Anthony Teague, Med Flory, Robert Nichols, Helene Winston, Kevin O'Neal, Frank Welker, John Rubinstein, Charles Briles, Patsy Garrett, Linda Sue Risk, Charles P. Thompson, Leonard Rumery, William Paris, Kathleen Rainey, Hal Pederson, Mike Wagner, Brett Parker, Duke Snider, Susan Olsen, William H. O'Brien, Joe Esposito, Jerry Schilling, the Pacific Palisades High School Madrigals
Songs (in the order performed):
"Almost" (written by Buddy Kaye; performed by Elvis Presley)
"Clean Up Your Own Back Yard" (written by Mac Davis and Billy Strange; performed by Elvis Presley)
"Swing Down Sweet Chariot" (written by Wallis Willis; performed by Elvis Presley)
"Violet (Flower of NYU)" (written by Steven Dueker and Peter Norton Lohstroh; performed by Elvis Presley)
"Signs of the Zodiac" (written by Buddy Kaye and Ben Weisman; performed by Elvis Presley and Marlyn Mason)
"Doodle Doo Doo" (written by Art Kassel and Mel Stitzel; performed by Linda Sue Risk)

> "Clean Up Your Own Back Yard" reached number 35 on the charts
> Released September 3, 1969
> Filmed October 28–November 29, 1968
> 97 minutes
> Metrocolor
> Aspect ratio: 2.35:1
> Released to DVD by Warner Home Video

It is ironic that one of the most delightfully entertaining Elvis Presley movies came along at the very end of his film career, and shortly after Elvis had completed a triumphant monthlong series of live shows at the International Hotel in Las Vegas. Elvis did 57 shows from July 26 to August 28, 1969, and *The Trouble with Girls* was released a week later, despite having been filmed nearly a year earlier.

Along with the successful live shows, Elvis had returned to the charts with "If I Can Dream" from the 1968 TV special; the song rose to number 12, the highest chart position for an Elvis single since "Crying in the Chapel" in 1965. The album *Elvis: TV Special* was even more successful, reaching number eight on the charts.

In the six months since the release of *Charro!*, Elvis returned to the recording studio in Memphis and recorded some of the finest music of his career. Along with the hits "In the Ghetto" (11 weeks on the charts, rising to number three), "Suspicious Minds" (13 weeks on the charts, rising all the way to number one), and "Don't Cry Daddy" (11 weeks on the charts, rising to number six), the albums that came from that session—*From Elvis in Memphis* and *From Memphis to Vegas/From Vegas to Memphis* charted at 13 and 12, respectively. Upon hearing that "Suspicious Minds" reached number one, a pleased Elvis stated, "I've been wrong for so many years, it feels good to be right again."

With top-selling albums and singles on the charts, and an important live show, Elvis Presley's movies were pretty much shunted aside in the realm of his career as well as pop culture. In fact they were of so little importance, *The Trouble with Girls* was not released until a full year after it was filmed. Despite having given up on a movie career and simply completing the rest of his contract, Elvis does not walk through his part with bored indifference. In fact, he seems enthused by his work in this period piece, enjoying the few songs and responding well to the other actors.

Director Peter Tewksbury, who helmed the awful *Stay Away, Joe*, does a significantly better job with this movie from the opening musical sequence to the film's conclusion. In fact, Tewksbury seems most comfortable with the grandiose entertainment scenes, using the widescreen image to offer a great deal of movement throughout the background while centering on action in the fore-

Press kit ad for *The Trouble with Girls*

ground. The entire opening is filled with movement, color, and sound, blending together to present the festive spirit that is maintained throughout the film.

The idea for this film dates back to 1959, with Glenn Ford set for the title role. By 1964, Dick Van Dyke was being considered for the lead. After a series of script changes, MGM sold the project to Columbia in 1965. When that studio could not get the project off the ground, it was sold back to MGM in 1968. It was finally dusted off as a vehicle for Elvis.

The plot is actually the most tangential aspect of the movie. The film is set in 1927 with Elvis playing Walter Hale, manager of a traveling Chautauqua[1] company that rolls into an Iowa town. The town has a scandal brewing with the murder of a local pharmacist (Dabney Coleman). A gambler is accused of the crime, but Walter realizes that it is one of the pharmacist's employees, Nita (Sheree North), with whom he's been having an affair. A subplot has Walter trying to prevent Charlene, the troupe's "Story Lady" (Marlyn Mason), from organizing the performers to form a union.

The relationship between Walter and Charlene fluctuates between romantic and volatile, with nicely choreographed argument sequences alternating with pleasantly shot romantic ones. Actress Marlyn Mason recalled in an interview:

> I had that scene where I am yelling at Elvis and Eddie Andrews, running about the room while Elvis stands and Eddie sits. I loved doing comedy, and this is a loud, fast-talking scene with a lot of movement. At one point, Elvis just breaks up laughing at me and the director Peter Tewksbury kept it in. It is one of my favorite moments in the movie. Later on we are in a scene where a bunch of fireworks are about to go off. Tewksbury wanted a certain reaction from Elvis and had him in close up as he was standing and I was sitting. While he was on camera, I was off camera and started to undo his belt and then his zipper. Elvis was so professional, he just went with it. And the director got the expression he wanted.

The cast is rounded out nicely with up-and-coming talent like Mason and Coleman, child performers like Pepe Brown and Anissa Jones,[2] and seasoned veterans like Vincent Price, Edward Andrews, and John Carradine to anchor the proceedings. The sprightly script, good direction, and strong cast combine to present a perfectly serviceable entertainment. It is not great cinema like *Flaming Star* or *King Creole* had been, but it compares comfortably with *Charro!* as the best movie Elvis had done since *Viva Las Vegas*. There are few songs in the movie and only some are performed by Elvis, and most of them are presented during the last half hour of the movie. They all benefit from the period flavor as well as Presley's renewed enthusiasm for his work.

The *New York Times,* often sharply critical of Presley's formulaic movies, was pleased with this one, stating:

> Peter Tewksbury's "The Trouble with Girls" is a charming though ineptly titled comedy with one fortunate murder, several pleasant songs, Elvis Presley, and a huge cast all of whom, down to the last extra, seem willing to act their fool heads off. The plot, which hinges on what a small-town hard-luck woman (Sheree North) rightly does to a lecherous druggist (Dabney Coleman), deserves little attention.

But the situation, a traveling Chautauqua making a small-town stand in the mid-1920s, deserves a lot of attention—which it gets in a film that succeeds so amiably in its parts that the relative weakness of the whole doesn't matter too desperately.

Variety, however, who had always responded open-mindedly to the Elvis movies, was unhappy with this feature, stating:

> Elvis Presley is lost in this one. Without star's usual assortment of 10 to 12 songs, and numbers cut down to a bare three, picture has little to offer. Title suggests a gay comedy but it's a mass of contrived melodramatics and uninteresting performances that do not jell into anything but program fare. All of the voltage of the Presley name will be required to get it over.

The Trouble with Girls is not completely without flaws. The erratic pacing, tangential plotline, and uneven structure can sometimes falter. At other times, though, the pace and structure are effective in context, maintaining a discernible rhythm throughout. Director Tewksbury seems especially comfortable with the material. Marlyn Mason recalled:

> I got the job because Tewksbury wanted me. He said if I didn't play Charlene he'd walk off the picture. He got along well with Elvis, and the set was always a lot of fun. I looked forward to going to work every morning. There was nothing fake about Elvis. He was very genuine and worked hard to do a good job. One thing I will never forget. We were talking on the set once, and he became very serious. He said, "all I ever wanted was to make one really great picture. I know people in this town laugh at me." It was heartbreaking. I am still sad when I think about it. Elvis was a lovely man, and a fine actor. If only he had more opportunity to show that in his movie career.

The Trouble with Girls continues the precedent set by *Charro!* wherein the three films Elvis made after his 1968 TV special were his best in years. They avoided the set formula, and provided ample opportunity for Elvis to exhibit talents that had been suppressed by the creative limitations of his other movies. Sadly, it was too late to matter.

CHAPTER 34
Change of Habit
(UNIVERSAL, 1969)

Director: William A. Graham
Screenplay: James Lee, S. S. Schweitzer, and Eric Bercovici, based on a story by John Joseph and Richard Morris
Producer: Joe Connelly
Assistant Director: Phil Bowles
Cinematography: Russell Metty
Editor: Douglas Stewart
Makeup: Bud Westmore
Hairstylist: Clair Holgate
Cast: Elvis Presley, Mary Tyler Moore, Barbara McNair, Jane Elliot, Leora Dana, Ed Asner, Robert Emhardt, Regis Toomey, Doro Merande, Ruth McDevitt, Richard Carlson, Nefti Millet, Laura Figueroa, Lorena Kirk, Virginia Vincent, David Renard, Ji-Tu Cumbuka, William Elliott, Rodolfo Hoyos, Jr., Tony DeCosta, Stella Garcia, Jim Beach, Timothy Carey, Robert De Anda, Linda Garay, Pepe Hern, Mario Aniov, Ray Ballard, Frank Corsentino, John Daheim, Paul Factor, Rita Conde, Steve Conte
Songs (as featured):
   "Change of Habit" (music by Ben Weisman and lyrics by Buddy Kaye; performed by Elvis Presley)
   "Rubberneckin'" (written by Dory Jones and Bunny Warren; performed by Elvis Presley)
   "Have a Happy" (written by Dolores Fuller; performed by Elvis Presley)
   "Let Us Pray" (music by Ben Weisman and lyrics by Buddy Kaye; performed by Elvis Presley)

"Rubberneckin'" was released as the B side of the hit single "Don't Cry Daddy," but it was the A side that charted.

Released November 10, 1969
Filmed March 7–May 2, 1969
93 minutes

Technicolor
Aspect ratio 1.85:1
Released to DVD by Universal Studios Home Video

Change of Habit was produced as part of the deal Colonel Parker arranged that also included the 1968 TV special. Elvis could no longer demand a million dollars a movie, his films no longer turning the level of profit that would warrant such an advance. However when Parker negotiated $1.25 million for the special and a movie, he was pleased to still be able to secure a million dollars for his star. Produced by NBC by longtime TV producer Joe Connelly (cocreator of *Leave It to Beaver* and *The Munsters*), *Change of Habit* was originally set to be a star vehicle for Mary Tyler Moore. However, when Elvis came on board, it became his movie, with Mary in support.

Mary Tyler Moore, Jane Elliot, and Barbara McNair portray nuns who come to the inner city to work incognito with the neediest people. Elvis is a ghetto doctor with the same idealism. The conflict deals with perspective. Elvis does not understand the nuns' approach, and they are unable to initially appreciate his methods.

As Elvis Presley's final acting role in a movie, the character of Dr. John Carpenter is effective, but director William A. Graham recalled in an interview for David Adams at the Elvis Australia website that there were portions of the performance where Elvis was lacking:

> When I first started directing I had gone to the Neighborhood Playhouse in New York, which was a famous acting school. So when I started working with Elvis, I went up to his house and we were running some scenes in the movie and I found he could handle humor quite well and he could also handle a fight scene. He could do an argument very well, very believably. But in certain other areas, like if it was a love scene or if there was some subtlety that was called for he was a little self-conscious. So I decided that we could do some work in that area. So I started teaching him some of the elements of what they called The Method, some of the things that I'd learned at the Neighborhood Playhouse.
>
> Well, the Colonel got wind of it and one day he called me into his office and he said, "I hear you've been going up to Elvis, Sonny." And I said, "Yeah, that's right. I've been working with him. We've been working on the acting and he's really coming along very well." So he said, "Well listen, Sonny," he said, "Let me tell you something. We make these movies for a certain price and they make a certain amount

Elvis, Barbara McNair, and Mary Tyler Moore in *Change of Habit*

of money, no less and no more." So he said, "Don't you be goin' for no Oscar, Sonny, because we ain't got no tuxedos." And so that was my reprimand. I kept on going up to see Elvis, but the Colonel was a little bit suspicious that we were gonna take the movie off in a little bit different direction from Elvis' normal stock in trade, and we did.

Change of Habit continues the style as presented by both *Charro!* and *The Trouble With Girls*: limited songs, a better script, and stronger direction. Elvis continued to enjoy working outside of the formula by which he'd felt creatively trapped, but it was still not enough to interest him in continuing with a movie career. Perhaps had this happened in 1965, it might have worked out. But director Graham's comments indicate that while Elvis continued to be interested in learning more about being a better actor, the Colonel continued to thwart any plans for Elvis to expand his range.

Elvis maintained a good attitude throughout the production, as Graham recalled for Adams:

> Elvis was wonderful to work with. Elvis was the nicest man I ever met in my life. He was the politest man I ever met. He called everyone sir or ma'am, you know, starting with the crafts service man with the guard at the gate, all the way up to the head of the studio. Everyone was sir. He was very responsive to direction. He didn't show any of the kind of ego, the kind of temperament that you would expect from

a big star—and he was a big star. He was wonderful with the crew. He didn't like to go into the commissary at lunchtime because people would pester him for autographs, so very often he would eat in his trailer. And then quite often he'd come out and sit around on the set and bring out his guitar and he would sing and play for us. You know, he'd play some of the old favorites like "Hound Dog," or "'Blue Suede Shoes" and this was wonderful for us. This was really a thrill.

Change of Habit works well alongside Elvis Presley's songs like "If I Can Dream" or "In the Ghetto," which took an idealistic, compassionate approach to the plight of the downtrodden, the latter song specifically centering upon those who are victims of a slum environment. These were the sort of issues Elvis avoided during much of the sixties, and now that he was confronting them, his perspective on such things became clearer.

The film also does not expect Elvis to carry the story alone. Mary Tyler Moore was a popular TV actress who'd done some films (this would be her last movie until *Ordinary People* in 1980, but she would score with her own TV series during most of the 1970s). As a love interest for Elvis, the romantic scenes were guarded because she is playing a nun whose status is not known by Dr. Carpenter. Their relationship builds slowly and tastefully, his romantic interest in her thwarted in a manner where he never catches on to her being a nun, until finally being told toward the end of the movie. (His response is, "I'll be damned.") Emotionally stirring scenes featuring the doctor using modern methods in response to the actions of an autistic child allow Elvis to do his most serious dramatic work since his films of the fifties.

This is not to say that *Change of Habit* is particularly good cinema. The situations are often too pat, while the characters show little depth. Strong emotional scenes such as Elvis with the autistic child, or Mary fending off an attempted rape by an angry and confused ghetto youth, allow the actors to stretch their abilities to some extent, but overall the movie remains fairly standard and its idealistic message is just part of the plotline. Still, it was the sort of thing Elvis would like to have done more frequently, and if a movie like *Change of Habit* had been an opportunity while he was slogging through the likes of *Harum Scarum* and *Paradise, Hawaiian Style*, it might have broken things up enough to keep the singer interested and engaged. However, as the Colonel told Graham, "Don't go looking for no Oscar."

Change of Habit's greatest accomplishment is establishing Elvis Presley beyond his formula films and presenting his significance to the modern era. He was no longer the relic from another time that he appeared to be in *Easy Come, Easy Go* or *Speedway*. He was now shown as aware of the bigger picture and able to confront and make his presence known in the realm of contemporary problems.

Variety stated:

> The Joe Connelly production carries humor to lighten its dramatic overtones, and its intriguing idea has a well-enough-constructed plotline to flesh out its premise for good family fare. Slight obscurity exists in the doctor's unawareness of the true identity of the girls assigned to him, but this is only a minor point for which subsequent action compensates. Presley displays his customary easy presence. He is strongly cast as the understanding medico.

By the time *Change of Habit* hit theaters toward the end of 1969, Elvis fans had clearly moved on from his movie career. Enthralled by the TV special and excited by his new recordings and live shows, the fans appeared to feel the movies were no longer a significant part of Elvis Presley's work. *Change of Habit* ended its initial week's box office at number 17 on *Variety*'s chart. However, it appears those who did see it were pleased. An exhibitor in Michigan wrote in *Box Office* magazine: "Of all the Elvis movies, I liked this one best. There as a good story behind it not a lot of singing and dancing. It was good entertainment." Another theater owner stated, "Good picture, good supporting cast. Elvis is lately showing that he is a very good actor and we hope to see him grow more with this type of performance."

There would, of course, no longer be any growth for Elvis as an actor. *Change of Habit* ended his career as a movie actor. Only documentaries of live shows would follow.

We can imagine what Elvis Presley's film career could have been, basing our thoughts on projects Elvis was forced to turn down such as *The Defiant Ones* and *Thunder Road*. The actors who worked with him, and whose own careers were not limited in scope, all seem to believe that had Elvis been allowed to stretch as an actor, he could have been an Oscar winner. The fact that Colonel Parker, even on what was already known to be Elvis Presley's last movie, reprimanded the director for spending extra time working with Elvis on his acting gives us a good idea why any growth was thwarted. To the anticreative Colonel Parker, Elvis Presley was a product.

His movie career over, his songs back at the top of the charts, Elvis Presley looked forward to the new decade of the 1970s as one of real promise. He returned to live touring and continued to record. His lifestyle also became more indulgent and excessive. As a result, this promising decade was one he would, sadly, not survive.

CHAPTER 35

The Concert Films

First there was *Elvis*, the 1968 TV special that triumphantly returned Elvis Presley to the forefront of popular culture. Then Elvis finished out his movie contract by making three movies that avoided the formula that was lightweight, creatively limiting, and, ultimately played out. His records were lurking at the top of the charts once again. At about the same time, he returned to the live stage.

In 1970, producer Howard F. Soklow and director Dennis Sanders put together a documentary entitled *Elvis: That's the Way It Is*. It allowed fans to look at the creative process at work. The movie showed Presley's preparation and various performances, in which he capitalizes on having fought his way out of the morass of forgettable movies and lackluster soundtrack albums that had defined his career for too many years.

Two years later, producer-directors Pierre Adidge and Robert Abel offered the similar documentary *Elvis on Tour*. These final two movies are not a part of Elvis Presley's filmography in terms of his acting, but they are Elvis films in the technical sense.

Elvis: That's the Way It Is seems a bit dated in its filmmaking style, with the sort of split screen, nonlinear structure that was popular at the time (it was recut in a 2001 "special edition" that serves its central figure much better). Fan comments, an Elvis convention in Europe, and other such tangents seem like dross (and are missing from the later recut). But when the film focuses on Elvis as a master showman or his creative process during rehearsals, it offers a sense of how hard he worked and how dedicated to the material he was. Of course the concerts offer a nostalgic nod to the classic rockers that made him such a phenomenon in the 1950s, but his choice to also include lesser-known rockers ("Patch It Up") or newer hits by others (Tony Joe White's "Polk Salad Annie") are even more interesting. When presenting his take on "I Just Can't Help

Believing," Elvis tells his audience, "B. J. Thomas has a new hit out. [pause during applause] And I don't much care for it," netting a big laugh from the capacity crowd and a chuckle from Elvis himself. An outstanding performance of Simon and Garfunkel's "Bridge over Troubled Water" might be the first concert film's highlight.

In order to better examine Elvis Presley's place in 1970, we have to remind ourselves that it was a strong decade for popular music. The albums released that year include the following:

Let It Be (the Beatles)
Willy and the Poor Boys (Creedence Clearwater Revival)
Deja Vu (Crosby, Stills, Nash, and Young)
Bitches Brew (Miles Davis)
Morrison Hotel (the Doors)
Workingman's Dead and *American Beauty* (Grateful Dead)
Volunteers (Jefferson Airplane)
All Things Must Pass (George Harrison)
Moondance (Van Morrison)

And this is only a small sampling of that year's releases. Some are the best albums by that particular artist or group. All have lived on as enduring classics in their field.

It was smart for RCA to release *Elvis: Worldwide 50 Gold Award Hits*, which is a box set collecting all of Elvis Presley's top singles, from his first RCA hits like "Heartbreak Hotel" and "Hound Dog" to songs from the Memphis sessions released only a year earlier, like "Suspicious Minds" and "In the Ghetto." Another song from the Memphis sessions, "Kentucky Rain," was also included in this box set, and that was a current hit, having reached number 16 on the charts. That same year the documentary hit theaters; an album featuring songs from the documentary was on the charts; and a song recorded live in concert, "The Wonder of You," became a Top 10 hit. While 1970 was an extremely prolific year for music, Elvis held his own and maintained the momentum of his comeback two years earlier. In 1971 he reached back into his country roots and released an album of traditional country songs featuring work by the likes of Bill Monroe and Ernest Tubb. *Elvis Country: I'm 10,000 Years Old* is one of the finest albums in Elvis Presley's career.

Elvis on Tour is probably the better concert film from a cinematic perspective, but it also shows Elvis evolving into the bloated, besequined Vegas entertainer that would consume his status by the end of the decade. A 1972 hit, "Burning Love," is perhaps Presley's last truly strong rock and roll recording, after which he settled a bit too comfortably as a performance icon whose grandiose readings

Press kit ad for *Elvis: That's the Way It Is*

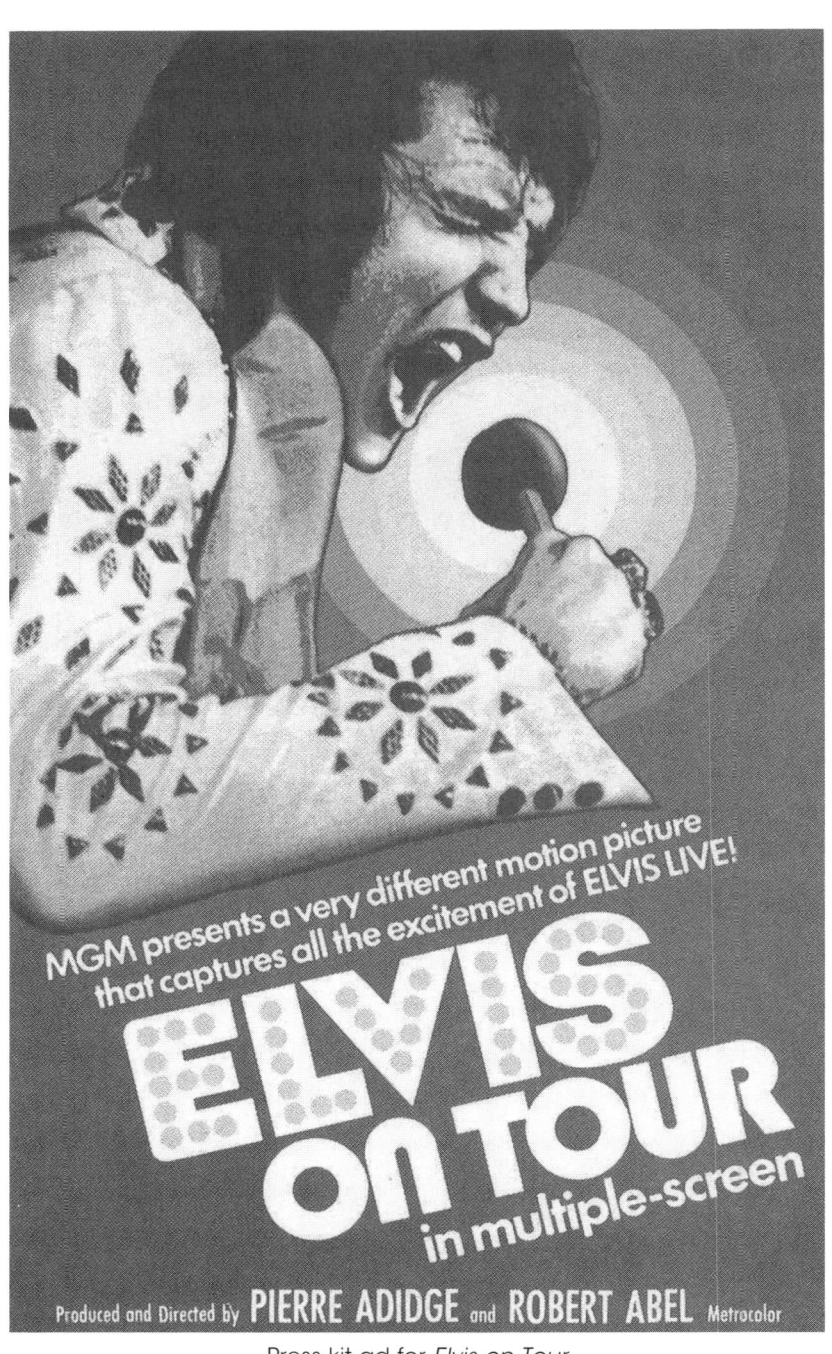

Press kit ad for *Elvis on Tour*

of "An American Trilogy" and "My Way" seemed at odds with the creator of the rock and roll attitude.

The next big event in Elvis Presley's career was a satellite hookup that was designed to broadcast a live show in Hawaii throughout the world—something unprecedented in 1973. Sadly, *Elvis: Aloha from Hawaii* was the beginning of the end.

CHAPTER 36
The Final Years

The idea of presenting an Elvis Presley concert throughout the world on TV via satellite was no doubt inspired by the use of satellite broadcasting for Muhammad Ali's prizefights. In the case of Elvis, an album of the event was produced and rushed into release shortly afterward.

Elvis: Aloha from Hawaii was an enormous event in its time, showing a smiling, passionate Elvis Presley completely owning the stage and fully committing to each song. It is heavy on his classic hits, but also features a few offbeat items. He does a beautiful job with George Harrison's "Something" and Hank Williams's mournful "I'm So Lonesome I Could Cry," which took on a deeper meaning, as his divorce from Priscilla was imminent.

Lamar Fike told Alanna Nash for her book, *Elvis Aaron Presley: Revelations from the Memphis Mafia*:

> We did it at the Honolulu Convention Center Arena. Even though it was a television show, the live audience was asked to donate what they could. Elvis wanted every cent—even from the merchandising—to go to the Kui Lee Cancer Center Fund. Kui Lee had written "I'll Remember You," one of Elvis's favorite songs. They raised three times what they expected.

Elvis also slimmed down for the concert, reportedly only consuming 500 or 600 calories per day. The resulting soundtrack album from this concert was on the charts for 19 weeks and made it all the way to number one. It was Elvis Presley's first number one album in nine years. It was also his last.

There have been many discussions about just what caused Elvis Presley's gradual meltdown after yet another recent triumph. Some believe he simply felt he had managed to reach all of his goals, to prove himself and his work as continually significant and timeless, and simply got tired of being Elvis Presley. Indulgences with prescription drugs had been a problem since the army years, and only escalated, resulting in mood swings that ended up in animosities among some of his longest and closest associates. He continued to tour, drugs and poor diet making this once-handsome man appear sweating and bloated. Even during his final years, when his weight gain had ballooned considerably, Elvis never lost his magnificent voice. Fans still attended his concerts, he was still able to pack large arenas, and when he would fog out on lyrics, he had the presence of mind to make a joke about it. His instinctive ability as a master showman never let him down.

Things got so bad by the middle of the decade, a group of disgruntled former employees wrote the book *Elvis: What Happened?* which revealed a side of Elvis Presley of which his fans were unaware. A paperback tell-all chronicling the prescription drug abuse, the dietary indulgences, and the sometimes violent mood swings became a popular best seller, leaving Elvis deeply hurt and feeling betrayed.

Elvis Presley died of a heart attack on August 16, 1977. In the wake of his death the scandalous stories that had been revealed just prior to his passing appear to have taken hold and tarnished his legacy. There are those who look upon Elvis Presley as a bloated, besequined, overrated relic whose work has not managed to retain its impact, and whose contribution was merely a stepping-stone to a much richer period that would follow. Of course this is nonsense. Elvis Presley is the single most important figure in the history of rock and roll and, as Dave Marsh wrote in his book, *Elvis*, "a true giant of the modern era." Presley's earliest work especially contains more than the seeds of the music—it holds every aspect of its power and appeal.

While *Change of Habit* was the final narrative movie Elvis made, he continued to get occasional offers, even as late as 1976, a year before the singer died. Barbra Streisand approached him to play the male lead in her production (with Jon Peters) of *A Star Is Born*, a part that eventually went to Kris Kristofferson after Elvis turned it down. Elvis was originally enthusiastic about the possibility of playing a solid dramatic lead in major motion picture opposite a top Hollywood star. However, Colonel Parker objected to the role of a washed-up singer who hits the skids as his wife's career flourishes, and the fact that Elvis would have to share top billing with Streisand.

Thus, the final chance Elvis had to offer one last dramatic performance in a major Hollywood production was again thwarted by the Colonel. At the end of Elvis Presley's life, very little had changed. The movies Elvis Presley left behind present several examples of how talent can be undernourished in show business. But, in retrospect, even the lightweight musicals offer a sense of campy fun that overshadows any creative limitations Elvis may have faced. And his best work displays another aspect of a brilliant entertainer whose talents were many and whose impact on popular music continues to resonate with every recorded song.

Notes

Chapter 1

1. Released on the Decca label in 1954 to little success, it was re-released in 1955 after being used in the movie and became a huge hit that has lived on.
2. Jerry Lewis told this writer that he recalls Elvis as one of the nicest people he met in show business, adding, "We had a lot of fun when we were both at Paramount." Elvis cited Dean Martin as one of his favorite pop vocalists and loved the Martin and Lewis movies. He was also a big fan of Lewis's solo ventures, especially *The Nutty Professor* (1963), which John Lennon also cited as his favorite American comedy film.

Chapter 2

1. Not to be confused with Joe DeRita, who is best known as Curly-Joe of the Three Stooges. Before joining the Stooges in 1958, he did appear in other films, including some westerns. But this is a different actor.
2. The songs, composed by Ken Darby, were credited to Darby's wife Vera Matson and Elvis Presley due to a contract arrangement.
3. An alternate ending where Elvis does not die was filmed but never used.

Chapter 3

1. It should be pointed out that this occurred during only one of the three appearances Elvis made on the program.
2. After his mother died, Elvis refused to ever watch this movie again.

3. Two versions of the song "Loving You" appear in the movie: an up-tempo version played over the opening credits, and a slower version that Elvis performs in the film. It is the slow version that is released as a single.

Chapter 4

1. His country-tinged "Blue Christmas" and his bluesy rocker "Santa Claus Is Back in Town" appeared on this album and have since become Yuletide staples.

Chapter 6

1. An eighth Top 40 hit was released posthumously.
2. Gilson was famously shot to death by his ex-wife in 1962 at the age of twenty-eight. The courts ruled it justifiable homicide.

Chapter 8

1. The songs "Britches" and "Summer Kisses, Winter Tears" were recorded but not included in the film.
2. Robert Wagner claimed to have been offered this role, but other accounts state that Elvis was the only one considered for the part after the Sinatra-Brando deal fell through.
3. During the one song sequence the character played by actor Richard Jaeckel does not have a dance partner, so he picks up a chair and dances with it. One of the lyrics in Elvis Presley's classic song "Jailhouse Rock" is "If you can't find a partner use a wooden chair."

Chapter 10

1. This was to be Maxwell's most prominent role in movies. In 1981, the thirty-nine-year-old actress and her husband were shot to death during a robbery attempt.
2. Although she was playing Presley's mother, Lansbury was only nine years older than Elvis. A year later in *The Manchurian Candidate* she would play the mother of Laurence Harvey, who was only three years her junior.

Chapter 11

1. Bruce Springsteen has occasionally performed "Follow That Dream" in concert as part of his encore.

Chapter 12

1. Ed Asner's film debut. He would later become famous on television for *The Mary Tyler Moore Show* and *Lou Grant*.
2. The 1937 film was, for years, retitled *Battling Bellhop* for television due to its similar title to the Presley movie.
3. Montgomery, Young's third of five wives, would divorce him a year later due to his alcoholism. Young shot his fifth wife, Kim Schmidt, to death in October 1978 after three weeks of marriage, then turned the gun on himself. No motive for the murder-suicide was ever made clear.

Chapter 16

1. There are actually two songs entitled "Kissin' Cousins" in the movie—the one that plays over the credits, and the up-tempo second cut that comes later in the movie.

Chapter 17

1. Penned by Presley associate and bodyguard, Red West.

Chapter 22

1. *The Sons of Katie Elder* was cowritten by frequent Elvis Presley screenwriter Allan Weiss. It is the only non-Elvis movie he wrote.

Chapter 29

1. Priscilla stated in *Elvis and Me* that while she realized there was some flirting between Elvis and Nancy Sinatra, she knew it led to nothing, and considered Nancy a friend. In fact, it was Nancy Sinatra who threw a baby shower for Priscilla.

Chapter 33

1. A circuit Chautauqua would travel about and set up tents, presenting entertainment and educational enlightenment to small-town people.
2. Jones was popular on TV's *Family Affair*. This was her only movie. She died of a massive drug overdose in August 1976, one year before Elvis Presley's death.

Bibliography

Books

Bartel, Pauline. *Reel Elvis*. Dallas, Tex.: Taylor, 1994.
Beatles. *The Beatles Anthology*. New York: Chronicle Books, 2002.
Brode, Douglas. *Elvis Cinema and Popular Culture*. Jefferson, N.C.: McFarland, 2006.
Carr, Roy, and Mick Farren. *Elvis: The Illustrated Record*. New York: Harmony Books, 1982.
Clayton, Rose, and Dick Heard, eds. *Elvis Up Close: In the Words of Those Who Knew Him Best*. Atlanta: Turner, 1994.
Cotten, Lee. *All Shook Up: Elvis Day by Day, 1954–1977*. Ann Arbor, Mich.: Popular Culture, 1998.
Goldman, Albert. *Elvis Presley*. New York: McGraw-Hill, 1981.
Guralnick, Peter. *Careless Love: The Unmaking of Elvis Presley*. New York: Back Bay Books, 2000.
Guttmacher, Peter. *Elvis! Elvis! Elvis!* New York: MetroBooks, 1997.
Hopkins, Jerry. *Elvis*. New York: Simon and Schuster, 1971.
Kanter, Hal. *So Far, So Funny*. Jefferson, N.C.: McFarland, 1998.
Lichter, Paul. *The Boy Who Dared to Rock: The Definitive Elvis*. New York: Doubleday Dolphin, 1978.
Marsh, Dave. *Elvis*. New York: Times Books, 1982.
Miller, Jim, ed. *The Rolling Stone History of Rock and Roll*. New York: Random House, Rolling Stone Press, 1976.
Nash, Alanna. *Elvis Aaron Presley: Revelations from the Memphis Mafia*. With Billy Smith, Marty Lacker, and Lamar Fike. New York: HarperCollins, 1995.
Noel, Chris. *Filming Girl Happy*. Create Space, 2012.
Presley, Priscilla Beaulieu. *Elvis and Me*. With Sandra Harmon. New York: Berkley Books, 1986.
Richards, Keith. *Life*. New York: Little, Brown, 2010.

Stanley, David E. *The Elvis Encyclopedia*. With Frank Coffey. Santa Monica, Calif.: General, 1994.
Wallis, Hal, and Charles Higham. *Starmaker: The Autobiography of Hal Wallis*. New York: Macmillan, 1980.

Periodicals

Billboard
Box Office
Classic Images
Films in Review
Jet
Memphis Press-Scimitar
Motion Picture Exhibitor
New York Times
New Yorker
Rolling Stone
Variety

Websites

Elvis History Blog: www.elvis-history-blog.com
Elvis Australia: www.elvis.com.au
Elvis Presley Official Site: www.elvis.com
IMDb (Internet Movie Database): www.imdb.com

Index

Acuff, Roy, 29
Adams, David, 253–254
Adams, Julie, 171, 174, 176, 177
Adams, Nick, 25
The Addams Family, 41
Adventures of Robin Hood, 39
Albertson, Jack, 138
"All Shook Up," 6, 22, 24, 37, 47, 114, 159, 269
American Bandstand, 214
Andress, Ursula, 127, 129, 131
Andrews, Edward, 250
Andy Griffith Show, 92, 95
Angels With Dirty Faces, 39
"Anna Lee," 12
Annie Oakley, 66
"Are You Lonesome Tonight," 60–61
Arnold, Eddy, 3, 29, 216, 220
Astaire, Fred, 229
Atkins, Chet, 2
Austin, Gene, 2

Bailey, Raymond, 43
Baker, Frankie, 187
Baker, Joby, 165
"Barefoot Ballad," 138
Barnum, P. T., 184
Beach Boys, 55, 120, 158, 212

the Beatles, 3, 4, 95, 133, 141, 151, 158, 161, 164, 165, 167, 176, 190, 196, 197, 198, 208, 210, 212, 219, 228, 238, 240, 258
The Beatles Anthology, 4, 197, 269
Beau James, 110
Beaulieu, Priscilla. *See* Presley, Priscilla
Becket, 87, 206
Belafonte, Harry, 229
Benedict, Billy, 187
Bergman, Ingrid, 43
Berle, Milton, 4, 7
Berman, Pandro S., 25
Bernds, Edward, 168, 171, 172, 173
Berry, Chuck, 4, 36, 49, 55
Betz, Carl, 199, 200
Beverly Hillbillies, 95, 137, 187
The Big House, 29
"A Big Hunk of Love," 50, 51
"Big Love, Big Heartache," 159
Billy Ward's Dominoes, 214
Bixby, Bill, 218, 229, 232
Black, Bill, 1, 2, 3, 4, 16, 19, 27, 36
Blackboard Jungle, 2, 25
Blackman, Joan, 80, 83, 86, 100, 104
Blackwell, Otis, 6, 37, 55, 109, 110, 114, 118, 120, 159, 171, 176
Blair, Nicky, 147

Blondell, Joan, 223, 226
Blue Hawaii, 72, 78, 79, 80–88, 92, 95, 96, 99, 104, 105, 108, 112, 113, 114, 116, 124, 126, 128, 130, 139, 158, 163. 168, 191, 193, 202, 214, 228
"Blue Suede Shoes," 6, 54, 55, 57, 255
Bogart, Humphrey, 13, 42, 96, 102, 153
Bonnie and Clyde, 208, 212, 228
Boone, Pat, 36
Bop Girl, 35
"Bossa Nova Baby," 128, 131
Bowery Boys, 103, 170, 172, 173, 174, 194
Bowery Boys Meet the Monsters, 174
Box Office, 14, 19, 23, 32, 59, 60, 86, 105, 184, 191, 204, 214, 256
Brand, Neville, 11
Brando, Marlon, 64, 131, 153, 220
Breathless, 49
Brennan, Walter, 182
Britt, Allen, 187
Brode, Douglas, 167, 232
Bronson, Charles, 100, 103
Brooks, Peter, 166
Brown, James, 214
Brown, Roy, 2
Brute Force, 29
"Burning Love," 258
Butch Cassidy and the Sundance Kid, 245
Butterworth, Donna, 193–195
Buttram, Pat, 157
the Byrds, 164, 240

Cagney, James, 42
Campbell, William, 9, 12–13
Canby, Vincent, 184
Cannon, Hughie, 187
"Can't Help Falling in Love," 80, 81, 83, 86
Cárdenas, Elsa, 127, 129, 131
Careless Love, 42, 139, 159, 208, 214, 239, 241, 269
Carradine, John, 250
Casablanca, 7, 39
Cash, Johnny, 1, 15

"Catch a Falling Star," 49
Change of Habit, 242, 252–256, 263
Chaplin, Charlie, 123, 138, 273
Charles, Ray, 143, 144, 20
Charro! 94, 242–246, 248, 250, 251, 254
Cisco Kid, 66
Clambake, 216–221, 246
Clark, Petula, 229
Classic Images, 12–13
"C'mon Everybody," 146
Cochran, Eddie, 55
Coleman, Dabney, 250
The Commancheros, 98
Como, Perry, 49, 108, 184
Connelly, Joe, 253
The Conqueror, 110
Cool Hand Luke, 212
Corey, Wendell, 16, 20, 22, 167
Cotton Candy Land, 118
Cowan, Jerome, 187
Craig, Yvonne, 118, 121, 134, 135, 139
Cramer, Floyd, 3, 36
the Crew Cuts, 36
Crosby, Gary, 165
Crowther, Bosley, 59, 96, 105, 131, 141, 220
Crudup, Arthur, 1–2
"Crying in the Chapel," 164
Curtis, Tony, 17
Curtiz, Michael, 38, 39, 40, 45, 57, 62, 64, 68, 98, 103

Daily News, 7
Darby, Ken, 12
A Date With Elvis, 50
Dave Clark Five, 161
Davis, Bette, 43
Day, Annette, 213, 214
Day, Doris, 110
Dean, James, 4, 12, 25, 37, 40, 87, 131, 153
Dean, Quentin, 223
Del Rio, Dolores, 63, 66, 68
Demarest, William, 143, 147
Dirty Harry, 64

"Do the Clam," 162, 163, 164
Dodge City, 39
Domasin, Larry, 127, 130, 132
Domino, Fats, 4, 36, 37
Donna Reed Show, 200
"Don't Be Cruel," 6, 8, 37, 47, 114, 159
"Don't Cry Daddy," 248
Don't Knock the Twist, 139
"Don'tcha Think It's Time," 52
Dooley, Bill, 187
Double Trouble, 62, 210, 211–215, 229
Douglas, Donna, 186, 187, 188, 189, 190
Drury, James, 11
Dunne, Phillip, 71, 72, 75, 78

Each Dawn I Die, 29
"Earth Boy," 113
Earth vs. Flying Saucers, 138
East Side Kids, 138
Easy Come Easy Go, 62, 206–210, 212, 214, 215, 231, 246, 255
Ebert, Roger, 231
Eden, Barbara, 63, 67, 68
Edington, Lyn, 164
Egan, Richard, 9, 11, 12
Eight on the Lam, 212
El Cid, 79
El Dorado, 188
Elliot, Jane, 253
Elvis (album), 7–8
Elvis (book), 5, 7, 22, 88, 263
Elvis, Cinema, and Popular Culture, 167, 232
Elvis Aaron Presley: Revelations from the Memphis Mafia, 24, 35, 51, 56, 70, 94, 99, 103, 106, 132, 141, 142, 150, 157, 161, 167, 176, 185, 196, 198, 220, 239, 241, 262
Elvis Country: I'm 10,000 Years Old, 258
Elvis is Back, 53, 55, 60, 151, 175
Elvis on Tour, 160, 163, 257, 258, 260
Elvis Presley (album), 5, 7
Elvis Presley: The Illustrated Record, 164, 269

Elvis: That's the Way It Is, 257, 259
Elvis: What Happened?, 263
Elvis: Worldwide 50 Gold Awards Hits, 258
Erickson, Leif, 152, 155

Fabares, Shelley, 162, 164, 165, 166, 168, 199, 200, 203, 204, 216, 217
Fabian, 55
"Fame and Fortune," 55
Farrell, Glenda, 134, 135, 137, 138
Faulkner, Edward, 171, 174, 175, 176, 177
"Fever," 55
Fike, Lamar, 27, 35, 50, 51, 59, 70, 78, 94, 95, 103, 141, 150, 185, 239, 262
Film Threat, 41
Flaming Lance. See *Flaming Star*
Flaming Star, 62, 63–70, 72, 77, 78, 83, 88, 94, 200, 223, 250
Flynn, Errol, 43
Follow That Dream, 72, 86, 89–99, 108, 124, 135, 137, 202
Fontana, D. J., 16, 19, 36, 54, 239
A Fool Such as I, 50
For LP Fans Only, 50
Ford, Glenn, 250
Ford, Paul, 50
Forte, Fabian. See Fabian
Fox, Frederick Louis, 242
Frankie and Johnny, 186–191, 203, 204
Freeman Joan, 152, 155
From Elvis in Memphis, 248
From Here To Eternity, 108, 203
Fun in Acapulco, 126, 127–133, 141, 176, 177, 215, 220

Gaer, Paul, 244
Gardner, Hy, 7
Garland, Hank, 36
Geller, Larry, 160, 190
Ghidrah, The Three-Headed Monster, 184
G.I. Blues, 54–62, 66, 69, 70, 72, 77, 78, 81, 83, 84, 86, 87, 88, 94, 105, 108, 112, 175, 196, 203

Gibbs, Georgia, 36
Gilson, Tom, 50
Girl Happy, 72, 160, 162–170, 176, 200, 202, 203, 225, 228, 239
Girls! Girls! Girls! 108, 109–117, 120, 194, 196, 215
Golden Laurel Award, 179
Gomez, Thomas, 225
"Good Golly Miss Molly," 49
"Good Rockin' Tonight," 2
Goodwin, Laurel, 109, 112, 114, 116
"Got a Lot of Livin' To Do," 19
Gottlieb, Alex, 187
The Graduate, 208, 212, 228
Graham, William A., 253–255
Green Acres, 95, 137
Griffith, Andy, 25, 92
Gross, Ben, 7
The Guns of Navarone, 79
Guralnick, Peter, 139, 208

Haley, Bill, 2
A Hard Day's Night, 167, 176, 239
"Hard Headed Woman," 45, 52
"Hard Knocks," 159
Harrington, Pat, 208
Harris, Wynonie, 2
Harrison, George, 197
Hart, Dolores, 19–26
Harum Scarum, 180–185, 187, 203, 204, 223, 239, 246, 255
Hathaway, Henry, 188
Hawkins, Jimmy, 165
Hawks, Howard, 188, 200
"Heartbreak Hotel," 3, 4, 47, 49, 108, 231, 258
Hee Haw, 135
Helm, Anne, 89, 91
Help! 176, 191, 212
Henderson, Douglas, 223
Hendrix, Jimi, 208, 212, 228, 238
Hepburn, Katherine, 7
Herman's Hermits, 161, 198
"He's Got the Whole World in His Hands," 49

High Noon, 2, 10
Hill and Range, 76, 161, 232
His Girl Friday, 90
Hitchcock, Alfred, 147
Holly, Buddy, 49, 55
Hootenanny Hoot, 139
Hope, Bob, 49, 110, 182, 212
"Hound Dog," 6, 7, 8, 25, 47, 55, 79, 114, 240, 255, 258
Howdy Doody, 35
Howlin' Wolf, 1
Hudson, Rock, 105, 117
Huffaker, Clair, 63, 64, 69
Hunt, Jimmy, 202
Hutchins, Will, 217, 219

"I Don't Care If the Sun Don't Shine," 2
"I Don't Wanna Be Tied," 112
"I Don't Want To," 113
I Dream of Jeannie, 68
"I Got a Woman," 6
"I Got Lucky," 103
"I Got Stung," 50, 51
"I Gotta Know," 61
"I Need Your Love Tonight," 50, 51
"I Want You, I Need You, I Love You," 6
"If I Can Dream," 241, 248, 255
"I'm a Roustabout," 159
In Cold Blood, 212
"In the Ghetto," 248, 255, 258
In The Heat of the Night, 226
Invasion of the Body Snatchers, 78
It Came From Beneath the Sea, 138
It Happened at the World's Fair, 72, 118–126, 130, 194
It's a Wonderful Life, 140
"It's Now or Never," 56

Jagger, Dean, 38, 41
Jailhouse Rock (movie), 25, 27–37, 40, 47, 53, 59, 72, 86, 88, 94, 108, 115, 116, 121, 124, 126, 128, 131, 137, 145, 154, 200, 203, 246
"Jailhouse Rock" (song), 79, 114, 131
The Jazz Singer, 147

Jet, 37
Jewison, Norman, 226
Jolson, Al, 147
Jones, Anissa, 250
Jones, Carolyn, 38, 41, 42, 45
Jones, L. Q., 223
Jones, Tom, 197
Jordanaires, 217
Jurardo, Katy, 225

Kansas City Confidential, 103
Kanter, Hal, 16, 19, 20, 22, 23, 25, 80, 87
Karlson, Phil, 100 103, 104, 105
Katzman, Sam, 134, 138, 141, 180
Keaton, Buster, 57, 138
Kennedy, John F., 132–133
The Kid, 123
Kid Galahad, 72, 86, 95, 96, 99, 100–108, 190, 207
King Creole, 37, 38–47, 52, 53, 57, 59, 62, 70, 72, 73, 75, 86, 88, 94, 108, 124, 137, 145, 154, 167, 200, 202, 219, 246, 250
King of Kings, 105, 182
"King of the Whole Wide World," 100, 103, 190
the Kinks, 161
Kirgo, George, 200
Kismet, 184
Kissin' Cousins, 134–142, 148, 151, 153, 176, 181, 207, 267
Klein, George, 214
Kovack, Nancy, 188

Lacker, Marty, 24–25, 99, 106, 132, 133, 167, 197, 198, 241
"The Lady Loves Me," 146
Laidman, Brad, 41
Lancaster, Burt, 7
Lanchester, Elsa, 207, 208
Lane, Joceyln, 171, 174, 177
Langdon, Sue Ane, 152, 157, 186, 187, 188
Lange, Hope, 71, 73, 74, 77

Lansbury, Angela, 80, 83, 86, 156
Laredo, 11
Leave it to Beaver, 253
Lederer, Charles, 89, 90
Lee, Peggy, 55
LeGault, Lance, 109, 139, 143, 152
Leiber, Jerry and Mike Stoller, 6, 7, 17, 25, 28, 38, 39, 47, 109, 110, 114, 128, 153, 158, 171
Lennon, John, 4, 198
"Let Me," 12
"Let's Have a Party," 21
Let's Make Love, 77
Letter from an Unknown Woman, 140
Lewis, Jerry, 7, 57, 193, 210
Lewis, Jerry Lee, 1, 15, 49, 55, 120
Life (book), 3
Life (magazine), 23
Lil' Abner, 96, 137, 138, 141
"Little Egypt," 153, 158, 159, 160
Little Richard, 4, 36, 49, 55, 120
Live a Little, Love a Little, 234–237
London, Laurie, 49
The Lone Ranger, 66
"Lonesome Cowboy," 21
"Love Me," 8
Love Me Tender (movie), 8, 9–15, 16, 21–22, 28, 64, 65, 94
"Love Me Tender" (song), 8, 9, 56, 241
Loving You (movie), 16–26, 28, 32, 154, 167, 202, 217, 266
"Loving You" (song), 21, 26

"Make Me Know It," 55
The Maltese Falcon, 7
"Mama," 113
Many Loves of Dobie Gillis, 77
Margret, Ann, 143–150, 164, 166, 189, 193
Marsh, Dave, 4, 7, 22, 88
Martin, Dean, 1, 7, 56, 57, 61, 79, 210
Marx, Groucho, 24, 57
Mason, Marlyn, 250, 251
Matthau, Walter, 38, 42, 45, 167
Maxwell, Jenny, 80, 85

"Maybe Baby," 49
McCartney, Paul, 4, 197, 198
McHugh, Frank, 208
McIntyre, John, 68
McNair, Barbara, 253, 254
McNear, Howard, 80, 86, 87, 89, 92, 127
"Mean Woman Blues," 21
Memphis Press Scimitar, 32
Meredith, Burgess, 223
Merrill, Gary, 218
Merry Mavericks, 174
"A Mess of Blues," 56
Midnight Lace, 110
Milhollan, James, 187
Mills, Hayley, 147
Miracle on 34th Street, 140
Mitchum, Robert, 35
Mobley, Mary Ann, 162, 166, 180, 184
Monroe, Bill, 2
Monroe, Marilyn, 78
Moore, Mary Tyler, 253, 254, 255, 267
Moore, Scotty, 1–2, 19, 36
Morgan, Harry, 186, 187, 188
Mr. Skeffington, 140
Mullaney, Jack, 171, 174, 177, 199, 202
The Munsters, 253
Murphy, Audie, 64
Mystery of the Wax Museum, 39
"Mystery Train," 2

Nash, Alanna, 24, 25, 35, 51, 132, 141, 143, 161, 176, 184, 185, 239, 258
Neal, Bob, 3, 6
Nelson, Gene, 134, 139, 140, 180, 181, 185
New York Times, 32, 45, 59, 69, 77, 96, 116, 131, 141, 147, 158, 168, 177, 184, 204, 214, 220, 231, 245, 246, 250
Nichols, Mike, 208
No Time For Sergeants, 25
Noel, Chris, 162, 164, 165, 167
None But the Lonely Heart, 73
Norton, Cliff, 187

O'Brien, Joan, 118, 121, 126,
O'Connell, Arthur, 89, 90, 91, 134, 135, 141
Odets, Clifford, 70, 71, 72, 73, 77
"Old Shep," 8
Once Upon a Time in the West, 245
"One Boy and Two Little Girls," 138
"One Night," 50, 51, 56, 241

Paget, Debra, 9, 11, 12
"Papa Won't You Please Come Home," 138
Paradise, Hawaiian Style, 191, 192–198, 203, 204, 239, 255
Parker, Tom, 2–8, 9, 15, 16, 22, 27, 35, 36, 47, 52, 53, 54, 61–62, 63, 69, 70, 71, 78, 80, 81, 86, 87, 88, 89, 95, 99, 100, 109, 119, 127, 133, 134, 138, 139, 140, 148, 150, 151, 152, 157, 161, 171, 172, 180, 184, 185, 186, 192, 197, 199, 203, 206, 208, 211, 216, 232, 239, 242, 246, 247, 253, 256, 263
Parrish, Julie, 194
Penn, Arthur, 212
Perkins, Carl, 1, 15, 54
Perkins, Millie, 71, 73
Peters, Jon, 263
Petticoat Junction, 95
The Phenix City Story, 103
The Phil Silvers Show, 50
Phillips, Dewey, 2
Phillips, Sam, 1–2, 3, 15
Pioneer Go Home, 89, 90
"Plantation Rock," 113
"Poison Ivy League," 153, 159
Pomus, Doc, 144, 163
"Poor Boy," 12
Powell, Richard, 89, 90
Presley, Gladys, 23, 50–51
Presley, Priscilla, 51
Presley, Vernon, 23, 50–51, 52
Price, Vincent, 250
Prince and the Pauper, 217

Princess and the Pirate, 182
The Prisoner of Zenda, 25
Prowse, Juliet, 56, 57, 59
Pryor, Alice, 187

Quarrymen, 3
Quillan, Eddie, 187
Quo Vadis, 25

Rafferty, Chips, 212
The Rainmaker, 7
Rains, Claude, 43
Range Rider, 66
RCA Victor, 1, 3, 6, 8, 24, 47, 50, 56, 79, 90, 151, 177, 190, 196, 197, 258
Ready Teddy, 8
The Rebel, 25
Rebel Without a Cause, 12, 25, 40
"Reconsider Baby," 55
Red Line 7000, 200
Reese, Tom, 63, 66
The Reno Brothers. See *Love Me Tender* (film)
"Return To Sender," 6, 109, 110, 114, 116, 120, 159
Rich, John, 152, 155, 157, 207, 208
Richards, Keith, 3
Riddle, Nelson, 49
Rio Bravo, 10
Riordan, Christopher, 143, 152, 160, 171, 175, 211, 216
"Rip It Up," 8
Robbins, Harold, 37, 41
Robinson, Edward G., 13, 96, 101, 102
Robinson, Louie, 37
"Rock-a-Hula-Baby," 81, 83, 86
Rock Around the Clock (movie), 139
"Rock Around the Clock" (song), 2
Rolling Stone (magazine), 68, 70, 241
Rolling Stones, 4, 161, 164, 176, 238
Romero, Alex, 27, 33
Rossington, Norman, 212

Roustabout, 72, 151, 152–161, 163, 174, 187, 207
Russell, Kurt, 118, 123

Sargent, Dick, 235
Schilling, Jerry, 159
Schwalb, Ben, 168, 171, 172, 179
Scott, Lizabeth, 19–26
The Searchers, 10, 65, 66
Sergeant Pepper's Lonely Hearts Club Band, 208, 212
Shadow of a Doubt, 147
She's Working Her Way Through College, 139
Shoals, Steve, 2, 6
"Shopping Around," 57
Sidney, George, 143, 144, 146, 148, 150
Siegel, Don, 63, 64, 65, 68
Silvers, Phil, 50
Sinatra, Frank, 1, 7, 52–53, 56, 57, 64, 203, 238
Sinatra, Nancy, 227–232, 244, 267
Slate, Jeremy, 54, 109, 113
Small, Edward, 189
Smith, Billy, 35, 161, 176, 196, 211, 220, 239, 269
Smith, Paul, 21
"Smoky Mountain Boy," 138
Snow, Hank, 2
So Far So Funny, 20
"Song of the Shrimp," 113, 118
Sonny Til and the Orioles, 164
Sons of Katie Elder, 188
Speedway, 223, 227–233, 255
Spinout, 199–205, 232
Stanwyck, Barbara, 152, 153, 155, 156, 158, 174
A Star is Born, 263
Starr, Kay, 49
Starr, Ringo, 197
Stevens, Stella, 109, 110, 112, 116
Stewart, Paul, 41
Stoller, Mike. See Leiber, Jerry and Mike Stoller

Stone, Harold J., 162, 164
A Stone for Danny Fisher, 37
Strauss, Robert, 109, 112, 116, 186, 187
Streisand, Barbra, 263
"Stuck On You," 53, 55, 56
"Such a Night," 55
Sullivan, Ed, 3, 19
Summer Magic, 147
Sun Studios, 1–2, 8, 36
"Suspicious Minds," 248
"Sweet Little Sixteen," 49
Sweet Smell of Success, 73

Taurog, Norman, 54, 57, 80, 83, 87, 109, 114, 116, 118, 119, 170, 171, 172, 173, 174, 175, 199, 203, 204, 206, 211, 227, 229, 231, 234, 237
"Teddy Bear," 17, 21, 23, 24, 25
Tewksbury, Peter, 223, 225, 248, 250, 251
"That's All Right," 1, 8, 36
"This is Living," 103
Thompson, Howard, 45
Thornton, Willie Mae, 6
Thorpe, Richard, 25, 27, 33, 126, 127, 128, 131
Three Stooges, 103, 165, 170, 172, 173, 174, 194, 202, 265
Thunder Road, 35
Tickle Me, 168, 170, 171–179, 194, 200, 229
Tiu, Vicki, 122, 194
"Today, Tomorrow, and Forever," 146
"Tomorrow is Such a Long Time," 203
Trosper, Guy, 25
"Trouble," 43
The Trouble with Girls, 247–251, 254
"Trying To Get To You," 6, 78
Twentieth Century Fox studios, 7
26 Men, 66
Two Mules for Sister Sara, 64
Tyler, Judy, 27, 32, 33, 35

Ullman, Ellwood, 168, 171, 172

Vallee, Rudy, 235
Van Dyke, Dick, 249
Variety, 47, 68, 70, 95, 116, 124, 126, 131, 141, 148, 158, 177, 184, 185, 188, 196, 203, 208, 209, 214, 215, 219, 225, 226, 231, 237, 244, 251, 256
Verocca, Frankie, 165, 204
Vincent, Gene, 55
The Virginian, 11
Viva Las Vegas (movie), 140, 142, 143–151, 153, 160, 163, 164, 167, 176, 177, 190, 193, 200, 203, 214, 215, 220, 232, 245
"Viva Las Vegas" (song), 143, 220

Wagon Train, 68
Walker, Ray, 217
Walley, Deborah, 202, 204
Wallis, Hal, 7, 25, 38, 59, 78, 80, 81, 83, 86, 88, 108, 109, 116, 126, 127, 130, 131, 152, 159, 191, 193, 195, 196, 206, 207, 210
Ward, Skip, 208
Warner Brothers, 39, 96, 101
Warren, Charles Marquis, 242, 244, 245
The Way of All Flesh, 140
Wayne, John, 64, 98, 110, 188
"Wear My Ring Around Your Neck," 52
Weaver, Tom, 12–13
Weiler, A. H., 69, 77
Welcome Home Elvis (TV show), 53, 56
Weld, Tuesday, 71, 73, 77
"We're Gonna Move," 12
West, Mae, 156
West Side Story, 79
Western World (magazine), 7, 53
"What'd I Say," 146
"Where Do You Come From," 113
A Whistling Tune, 13
"White Christmas," 36
the Who, 164
"Who Needs Money," 217
Wild in the Country, 70, 71, 72, 73, 74, 75, 76, 77, 78, 79, 83, 87, 88, 157

Williams, John, 212
Wilson, Jackie, 214
"Witchcraft" (Sinatra song), 56
"Won't You Come Home Bill Bailey," 187, 194
Wray, Fay, 43
Wuthering Heights, 140

Yankee Doodle Dandy, 39, 57
the Yardbirds, 164
Yarnell, Celeste, 235–237

"Yellow Rose of Texas," 146
"Yoga is as Yoga Does," 206, 207, 239
York, Francine, 171, 174, 175
You Bet Your Life, 24
"You Gotta Stop," 207
You'll Never Get Rich. See The Phil Silvers Show
Young, Gig, 100, 101, 104
"(You're So Square) Baby I Don't Care," 33

About the Author

James L. Neibaur is a film historian and retired educator whose books include *The Fall of Buster Keaton*, *Early Charlie Chaplin*, *The Silent Films of Harry Langdon*, *Buster Keaton's Silent Shorts* (with Terri Niemi), and *The Charley Chase Talkies*, all published by Scarecrow Press. He also regularly reviews books and DVDs as a freelance writer, writing nearly 100 articles per year, and has over 40 essays in the *Encyclopedia Britannica*.

JUN 1 0 2014

3 1327 00587 5182

14

28 DAY

Hewlett-Woodmere Public Library
Hewlett, New York 11557-0903

Business Phone 516-374-1967
Recorded Announcements 516-374-1667